reel to real

bell hooks

reel to real

race, sex,

and class

at the movies

Published in 1996 by

Routledge
29 West 35th Street
New York, NY 10001

Published in Great Britain in 1996 by

Routledge
11 New Fetter Lane
London EC4P 4EE

Copyright © 1996 by Routledge

Printed in the United States of America
Design: Jack Donner

For permission to reprint materials first published elsewhere, the author would like to thank the following: *Sight and Sound* for "*Crooklyn*: The Denial of Death" (Vol. 4, Issue 8, August 1994) and "Neo-Colonial Fantasies of Conquest: *Hoop Dreams*" (Vol. 5, Issue 4, April 1995); *Artforum* for "Cool Cynicism: *Pulp Fiction*" (Vol. 33, Issue 7, March 1995): Routledge for "What's Passion Got to Do with It?" from *Outlaw Culture: Resisting Representations,* bell hooks (1994); *Bomb Magazine* for "The Cultural Mix: Interview with Wayne Wang" (Vol. 53, Fall 1995); South End Press for "The Oppositional Gaze" and "Is Paris Burning?" from *Black Looks: Race and Representation,* by bell hooks (1992) and "Whose Pussy Is This: A Feminist Comment" from *Talking Back: Thinking Feminist Thinking Black,* by bell hooks (1989).

Library of Congress Cataloging-in-Publication Data

hooks, bell.
Reel to real / bell hooks.
    p.   cm.
  Includes index.
  ISBN 0-415-91823-5 (HB: acid-free cover). — ISBN 0-415-91824-3 (PB: acid-free cover)
1. Motion pictures—Social aspects—United States. 2. Motion pictures—Political aspects—United States. 3. Motion picture producers and directors—United States—Interviews. 4. Afro-American motion picture producers and directors—Interviews.
I. Title.
PN1995.9.S6H66 1996
302.23'43—dc20
96–26474
CIP

for the filmmaker who still dreams . . .

"We used to dream the same dreams.

That was how I knew you would

love me in the end."

contents

1

introduction

making movie magic

Movies make magic. They change things. They take the real and make it into something else right before our very eyes. Usually when I critique a movie lots of folks like, they tell me, "It was just showing the way things are. It was real." And they do not want to hear it when I make the point that giving audiences what is real is precisely what movies do not do. They give the reimagined, reinvented version of the real. It may look like something familiar, but in actuality it is a different universe from the world of the real. That's what makes movies so compelling. Talking about the need for an "aesthetic ecology" wherein the artistry of films is not submerged by any other agenda, visionary filmmaker Stan Brakhage shares this insight: "All this slavish mirroring of the human condition feels like a bird singing in front of mirrors. The less a work of art reflects the world the more is being in the world and having its natural being like anything else. Film must be free from all imitations, of which the most dangerous is the imitation of life."

Most of us go to movies to enter a world that is different from the one we know and are most comfortable with. And even though most folks will say that they go to movies to be entertained, if the truth be told lots of us, myself included, go to movies to learn stuff. Often what we learn is life-transforming in some way. I have never heard anyone say that they chose to go to a movie hoping it would change them utterly—that they would leave the theater and their lives would never be the same—and yet there are individuals who testify that after seeing a particular film they were not the same. Much of what Jeanette Winterson attributes to the power of the literary texts in her collection *Art Objects: Essays on Ecstasy and Effrontery* is equally true of cinematic narratives. She contends: "Strong texts work along the borders of our minds and alter what already exists. They could not do this if they merely reflected what already exists." As cultural critics proclaim this postmodern era the age of nomadism, the time when fixed identities and boundaries lose their meaning and everything is in flux, when border crossing is the order of the day, the real truth is that most people find it very difficult to journey away from familiar and fixed boundaries, particularly class locations. In this age of mixing and hybridity, popular culture, particularly the world of movies, constitutes a new frontier providing a sense of movement, of pulling away from the familiar and journeying into and beyond the world of the other. This is especially true for those folks who really do not have much money or a lot of time as well as for the rest of us. Movies remain the perfect vehicle for the introduction of certain ritual rites of passage that come to stand for the quintessential experience of border crossing for everyone who wants to take a look at difference and the different without having to experientially engage "the other."

Whether we like it or not, cinema assumes a pedagogical role in the lives of many people. It may not be the intent of a filmmaker to teach audiences anything, but that does not mean that lessons are not learned. It has only been in the last ten years or so that I began to realize that my students learned more about race, sex, and class from movies than from all the theoretical literature I was urging them to read. Movies not only provide a narrative for specific discourses of race, sex, and class, they provide a shared experience, a common starting point from which diverse audiences can dialogue about these charged issues. Trying to teach complicated feminist theory to students who were hostile to the reading often led me to begin such discussions by talking about a particular film. Suddenly students would be engaged in an animated discussion deploying the very theoretical concepts that they had previously claimed they just did not understand.

It was this use of movies as a pedagogical tool that led me to begin writing about films as a cultural critic and feminist theorist. Centrally concerned with the way movies created popular public discourses of race, sex, and class, I wanted to talk about what these discourses were saying and to whom. Particularly, I wanted to interrogate specific films that were marketed and critically acclaimed as progressive texts of race, sex, and class to see if the messages embedded in these works really were encouraging and promoting a counterhegemonic narrative challenging the conventional structures of domination that uphold and maintain white supremacist capitalist patriarchy. Even though many traditional academic film critics are convinced that popular art can never be subversive and revolutionary, the introduction of contemporary discourses of race, sex, and class into films has created a space for critical intervention in mainstream cinema. Often multiple standpoints are expressed in an existing film. A film may have incredibly revolutionary standpoints merged with conservative ones. This mingling of standpoints is often what makes it hard for audiences to critically "read" the overall filmic narrative. While audiences are clearly not passive and are able to pick and choose, it is simultaneously true that there are certain "received" messages that are rarely mediated by the will of the audience. Concurrently, if an individual watches a film with a profoundly politically reactionary message but is somehow able to impose on the visual narrative an interpretation that is progressive, this act of mediation does not change the terms of the film.

A distinction must be made between the power of viewers to interpret a film in ways that make it palatable for the everyday world they live in and the particular persuasive strategies films deploy to impress a particular vision on our psyches. The fact that some folks may attend films as "resisting spectators" does not really change the reality that most of us, no matter how sophisticated our strategies of critique and intervention, are usually seduced, at last for a time, by the images we see on the screen. They have power over us and we have no power over them.

Whether we call it "willing suspension of disbelief" or just plain submission, in the darkness of the theater most audiences choose to give themselves over, if only for a time, to the images depicted and the imaginations that have created those images. It is that moment of submission, of overt or covert seduction that fascinates me as a critic. I want to critically understand and "read" what is happening in that moment, what the film tries to do to us.

If we were always and only "resisting spectators," to borrow a literary phrase, then films would lose their magic. Watching movies would feel more like work than pleasure. Again and again I find myself stressing to students, to nonacademic readers, that thinking critically about a film does not mean that I have not had pleasure in watching the film. Although the movie annoyed me intensely, I enjoyed watching Quentin Tarantino's *Pulp Fiction*. I left the theater at midnight, came home, and sat writing into the dawn. My hands were cold, as the heat in the building had long since been turned off. My feet were numb, but as long as I was writing I did not notice, I was trying to capture the fierce intense impressions the film had made on me. It's awesome when a creative work can charge my critical batteries in this way.

Rarely do I write about work that does not move me deeply. And I hate to write about a film when I think it's just "bad." There are two exceptions in this collection. Larry Clark's *Kids* did not move me at all; it enraged me. And because so many progressives critiqued the work in discussion but did not want to go public for fear of censure, I decided to write an essay. *Waiting to Exhale* is the one bad movie I write about. It is not bad because of the genre. There are some great popular films made solely to entertain, and this is not one of them. I chose to write about *Waiting to Exhale* as a way to critically reflect on the notion of "black film," to critically examine the way blackness as commodity is appropriated by mainstream media and then marketed as fictive ethnography, as in "this is about black life."

At its best cultural criticism of movies illuminates, enabling us to see a work in a new way. It enhances the visual experience. Quentin Tarantino is fond of declaring: "If I wasn't a filmmaker, I'd be a film critic.... I would rather get a well-written, thoughtful review, even if it be negative than a badly written gushy review. I they're coming from somewhere, that's interesting, it's all food for thought." The critical essays I have written on films usually provoke and cause a stir precisely because I write about work that has passionately provoked and engaged me. Spike Lee has done many films since *She's Gotta Have It* came out in 1985, but what a stir that picture caused. At the time, it was really remarkable that a black male filmmaker was perceived as offering a vision in cinema of a sexually liberated black woman. This film generated more discussions of the politics of race and gender, of rape and violence against black women, than any feminist article or book on the subject at the time. Naturally, I was moved to write a critical piece. This was the first essay I had ever written about a film. It was called "'Whose Pussy Is This?' A Feminist Comment." Published first in my column in the left magazine Z, it reached audiences both inside and outside the academy. Later I included it in *Talking Back*, my first collection of essays. It became the most xeroxed, the most talked-about piece, serving as a critical intervention challenging viewers to look at the film in a new way. To be honest, I was stunned by the feedback. Not only was I awed by the way folks managed to get ahold of this piece, I was moved on hearing story after story about the intense discussions that followed a viewing of the film when audiences had also read the essay.

I kept waiting for a Spike Lee film that would really have a complex awareness of sexual politics. Finally, after eight films, he made *Girl 6*. Ironically, many critics missed the shift in perspective in this movie. Unlike Lee's other work, this film critically examines sexism and misogyny. Excited to see the influence of feminist thinking, I was shocked that so many viewers failed to grasp this shift and decided it was necessary to write a feminist critique celebrating and exploring this change.

As a critic who has always worked to address audiences inside and outside the academy, I recognized that oral critical discussions of films took place everywhere in everyday life. Across class, race, sex, and nationality, people would see a film and talk about it. As a black woman intellectual working overtime to call attention to feminist thinking, to issues of sexism, one who wanted to talk about the convergence of race, sex, and class, I found films to be the perfect cultural texts. I was particularly pleased to have the opportunity to write about Atom Egoyan's work, because I had been a fan of his films since the beginning. When *Exotica* was made it was exciting to see that an interesting independent filmmaker could make a work that proved to have such wide appeal. Then there is Isaac Julien's short video/film *The Attendant*. When I showed it to my class of women students at City College, who were reading the essays of cultural critic Stuart Hall, they felt that they just could not grasp what was happening. I wrote this essay for them and for everyone else who wants to have a way to think about this film. Similarly, I was moved to write about the connections between eroticism and death in Mike Figgis's recent film *Leaving Las Vegas* because of the ways that film speaks to the issues of power and desire, pleasure and danger, reconfiguring tropes of female masochism in ways that may or may not be liberatory.

Seeing movies has always been a passion in my life. When I first met movie "aficionado" A. J.—Arthur Jaffa (a director and cinematographer)—he was pretty amazed that I could name and had seen movies he did not know about and vice versa. Some of the flavor of our ongoing dialogue is captured here in the critical conversation we have about film. This project began when Caleb A. Mose asked us both to come and be interviewed for a film he was making. This dialogue was spontaneous — unstructured. It was different from an interview. When I interviewed Charles Burnett, Julie Dash, Camile Billops, and other filmmakers, I went to them with a set of specific questions that formed the basis of our discussions. With Billops I wanted to talk about the place of confession and the autobiographical, with Dash her use of archival material and ethnographic research. Individuals who love Dash's *Daughters of the Dust* may have read our conversation in the book that focuses on the film.

When the subject is race I am particularly concerned with questions of race and black liberation. Many of the essays and discussions in this collection focus on the work of black filmmakers. In critical essays I reflect on the issue of aesthetic accountability and how the burden of representation informs this work. Exploring the issues of resisting images, I raise questions about what is required to imagine and create images of blackness that are liberatory. Changing how we see images is clearly one way to change the world. The work of black filmmakers receives much attention in *Reel to Real* precisely because the multiple narratives it constructs revitalize contemporary critical discussions of the way blackness is represented and seen in this society. Despite progressive interventions (there are certainly more black filmmakers making films, both Hollywood and independent films, than ever before), there have not been sustained major visual leaps in the nature of black representation. Concurrently, the essentialist belief that merely the presence of larger numbers of visible black filmmakers would lead to a more progressive and/or revolutionary cinematic representation of blackness has been utterly challenged by the types of films that are being made.

In keeping with the critique of essentialism suddenly we are compelled to think more deeply about the standpoint of the black filmmaker. Interviewing Isaac Julien after the premiere of his feature film *Young Soul Rebels*, we spoke about the ways black audiences can be as uncomfortable with diverse and/or radical representations of black subjectivities as any other group. Julien reminded us then that "blackness as a sign is never enough. What does that black subject do, how does it act, how does it think politically? ... being black isn't really good enough for me: I want to know what your cultural politics are." The interrogation of the very sign of blackness by contemporary left cultural workers ruptured the critical complacency surrounding fixed assumptions about the black aesthetic that had for the most part constituted the conceptual framework within which most critical writing by black thinkers about film took place.

Often the new critical writing done by folks, like myself, who are not traditionally trained as film critics is viewed suspiciously. Indeed, our work interrogates the very assumptions about the nature of black representation that a preexisting body of film theory had helped to put in place and sustain. In the essay "What Is This 'Black' in Black Popular Culture?" Stuart Hall defined the subversive standpoint as one that refuses to see everything via the logic of binary opposition: "The essentializing moment is weak because it naturalizes and dehistoricizes difference, mistaking what is historical and cultural for what is natural, biological, and genetic. The moment the signifier 'black' is torn from its historical, cultural, and political embedding and lodged in a biologically constituted racial category, we valorize, by inversion, the very ground of the racism we are trying to deconstruct." Dialogues with black British cultural critics and filmmakers were important critical interventions. These discussions challenged us all to think differently about black identity, to more forcefully engage critiques of essentialism and to focus on diasporic representations.

For individual traditional black film critics and many of us "new kids on the block" it was difficult to face that in some rare moments there were more progressive representations of blackness in the work of exceptional visionary white filmmakers (cultural workers like John Sayles and Jim Jarmusch) than in the work of individual conservative black filmmakers. Their representations of blackness, along with others, were the positive interventions providing concrete interrogative evidence that it was not so much the color of the person who made images that was crucial but the perspective, the standpoint, the politics. For so long most white filmmakers were interested in using black images only as a backdrop reinforcing racist paradigms that it was easy for a black essentialist aesthetic to emerge, since it appeared that most white artists were incapable of seeing blackness from a decolonizing standpoint. Now that more white filmmakers, both mainstream and independent, centralize black characters in films, diverse white perspectives and standpoints are more obvious.

Even though so much critical work has emerged in cultural studies and/or film studies interrogating old colonizing racial imagery, particularly the representation of blackness, creating new awareness of standpoint and accountability, some filmmakers still don't get it. Ironically, the focus on diversity has inspired some white filmmakers (for example,

Quentin Tarantino and Larry Clark) to exploit mainstream interest in the "other" in ways that have simply created a new style of primitivism. While these filmmakers made use of border crossing and themes of cultural hybridity, they did not do so in any way that was particularly subversive and/or enlightening. The essays on Tarantino and Clark in *Reel to Real* explore the ways transgressive imagery of a nonwhite "other" is used in the work of these filmmakers without challenging stereotypes or the existing structures of domination. All too often artists fear that thinking politically about their work will interfere with some "pure" vision. Yet it is this very notion of visual purity that is a distortion. We often have too narrow a notion of what it means to be political. Even though much of Stan Brakhage's work was very personal, in relation to gender he was making incredible interventions. This work was political. It was thrilling to hear Brakhage affirm that standpoint in the interview Suranjan Ganguly published in *Sight and Sound*, "All That Is Light." When asked to respond to critiques that his works are not that politically relevant, Brakhage insists that his works address sociopolitical realities emphasizing: "I think my films address that constantly. I don't think there has ever been a film that I wished to make that wasn't political in the broadest sense of the term, that wasn't about what I could feel or sense for better or worse from the conditionings of my times and from my rebellions against those conditionings." These issues are constantly relevant to black filmmakers, who are consistently made to feel that their work can have a profound meaning only if it is overtly political. Issues of accountability as they affect both filmmakers and critics are discussed in *Reel to Real: Race, Sex, and Class at the Movies.*

This collection of essays brings together new and old work. I am reprinting only previously published work that often finds its way into classroom discussions. Hopefully, this book will simply make that work more accessible. Much of the cultural criticism I wrote on film appeared first in small magazines with not a large readership. To make that work more available I have begun to include individual essays in other books of collected work. Over time it became evident that the work was piling up and that indeed it was possible to do a collection of my work that focused just on film. Rather than include all the essays on film I have written, this collection includes only those previously published essays that received lots of attention and continue to be read and discussed. That work stands both in juxtaposition and in contrast to my new work. The conversations and interviews are important because they allow for feedback between critic and filmmaker. Contrary to Tarantino's declaration that if he were not a filmmaker he would be a film critic, I could never imagine making films—largely because it is a process that is the complete opposite of critical writing, which one does alone. Filmmaking is an awesome collaborative process, even though we still hold the individual filmmaker responsible for the final product. This is especially true of Hollywood films made with huge budgets. Hopefully, future discussions of race, sex, and class at the movies will expose and analyze more of what happens behind the scenes.

At different public events when questioned about either the homophobic images of gay characters in his films or the misogynist portrayals of women, filmmaker Spike Lee has mocked the issue of artistic accountability by suggesting he is merely documenting life "as is." His unwillingness to engage critically with the meaning and messages his work conveys (whether the content does or does not reflect his belief system) undermines the necessity for both critical spectatorship and critical thinking about representations. Certainly everyone who has ever exploited depictions of racial stereotypes that degrade black people and perpetuate white supremacy could argue that they are merely showing life as is. Thinking in a constructive way about accountability never diminishes artistic integrity or an artistic vision, it strengthens and enhances.

Much of the magic of cinema lies in the medium's power to give us something other than life as is. I have written more critical essays about Spike Lee's work than about that of any other filmmaker. Often readers wrongly assume I do not find his work engaging. Indeed, there is a magical moment in every film Spike Lee has made, and I am always eager to see the work, to see that moment. I tell audiences, particularly nonacademical folks, when they question me about Spike Lee's work, that my desire is not to "trash" his work but to provide a critical perspective that could be useful to audiences and to him by enabling us to see Lee's work in new ways, to reimagine and reenvision. Indeed, all the critical writing and discussion in *Reel to Real: Race, Sex, and Class at the Movies* is meant to be constructive, to critically intervene in a way that challenges and changes. Movies do not merely offer us the opportunity to reimagine the culture we most intimately know on the screen, they make culture. These essays, conversations, and interviews rigorously and playfully examine what we are seeing, ways we think about what we are seeing, and ways we look at things differently. This work interrogates even as it continually celebrates cinema's capacity to create new awareness, to transform culture right before our very eyes.

2

good girls look
the other way

A page in the book *Her Tongue On My Theory* has a single photographic image of a woman's closed painted lips. Next to it the caption raises the question: "Stripped of history?" Desire has the power to do just that, to make us forget who we are. It both disrupts and deconstructs. It dismembers and disembodies. The power of desire to seduce, to lead us in dangerous directions is explored in Spike Lee's moving film *Girl 6*. Offering audiences intense close-up shots of lips—closed, moving, talking—the passion of this film is there in the mouth, the voice. Contrary to what most viewers imagine before they see *Girl 6* this is not a film that exploits the objectification of women. This is a film that explores the eroticization of stardom, of attention. It is a long slow narrative about lack, about where the inability to feel pleasure can take one. The film keeps telling us over and over again that there are spaces in our lives, spaces of longing where nothing matters but the quest to fulfill desire.

The longing of women and men in this film is not for sexual satisfaction but for undivided, unconditional attention. It is the desire to be seen, to not be erased or rendered invisible that fuels individual longings.

A really sad and tender film, no wonder it is misunderstood, seen by many as a "bad" movie. It is not as some critics have suggested a failed comedy. While the film has witty, satiric moments that are incredibly funny, it is a serious film. Unlike other Spike Lee films the narrative is not carried along by the persistent humor of vernacular black culture. Race and racism are backdrops, they are not the issues that have center stage. The poetics of unrequited desire is foregrounded in this film. No wonder then that most audiences cannot handle it. And more is the pity that women, many of them feminist in their thinking, want to dismiss it as just sexism all over again.

Sometimes advertising can kill a movie as much as it can make everyone want to go out and see it. Before anybody sees *Girl 6* the rumor is out that Spike is making a film about phone sex. The previews we see at other movies aim to titillate. Exploiting hidden pornographic longings in the viewer, they imply that the film will be shallow, light, all surface just like your everyday run-of-the-mill heterosexual bad porn. Provocative advertising may lead audiences to the film, but most will not be satisfied with what they see on the screen. Of the nine films that Spike Lee has made this is the most serious, the one that really does not centrally focus on race and racism, the one that uses a lot of technical experimentation in the cinematography.

Before I see *Girl 6* everyone is telling me that this film is "Spike's answer to the feminists." As a cultural critic and feminist thinker who began writing on film in response to *She's Gotta Have It*, I wondered what the question was that feminists had asked Spike. In my critical writings on his work I have called for a broader, more complex vision of womanhood in general, and black womanhood in particular, in Lee's work. And of course in the essay "Whose Pussy Is This" I suggested that it might be great to have a film where when asked that question, an empowered black woman would be seeking her own answer and speaking it with her own sexual voice. In many ways *Girl 6* shows that Spike Lee's artistic vision regarding the representation of female sexuality has expanded. His maturation as a filmmaker is evident, and with it his capacity to represent women characters in more complex ways. This film is not an orgy of pornographic sexism. Audiences voyeuristically enter a world where men "act out" their patriarchal fantasies, through enlightened commentary by both the phone sex operators and the male characters. The women working in the sex industry whose job it is to respond to those fantasies are never portrayed as victims.

From the get-go, *Girl 6* lets audiences know that women working in this aspect of the sex industry, as in so many other areas, are doing it for the money. And that sometimes it can be pleasurable work like any other job any other worker does for the money, while at other times it is dehumanizing, degrading labor. Headed by a sexy, powerful, full-figured black woman, the team of women Girl 6 joins are depicted as completely detached from their jobs and fairly contemptuous of the men who are seeking phone sex. Everyone is clear that it is boring, tedious work. Mostly, they are doing other things while they talk to the guys on the phone—reading, drawing, eating. Even though undivided attention is what the callers seek, and appear to be getting, the truth is, the operators are only pretending.

The lead character, Girl 6, seeks work in the sex industry only after failing to find gainful employment as an actress. Ironically, it is her refusal to let her naked body be exploited for visual pornographic pleasure that leads her to lose jobs. Blatantly the film reminds audiences that women's bodies are subordinated to patriarchal pleasure in ways that are similar in the movies and on the streets. A critique of sexism in the film industry is made when the movie begins. In a masterfully satiric moment filmmaker-actor Quentin Tarantino plays the role of Q.T., the hottest director in Hollywood. When Girl 6 tries out for a role in his latest film, he humiliates her. He silences her. Basically he tells her to shut up and listen, to be obedient, to do as she is told. When she submits exposing her gorgeous full rounded breasts, shame overwhelms and she leaves. Later her agent admits that he has not informed her that she must audition and possibly work in the nude because he knows she would protest. His deceit and betrayal are part of the seduction. He attacks her principles, pointing out that Sharon Stone has had no such inhibitions. Again and again Girl 6 gets the message that success depends on her willingness to exploit her body, her being. To be a film star she must be willing to go all the way. When she refuses she ends up with no money, no skills, and turns to phone sex.

Girl 6 is utterly seduced by the magic of Hollywood. Her seduction begins in a childhood spent watching television and movies. The filmic heroine whose footsteps she hopes to follow is Dorothy Dandridge, the first black woman ever to be considered for an Academy Award. Dandridge broke down color barriers, and tantalized audiences with her portrayal of a sexually liberated, independent woman in *Carmen Jones*.

Dandridge wanted to achieve stardom walking the same path as her white female contemporaries, Grace Kelly, Audrey Hepburn, Judy Garland to name a few. She not only slept with white men, when a newspaper reported that she had slept with more than a thousand men, she threatened to sue and received a public retraction.

Certain aspects of the film industry, especially the history of black film, are subtly conveyed by the focus on Dorothy Dandridge. And even though *Girl 6* overtly deals with the issue of racism, everyone understands that in the world of representations whiteness is the essential ingredient necessary for ultimate fulfillment. This is true of both movie culture and the realm of phone sex. The head of the agency reminds all the women that they must all describe themselves as "white" unless they are assuming a role in a requested fantasy. Sallie Tisdale's *Talk Dirty to Me* documents the longing for young white, blonde flesh that abounds in the sex industry. The same holds true for Hollywood. At the very same time that critics are unable to see the deeper dimensions of Lee's film, works by white male directors *Casino* and *Leaving Las Vegas* with female leads who are white and blonde working in the sex industry receive critical acclaim. Lee's film subtly critiques the hegemony of white images of glamour even as he explicitly shows the way black women enter a movie industry where their beauty marks them for roles as sexual servants.

Exposing the way in which black female sexuality is imaged in television and movies in all-black productions, Lee reenacts a hilariously funny scene from the sitcom *The Jeffersons* where the daughter is protected from the racy phone calls of a male admirer by her patriarchal dad, who literally shoots the phone. Nuclear-family values intact, the characters dance to celebrate. Yet this image suggests that within the context of conservative black family values sexual repression is the order of the day. This is no more a location where a liberatory black female sexuality can emerge than in the context of whiteness.

The black woman character who is the movie's embodiment of sexual power and agency is the police officer Foxy Brown, whose name, "Lovely," Girl 6 assumes for her phone callers. Since they are white, she can rely on them to be unfamiliar with this cultural reference. Lee incorporates footage from a black exploitation film featuring Foxy. In the scene we see, Lovely gains power only by destroying black men. She becomes a pseudo male in drag, hence her ability to assert sexual agency. By relying on mass-media images to structure her sense of self and identity, Girl 6 can find no representations of liberatory sexuality. She must be either victim, vamp, or castrator. All of these roles still require that she shape her sexuality in response to the eroticism of the patriarchal phallic imaginary. For that imaginary controls the world of media images—of representations.

Black males, the film suggests, can rely on the realm of sports to constitute a space where they can perform and shape an empowering identity. Jimmy, the friendly neighbor who lives in the same building with Girl 6, collects baseball cards with black players. While he borrows money to survive from Girl 6, he is able to use his childlike fantasies to ensure a future. The imagery that he engages does not require a negation of blackness. Whereas any black actress who wants to make it in Hollywood has to confront a world where glamour, beauty, sensuality and sexuality, desirability are always encoded as white. Therefore the black female who wishes to "make it" in that cultural sphere must be prepared to disidentify with her body and be willing to make herself over. As the film progresses we witness the myriad ways Girl 6 makes herself over to become the desired object. Her constant changing of outfits, hairstyles, and so on, reminds viewers that femininity is constructed, not natural. Femininity, like phone sex, was invented to satisfy male fantasy. It is there to affirm the realm of the masculine, of phallic power. The bodies of real women must be sacrificed on the patriarchal altar.

Sexism and racism converge to make this sacrifice all the more tragic and horrific for black women. These factors ensure that Girl 6 and the male friends who are her comrades (her ex-husband, her buddy Jimmy) are likely to be poor. They are psychically damaged. The one black adult male who calls for fun sex is as obsessed with baseball as Jimmy. His clinging to fantasies of phallic stardom contrasts with his flabby body and his lack of a real team. All the major black characters in the film are thwarted in their desire to achieve economic prosperity and stardom. Fantasy is the catalyst for their desire. Even if they cannot make it to the top, they can sustain themselves with fantasies of triumph—of stealing power back from the conquering forces of whiteness (the ex-husband bases his identity on Robin Hood). The white woman with whom Girl 6 bonds warns her not to become addicted to fantasy. She does not listen. All her dreams are rooted in fantasy. Addictively attached to the attention she receives from callers, she agrees to meet with Bob, the well-to-do white male businessman who usually talks with her about his mother's impending death. Dressed as though she is starring in a movie, Girl 6 waits for Bob to show up, only he never comes. When a white male walks by not even noticing her, she calls out to him. He does not turn and look her way. Invisible within the realm of whiteness, Girl 6 is powerless to fulfill her fantasies.

Rejection only intensifies the shame that has already been central to the formation of Girl 6's identity. Philosopher Sandra Bartky in her insightful work *Femininity and Domination: Studies in the Phenomenology of Oppression* emphasizes that "Shame is profoundly disempowering," as "the need for secrecy and concealment" it creates leads to isolation. Certainly, Girl 6 seems unable to share with anyone the extent to which she is trapped by her longings for stardom and her understanding that she cannot really fulfill those longings without destroying parts of herself. Both her shame and her sense of woundedness lead her to identify with the pretty little black girl growing up in Harlem who falls down the broken elevator shaft. Overidentified with the television image of this little girl whose tragedy brings stardom, Girl 6 bandages her head as though she, too, were suffering.

Media images have so much power that they distort reality. They encourage children to seek solace in fantasy. Commenting on her relationship to media images in an interview in *Essence* magazine, Theresa Randle remembers: "I loved Shirley Temple movies. I used to watch this little girl go in and out of all these different experiences and I hoped to be able to do the same thing." Throughout the film, Lee suggests that individuals who are psychically wounded are trapped in infantile states. Addiction to fantasies begins in childhood as a way the self is nurtured when there is no real nurturance, when life is without substance or meaning. The mother and aunt of the little girl who is hurt use God as their solace, whereas the wounded "inner child" relies on fantasy—on dreams of power and glory.

No matter how powerful and materially successful the corporate white men are in *Girl 6*, they are also emotionally wounded, stuck in infantile stages of development. Exploring the origin of male sexual fantasies in *Vogue* magazine, a white male writer comments: "It seems to me that many men fix on their object of desire at a place that is deep in the recesses of childhood; their libidos are coded at an early age. The childish aspect of lust is for most men the hardest to admit or to come to terms with. It is the childishness that all prostitutes and role-players know. For many men, the mere fact that something regarded as infantile is a stimulus makes them reluctant to disclose it." Anonymous phone sex enables these men to speak their desires, however strange or perverse. This discharging of the repressed emotion (culminating in jerking off) allows them to reenter the space of real life.

Despite interventions made by contemporary feminist movement, women are still struggling to find a sexual voice, to find places where our desires and fantasies can be articulated in all their strangeness and perversity. One of the most powerful collections of feminist essays about sexuality, *Pleasure and Danger* edited by Carole Vance, contains work where women talk about the difficulty of naming what we desire sexually. In "The Forbidden: Eroticism and Taboo" Paula Webster talks about the nature of female fear, the failure to find a sexual voice: "Like strangers in a strange land, we ask ourselves these poignant questions when we admit our confusions to consciousness. The responsibility of creating a sexual life congruent with our often mute desires seems awesome and very likely impossible.... Going beyond, the erotic territory that is familiar feels forbidden; we stop even our imaginings when confronted with taboo. Our hearts race, the world seems fragmented and threatening; we say 'no' over and over again, convincing ourselves that to act or even to dream of new pleasure would be devastating. We meet the taboo head-on, and we are immobilized." Girl 6 finds herself voyeuristically drawn to phone sex, getting deeper and deeper into the world of misogynist pornographic male fantasy. Following the lead of the female "pimp" played by none other than Madonna, she goes where the male imagination takes her. And it is only when the anonymous caller who is into "snuff" fantasies actually threatens to actualize the fantasy, to really kill her, that she awakens from the seductive trance her erotic voyeurism has lured her into. Patriarchal fantasies require that female desirability be constructed in the space of self-negation, of lack. To be subordinated fully Girl 6 (and all women) must die to her longings and be willing to act as a mirror reflecting male desire. This is what Spike Lee shows us in the film.

When Girl 6 performs her "sex roles" for her ex-husband only to find that he then expects her to act the role of freak, she steps back into the conservative realm of family values where repression is the sign of respectability. Acting like an outraged virgin, she sees no connection between her performance and his assumption that she will do anything to pleasure him. Despite his addiction to stealing, he is the one person depicted in this film who constantly resists dehumanization in the realm of the sexual. Valuing touch, connection, face-to-face encounters, he expresses emotions. He is the real romantic in the film, bringing flowers to Girl 6, giving her the old magazine with Dorothy Dandridge on the cover. In the end he calls her by the name Judy, reminding her of her real identity. Yet even their farewell scene is life imitating the movies. In reality their marriage has failed. In the fantasy they can still be close.

Like newlyweds, dressed in white, they reunite only to part. This is the culture movies create in real life. Jimmy carries the suitcases, looking on, genuinely disappointed that he is losing a friend but pleased that she has awakened from her trance.

Girl 6 has no time for emotional feelings. She is stuck, unable to feel pleasure, swept away by her longings for attention, for stardom. Losing touch with caring black male friends, subtextually she symbolically follows the path of Dorothy Dandridge, who late in her career was repulsed by the touch of black men. White men matter more to Girl 6 because they have the power to give her the career she so desires. Once again this signals a symbolic doubling with Dandridge, who was often sexually involved with the white men who helped advance her career. In the last black-and-white "dream" sequence, Girl 6 is in Hollywood. This scene dramatizes her desire to inhabit a visual universe where she can be center stage, the glamorous star. The powerful white male who receives her in full diva garb is flanked by servants: Girl 6 is led to the "cinematic massa" by a fawning black secretary. Enchanted by her presence, he lavishes her with attention. In this fantasy racism does not exist and all is possible. Definitely the perfect actress for the part, Theresa Randle admits in *Interview* magazine that she is totally obsessed with "old-style movie glamour." "I want to be Dorothy Dandridge or Marilyn Monroe walking down a red carpet looking fabulous." Willingly embracing fantasy, Randle, like her character, apparently finds it easy to look the other way when it comes to the fate of these two stars, whose lives end tragically. They were glamour girls who made it and died young. They were women who wanted sexual agency and never found a way to have it. Even when their dreams of stardom were fulfilled, it was not enough.

In many ways *Girl 6* is a satiric comment on the theme of insatiable female sexual desire that Spike Lee fixated on in *She's Gotta Have It*. Like Nola Darling, Judy claims that she is speaking to clear her name. At this moment she seems to be doubling for Spike Lee, who is also clearing his name with this film, wiping away the charges that he can only create sexist representations of black women. With wry wit, his satiric comment is that he had it wrong in *She's Gotta Have It* by suggesting that sexual desire really mattered to the "liberated" woman. Now he tells us that what sexy black women (and all women) really want is power and stardom—and if they have to, they will prostitute themselves to get it. And of course the white world of cinematic cool (quintessentially embodied in this film by Quentin Tarantino and Madonna) says, What's wrong with a little prostitution between friends? It's all performance.

Like Nola Darling, Girl 6 is conflicted. She wants to go all the way to stardom, but she is not sure she is ready to make the sacrifice especially if in the end she must sacrifice her life. If she does not play the game, if she is not willing to go all the way, she can never be a big success. When Judy resists in Hollywood, refusing to take off her clothes, she leaves with her integrity intact, celebrating by dancing on Dorothy Dandridge's star. In the distance we see that there is no crowd waiting outside to see the movie that is showing. The marquee gives its title — Girl 6. Once again Spike Lee signifies on his own work in Hollywood. Up to a point he has played the game and made it, doing more feature films than any other black director to date. Yet he has refused to go all the way. Girl 6 is his gesture of resistance. Combining strategies of experimental filmmaking, refusing to give us race as we conventionally see it at the movies, or sex, or class, he risks that audiences will be unable to appreciate the significance of this work. He has the power to reclaim the space of artistic integrity. Working against the requirements of Hollywood, Spike Lee offers viewers the most diverse images of black female identity ever to be seen in a Hollywood film in Girl 6. Represented as mothers, newscasters, business executives, phone sex operators, black women have center stage in this film.

This does not mean that the story told is not a sad one. When the movie ends Judy's dreams are not fulfilled. They remain fantasy. Girl 6 never finds a sexual voice. We leave her as we find her, swept away by desire. It seems fitting that the sound track to this film would be created by the musical genius of the artist once known as Prince. For he eroticizes the voice in music, making a realm of sexual promise and possibility, of articulated anguish and unfulfilled desire. At times the sound track brings an operatic sensibility to Girl 6. Like the world of movies, from Hollywood to bad porn, the tradition of opera has given us a space of performance where women's longings are always betrayed, where negative representations of women abound. At the end of her book Opera, or the Undoing of Women, Catherine Clement seduces readers with the promise of a world where women can live without betrayal. "Singing there, scarcely audible, is a voice beyond opera, a voice of the future. A voice from before adulthood: the voice of tenderness and cuddling. The voice of a sweet body, one with no distance, one only a real body can make appear. Sleep will no longer awake to a little girl who is dead. Just as you always stretch your arms when you leave the darkness, these women will always sing." There is this spirit of hopefulness in Spike Lee's Girl 6. It lies not in the narrative but in the representations.

The film acts as critical intervention, opening up a cinematic space where women can disinvest from and disengage with old representations. Importantly, this exciting critical intervention will be overlooked if we see the film through the eyes of a narrowly formed feminism that clings to what Drucilla Cornell calls in *The Imaginary Domain* "the configuration of the masculine imagery." Another way to state this would simply be to say that if audiences are hung up about a black male representing female sexuality, using female nakedness and objectification, than they cannot see the whole picture. Oftentimes when the context of a film is the sex industry, that is all anyone sees. So far reviews of *Girl 6* suggest audiences are unwilling to look past the phallic cultural preoccupation with outlaw sex to see what is really happening in the movie. Surely some of this resistance has to do with the fact that audiences in our culture have yet to learn how to see race and sex while simultaneously looking beyond them. In other words, we still live in a culture where black female bodies are stereotypically "seen" in a sexual light so that it becomes difficult for audiences of any race to see our image standing for universal themes of identity formation, sexual agency, feminist resistance, unrequited longing, etc.

The cover of *Essence* magazine that highlights the female star of *Girl 6* carries the caption "Spike Lee Does Phone Sex: Has He Gone Too Far?" This caption misleads. The film takes us into the world of the phone sex industry and beyond it. All the other journeys in the movie seem to be the ones audiences refuse to go on. The temptation to see *Girl 6* as only about the way men sexually exploit female bodies in the sex and movie industries must be resisted if we are to embrace the artistry and vision of this film. Spike Lee gives us new cinematic terrain with this movie, reminding us that resistance is vital if we want to see Hollywood change its ways of doing race, sex, and class. Girl 6 resists. Drucilla Cornell reminds us that women are still struggling to create a space where our sexuality and our sexual voices can speak freely, where female sexual identity and performance can be represented in their diversity and difference. That space has to be imagined and created by both progressive, visionary women and men. Affirming our need to make this cultural journey she writes: "There is space for the woman with glory in her heart as long as we insist that we are already dwelling in it. We must write that dwelling into being as a place for us to 'be' differently, to be beyond accommodation." This is the cultural space Judy longs for, a world where she will not have to accommodate the desires of others. Spike Lee's *Girl 6* gives us a glimpse of glory. Don't look the other way.

3

transgression

and transformation

Leaving Las Vegas

Six years ago I published a book of essays, *Yearning: race, gender, and cultural politics*, which included this dedication: "for you to whom i surrender—to you for whom i wait." When the book was about to go to press, several feminist editors working on the project expressed concern about this dedication. They found the use of the word "surrender" problematic, disempowering to women. It suggested for them a loss of control, power-lessness. While I agreed that the word "surrender" has this connotation, it also means to give up, to submit. I argued that there are moments when submission is a gesture of agency and power, that a distinction has to be made between conscious surrender, an act of choice and the submission of someone who is victimized and without choice. It seemed to me then, as it does now that women would need to know the difference if we were ever to be capable of self-actualization within patriar-chal culture.

To love fully one must be able to surrender—to give up control. If we are to know love, then we cannot escape the practice of surrender. In patriarchal culture women who love men take a risk that our willingness to surrender may create a space of vulnerability where we can be wounded, violated. This is why there was such a critique of romantic love in early radical feminist discussions and why it was believed that it was difficult for any woman to fully realize feminist practice in a heterosexual relationship. Hence the saying: "feminism is the theory and lesbianism is the practice." Women active in the feminist movement who continued relating to men sexually had to grapple with the meaning of a politics of surrender in the context of heterosexual love in patriarchal society.

Unfortunately, feminist thinkers have to a grave extent abandoned radical discussions of sexuality and the meaning of love in heterosexual relationships. At times these concerns are dismissed as irrelevant and the issues are addressed by simply calling attention to male sexism as though acknowledgement of that reality precludes any need to understand the construction of female and female sexual agency within this context. These issues are raised by Mike Figgis's film *Leaving Las Vegas*. Many feminist viewers simply dismissed this film as another example of the male pornographic imagination at work. Despite the ways in which sexism informs female sexuality is in this film, *Leaving Las Vegas* is a daring work in so far as it suggests that within patriarchy female masochism need not be disempowering, that it can be the space of abjection and surrender wherein the powerless regain a sense of agency. However utopian, this vision does not condemn women to play forever the role of victim.

Leaving Las Vegas chronicles the story of Sera, a prostitute who falls in love with a washed up movie executive named Ben who is drinking himself to death. Ben chooses to travel to Las Vegas to abandon himself to dying. When the film begins we witness him bottoming out at work and in relationships. The film makes it clear that he is not seeking help (this is not about recovery). Addressing the issue of alcoholism in his popular work *Further Along the Road Less Traveled*, psychologist M. Scott Peck contends: "Alcoholics are not any more broken than people who are not alcoholic. We all have our griefs and our terrors, we may not be conscious of them, but we all have them. We are all broken people, but alcoholics can't hide it anymore, whereas the rest of us can hide behind our masks of composure. We are not able to talk with each other about the things that are most important to us, about the way our hearts are breaking. So the great lesson of alcoholism is the nature of the disease. It puts people into visible crisis." Yet Figgis creates an alcoholic in crisis who is not seeking redemption. He has surrendered to his fate. He is courting death.

In the midst of this flirtation, he seeks community and finds it with Sera. Mistakenly, reviewers of the film talk about it as a romantic love story between two individuals who are both broken. The sign of Sera's brokenness is presumably that she is a sex worker. However, audiences and critics arrive at this assessment of her through the lens of their own morality, their own sense that to work as a prostitute means that one is a loser. In actuality, the film disturbs many feminist viewers precisely because Sera is not presented as a victim. In *Leaving Las Vegas* Sera is depicted as a prostitute who enjoys her work. She likes the power to take charge, to use sexuality as a means of making money. Like the actual prostitute in Sallie Tisdale's *Talk Dirty to Me* who states that she would like to be able to display the material comforts of her life and say to people: "See? I am really good in bed! Look at this apartment! Look at what my pussy got me!" It is this assertion of female agency in relation to her body that Sera's character exhibits in the film that is so unsettling for viewers. Many of them choose to see this characterization as male fantasy rather than accept that there are women in the sex industry who feel this way about their work.

Unlike Ben, the alcoholic male, Sera is not washed up. Her vulnerability lies not in her profession but in her longing to be seen as more than her job. In fact, she is resisting the dehumanization that working as a prostitute in patriarchal culture would have her succumb to. It is this resistance, this refusal to be a victim, or object without choices that attracts her to Ben. He seduces her by recognizing her humanity, by seeing that she is not defined by her work and the stigma attached to it. This recognition enables Sera to share with someone critical awareness of the burden of having other people treat you as a loser when you do not see yourself that way. Sera responds to this recognition, to Ben's willingness to address her in the complexity of her being, by falling in love. Yet later, once she has trusted him, he continually reminds her, "We both know that I am a drunk and you are a hooker." Love matters to Sera more than to Ben.

Wary of her and love, instead of returning that love fully, Ben violates the trust she shows him by swiftly becoming an intimate terrorist. While Sera can express her need for Ben without shame, he resists. It is his resistance that turns the potential love relationship into a torturous sadomasochistic bond. Michael Miller argues in *Intimate Terrorism* that when the psychological fate of the self becomes enmeshed with erotic passion, individuals panic: "When people fear what they need, they become angry both at themselves and at those from whom they seek to get their needs met ... Often you see a man and a woman in an intimate relationship ... treat one another with cruelty that they would never consider directing toward anyone who meant less to them." This is precisely what happens with Ben in *Leaving Las Vegas*.

Having made the decision to surrender to death, Ben resists the pull of eros—the call to return to life that sexual longing and connection make on his psyche. His impotence is the sign of that resistance. Hence his insistence that Sera never suggest that he seek help. He demands that she completely surrender any longing for him to be well—to stay alive. It is the unequal demand in the relationship that creates the sado-masochistic dynamic. Sera becomes the slave of love. In the end it is she who confesses in therapy that" "We realized we didn't have much time and I accepted him for what he was."

Throughout the film, Ben remains enthralled by his flirtation with death. In the forward to *The Tears of Eros* Georges Bataille celebrates a love affair like Ben's, declaring: "The essence of man as given in sexuality— which is his origin and beginning—poses a problem for him that has no other outcome than wild turmoil. This turmoil is given in the 'little death.' How can I fully live the 'little death' if not as a foretaste of the final death? The violence of spasmodic joy lies deep in my heart. This violence, at the same time, and I tremble as I say it, is the heart of death: it opens itself up to me." To a grave extent, Ben the wasted lost male soul, is the personification of the patriarchal betrayal of masculinity. Before he leaves for Las Vegas, everyone he reaches out to for connection is male. His friend Peter tells him "Never contact me again." Once he is broken, the world of homosocial patriarchal bonding that once sustained him shuns him. Lost to himself and others precisely because his lust for death is the extreme living out of the patriarchal masculine ethos, he is naked and exposed.

As Sera's sense of wholeness is restored by the act of loving Ben, he loses his power over her. She begins to long for him to be well. When she expresses that longing he violently rejects her. Later he violates her home by bringing another woman prostitute there and sharing with her the erotic passion he withholds from Sera. Even though she has willingly surrendered to love, Sera refuses violation, especially in the domestic space that is her sanctuary and refuge. Despite her love for Ben, she demands that he leave. It is at this filmic moment that the misogynist pornographic imagination rears its ugly head and we see that Sera's refusal to be a victim in romantic love sets the stage for her to be brutally raped. This is the sequence in the film that appears as pure, unadulterated sexist male fantasy. Up until this point in the movie, Sera has been a savvy, tough woman of the streets who can take care of herself. Suddenly, she is portrayed as dumb, as blinded by the sight of three college males with money seeking sexual servicing. In this sequence Sera is triply betrayed: First by the men who rape her, then by the lover who has violated her in the first place, and ultimately by the filmmaker who succumbs to the usual stereotypes and has the "bad" girl punished. This male punishment of the sexually assertive woman who refuses to be a victim gives the film a conventional, predictable patriarchal pornographic slant.

Indeed, this brutal anal rape sequence undermines the more progressive narrative in the film wherein Sera's sense of self is restored by having a healthy interaction with a male she loves. Interviewed in *The Power to Dream*, writer Maxine Hong Kingston states: "I believe that in order to truly grow up, women must love men. That has to be the next stage of feminism. I can't believe that feminism just breaks off at the point where we get to join the Marines." Significantly, Sera is the quintessentially sexually liberated woman in modern society. Her overactive sexuality serves to mask her desire to be loved. It is in the act of loving that Sera risks vulnerability, not in being sexual with men. In sex she can be indifferent—in control. To love she must let go. It is this letting go that makes it possible for her to be redeemed. Unlike Ben, she begins a love affair with life. Loving him makes her want to live. In *Rituals of Love* Ted Polhemus and Housk Randall suggest that in the sadomasochistic power ritual the submissive believes that by "submitting to humiliating indignity she will discover in herself a 'sublime dignity' and that by the loss of control over her own actions (the will that wills self-abandon) she will discover a greater self-hood." This is Sera's quest.

After she has gained recognition of her selfhood through the reciprocal bond she forms with Ben, she finds it impossible to reinhabit a social space where she is not being truly seen. Although she has asked Ben to leave, she continues to love him. Throughout their affair she has felt powerless because she cannot sexually seduce him. Seduction is the way that she previously controlled men. Describing the power relations embedded in the process of seduction, Jean Baudrillard in *Seduction* states: "There is something impersonal in every process of seduction, as in every crime, something ritualistic, something supra-subjective and suprasensual, the lived experience, whether of the seducer or his victim, being only its unconscious reflection." Sera the experienced seducer is seduced. Baudrillard claims that "seduction always seeks to overturn and exorcise a power. If seduction is artificial, it is also sacrificial. One is playing with death, it always being a matter of capturing or immolating the desire of the other." When Ben calls Sera, like the slave of love she is, she obeys. Entering the sleazy hotel room where he lies in the throes of death, she gives him the mingling of tears and eros Georges Bataille extols in his work. For Ben ecstasy is merely a preparation for death. Meditating on death, on the "last instant," Bataille observed: "When there is physical pain, a high degree of what may be termed narcissistic cathexis of the painful place occurs: this cathexis continues to increase and tends, as it were, to 'empty' the ego." It is this state of emptiness that gives Ben his aura of blissful indifference. That bliss would be eradicated at the moment of death, were it not for Sera's presence. As Bataille testifies: "In myself, the satisfaction of a desire is often opposed to my interests. But I give in to it, for in a brutal way it has become for me the ultimate end ... the end of reason, which exceeds reason, is not opposed to the overcoming of reason! In the violence of the overcoming, in the disorder of my laughter and my sobbing, in the excess of raptures that shatter me, I seize on the similarity between a horror and a voluptuousness that goes beyond me, between an ultimate pain and an unbearable joy!" Ben fails in his quest to meet death alone. The desire for connection triumphs. He is able to go—to truly leave Las Vegas—only when he is connected, only when he has a witness.

Sera gives him the recognition he needs before dying, just as he has given her the recognition that restores her to full humanity, that brings her back to life. Coming back to life for Sera means acknowledging pain and suffering. To cope with the very realties Ben has failed to cope with, she seeks connection and healing. The wounds of passion in her life become the source of that healing.

As a witness to death, Sera is ultimately transformed. She experiences a world that is deeper than the one she knows every day. All experiences are essential for self-actualization, including those of suffering, degradation, and pain. Through her acceptance of Ben and of herself, Sera finds a way to experience unity. In On the Way to the Wedding, the Jungian therapist Linda Leonard shares this insight: "As Heidegger has said, our being is to 'be there' where Being opens up and reveals itself, and our task is to open to the revelation and to try to preserve it through expression. For Heidegger, the fundamental opening-up of experience for the human being occurs when one is able to accept and affirm the mystery of death within one's being. For in the acceptance of our 'being-unto-death' we surrender our desire to control reality and thus are able to accept whatever offers itself to us.... For death is the ultimate transformation and threshold." Sera crosses the threshold of death and enters life. She is born again through her redemptive love. The tragedy of *Leaving Las Vegas* lies in the way in which Ben's transgression of boundaries does not lead to redemption. This is the danger of being seduced by transgression. At the end of her essay "Is Transgression Transgressive?" Elizabeth Wilson concludes: "We transgress in order to insist that we are, that we exist, and to place a distance between ourselves and the dominant culture. But we have to go further—we have to have an idea of how things could be different, otherwise transgression is mere posturing. In other words, transgression on its own leads eventually to entropy, unless we carry within us some idea of transformation. It is therefore not transgression that should be our watchword, but transformation." If audiences watching *Leaving Las Vegas* are merely enthralled by sexual scenarios of pleasure and danger, by alcoholic hedonistic excess, by the various tropes of transgression, they will feast on the tragedy and ignore the call to love—to be transformed utterly. To love is to endure.

4

Exotica

breaking down

to break through

Few films in the United States address the issues of race, sex, and class in an inclusive manner, from a critical location where diverse standpoints are revealed. In our culture one issue usually takes precedence over the others. Spike Lee can give us progressive cinematic messages about race but reactionary visions of gender. Oliver Stone can focus on national identity and imperialism but ignore race. Artists in this culture have difficulty imaginatively seeing the whole picture because we have all been socialized to learn in parts—to see only fragments. This fractured mode of seeing leads most critics in the United States to see a film like Atom Egoyan's *Exotica* and never notice the way it raises issues of race, class, nationality. Looking through a narrow lens, they see the film as exclusively about sexuality. In this culture most audiences were voyeuristically fascinated by the strip joint, while they found the various plots of the film that did not address sexual issues uninteresting.

Introducing an interview with Egoyan titled 'Atom's ID" (published in *Artforum* magazine) Lawrence Chua begins: "It is a young stripper in schoolgirl drag who ushers us into Atom Egoyan's heart of darkness . . ." One might think from this statement that the film opens at the strip club, when in actuality we end up there only after we have visually moved through various locations. And once we get to Club Exotica, even before we focus on the table dancer Christina, we hear the sounds of this place—the Middle Eastern music, the seductive voice of the club's emcee. We see the lush decor designed to evoke the jungle—the realm of the exotic. A sharp contrast emerges from the outset between the "exotic" setting and the mundane activities happening here—the same stuff that goes on in any strip joint anywhere in the world. From "jump," then, Egoyan merges the specific and the universal. You are in the land of the familiar and the strange at the same time. And this becomes the prevailing metaphor for the postmodern psyche. Indeed, *Exotica* is the quintessential postmodern film.

Club Exotica is a diasporic landscape, a place where individuals meet across boundaries of race, sex, class, and nationality. In the film, identity is always up for grabs, nothing is ever the way it seems. Stuart Hall's essay "Cultural Identity and Diaspora" reminds readers that identity is "a matter of 'becoming' as well as 'being.'" Hall contends: "It belongs to the future as much as to the past. It is not something which already exists, transcending place, time, history, and culture. Cultural identities come from somewhere, have histories. But like everything which is historical, they undergo constant transforation. Far from being eternally fixed in some essentialized past, they are subject to the continuous play of history, culture, and power." The power of nation and state is registered in the opening scenes of *Exotica*.

When the film begins we enter the world of border crossing by watching a young black man being trained as a customs inspector. He is being taught to interrogate with both his eyes and his mouth, to question what he sees, to see that which must be questioned. He must judge appearances, yet the film constantly reminds us that those judgments will always be faulty, for nothing is ever the way it seems and everything is always changing.

From the onset cultural hybridity is the landscape of this film. The signs of border crossing and cultural mixing are everywhere. Right away it is obvious that we are not in the good old U.S. of A. Strip joints in this country do not play Middle Eastern music, no matter who owns them. The culture we watch on Egoyan's screen, where difference is tolerated and border crossing more a norm than a contrived spectacle, has been created by immigration, mingling, and integration. It is a fact of life, not a fantasy.

The mundanity of this cultural mixing is marked by the absence of any heavy-handed focus on difference. While we see photographic images of the black wife of the white lead character, Francis, a tax auditor, this interracial liaison is normalized, as are all the border crossings in the film. There is little tension between gay and straight, black and white, or immigrant and nonimmigrant populations. In this fictive world of difference Egoyan suggests that desire—the longing for connection and the fear of loss—is the thread that connects, the common experience. The introduction to my *Yearning: Race, Gender, and Cultural Politics* concluded with a statement that mirrors Egoyan's insight: "All too often our political desire for change is seen as separate from longings and passion that consume lots of time and energy in daily life. Particularly the realm of fantasy is often seen as completely separate from politics.... Surely our desire for radical social change is intimately linked with the desire to experience pleasure, erotic fulfillment, and a host of other passions....The shared space and feeling of 'yearning' opens up the possibility of common ground where all these differences might meet and engage one another. It seemed appropriate then to speak this yearning." Throughout *Exotica* emotional intensity is marked by unrequited states of yearning.

The inability to speak yearning—the power of repression—is articulated by the two prominent male characters, the straight white male Francis and the inarticulate gay white male Thomas, a pet shop owner. Both men carry around bottled up passions that they can unleash only in encounters with an "other." The unconscious desire for an encounter with "otherness" Egoyan suggests emerges from that inner space where we are uncomfortable with our longings, where we deny them power, even as we transfer and transpose them via fantasy onto an other. We then seek that other to gain fulfillment.

Vulnerable in the act of seeking, we wander into strange locations, exposing the very parts of ourselves that we seek to hide in the space of the familiar. By transgressing the boundaries of the norm, we hope to overcome feelings of loss and rediscover the way home. Turning the colonial paradigm of conquest and domination on its head, Egoyan suggests that the lost and lacking white colonizer seeks to divest of the colonizing impulse by submerging his identity in the world of the other and in the hopes that he will be transformed. It is this redemptive transformation Francis seeks when civilization and the family as he has constructed them break down. No longer on "top" of the situation, no longer behind the camera making home movies, Francis has been violated. It is that sense of shared violation which connects him and the lap dancer Christina.

To experience recognition he must leave the world of home and find a place of refuge. Club Exotica provides him sanctuary. The pristine aura of material privilege in Francis' home contrasts with the tacky, decadent decor of Club Exotica. Yet it is "on the down low" that Francis hopes to find satisfaction for his yearning. Listening in on his dialogue with Christina, we hear him lay out a patriarchal paradigm of masculinity, of fatherhood: We hear him seek confirmation of his ability to protect those he loves. We hear him affirm that he would never abandon them. When his daughter is murdered, when his wife dies in a car accident he must come face to face with the reality of his own powerlessness. While the drama he enacts with Christina is meant to affirm and reaffirm his sexual potency, in actuality it is merely the act of regression that enables him to repress the truth of impotency and powerlessness. The family as he has previously known it is no more. This is the truth that he cannot accept. Betrayal and death underscore the fragility of the myth of intactness. Even the family video in which we see the hand of the black wife protecting her child from the invasive, potentially violating gaze of the white father stands as testimony that the happy go lucky family Francis nostalgically longs for may have existed only in the realm of fantasy. His need to cling to the fantasy leads him to repress the memory of trauma (i.e. loss) by pretending with Tracey, the baby-sitter, that nothing has changed, by trying to recreate the bonds of love he has shared with his daughter with Christina. She understands because of her own memory of violation.

Without consciously registering it, they seek each other for healing. When interviewed by Lawrence Chua, Egoyan acknowledged that he is "fascinated by characters who don't have access to or contact with a professional, sanctioned form of therapy and therefore have to create their own." Yet the site of healing is not that of the interaction between Christina and Francis. Healing happens only when Eric, the seductive emcee who has been Christina's lover, disrupts the make-believe dialogue, ruptures the denial. By so doing Eric re-creates the trauma of loss, enabling Francis to express both anger and grief. As psychologist Judith Viorst maintains in her book *Necessary Losses*, the failure to acknowledge aggression can lead to an absence of love. Francis must move from the narcissistic self-involved state wherein he idealizes his wife and child into the real world, where he must face disappointment and loss. Reconciliation comes to him away from the space of denial. When Francis comes face to face with Eric in the dark shadows of night, facing the dragon, he sees there the mirror of his own pain and is able to find release. The moment when Eric acknowledges the pain of the past giving him the recognition he needs to be well through shared memory, Francis can be made whole. Their embrace is the moment of redemption and reconciliation.

Concurrently Christina regains her subjectivity not through the relationship with Francis but via her encounter with Thomas. Unlike all the other men who come to her seeking the fulfillment of their longings, of their sexual desire, Thomas is there only as a witness. When the two characters meet, theirs is a dialogue of mutuality. They both understand what has taken place. The witnessing of Francis's suffering has made them compassionate and open-hearted. With Thomas, Christina can give and he can receive. Between them, there is no possibility of betrayal.

The theme of betrayal in one's family of origins is constantly evoked in *Exotica*. Even though Francis idealizes his relationship with his daughter, his compulsive longing to "possess" her is a desire that could easily have led to violation. When he transposes his feelings onto the young Christina, who is actually being abused in the family context by assuring her that her father feels towards her the way he feels towards his daughter, the possibility of violation is highlighted. Whenever there is intense connection, there is the potential for violation. Again and again in *Exotica* we encounter the theme of abuse in childhood. That early "trauma" is represented by the schoolgirl striptease. The "symbolic" fathers, grown men who are aroused by this fantasy, remind us of this tension, of what can happen between the powerful and the powerless. And if audiences fail to "get it," because they are so tantalized and sexually turned on by the schoolgirl striptease act, the pregnant body of Zoe is there to remind us where it all begins. Her child is conceived in an act of betrayal. She is the daughter of a mother who has betrayed her and other females. It is Christina who names the mother's betrayal, who articulates that masking and deceit was the foundation of the mother/daughter bond both real and symbolic and not love. It is she who remembers the time when Zoe repudiated her mother's life and longed for a different fate. Christina indicts Zoe for failing to invent a self apart from her mother's fantasies.

The bond between Eric and Christina is broken by betrayal. Betrayal is always about abandonment. This is a central theme in the film. It is there in the relationship between Thomas and the customs officer who gaslights him. Voyeuristically, we witness the tenderness of their seduction knowing that it will lead to betrayal. It is present in the relationship between Francis and his brother. Despite their various differences, race, class, sex, nationality, all the individuals in the film are wounded by abandonment, by violation. These wounds of passion are the result of childhood trauma, the memory of irreconcilable loss. In *Necessary Losses*, Judith Viorst suggests that the fear of abandonment surfaces in childhood once the bliss connection between mother and child is severed. Our pain lies in the fact that growth demands renunciation, the letting go of paradise. Viorst contends: "We acknowledge a paradise and a paradise lost. We acknowledge a time of harmony, wholeness, unbreachable safety, unconditional love, and a time when that wholeness was irretrievably rent ... We acknowledge it as reality or dream ... we also yearn to recapture the lost paradise of that ultimate connection." Egoyan shows us that fantasy is one place where we continue to search for paradise.

Ultimately, however, he shows that even the fulfillment of fantasy will not bring an end to our yearning. In the culture of *Exotica*, the end of desire is not fulfillment but the recognition of the place of suffering. To become whole we must be willing to come to consciousness by feeling the pain. The forces of evil surround us when we remain unable, as Carl Jung reminded us, to meet the shadow. To know salvation the characters in *Exotica* must face the truth. They must stop lying to themselves and to others.

The call to break through denial and face reality—the truth is marked by the haunting taunting lyrics of Leonard Cohen's song "Everybody Knows," played over and over again when Christina performs her schoolgirl act. The knowledge we all share is the truth of our collective woundedness. Everybody knows that much of that woundedness occurs in our families of origin, in the space of childhood. The innocence we yearn for, Egoyan suggests, was always and only a fantasy. To return to truth, to save ourselves—we must have the courage to remember.

By the end of *Exotica* we are taken on a journey that goes all the way back to Christina's childhood. We witness her longing to be loved and protected. We see her desire to live in a world where she will not be violated or abused. We see her need to have her sorrow recognized. And we also confront the painful reality that no one comes to release her from the space of trauma, that she has no choice but to get out of the car (the space of intimacy she shares with the symbolically loving father) and return, broken-hearted, home.

It is the image of her pain that stays with us. An image so intense that we find release only by remembering the movie in our minds, so that we can see that Christina moves from the wounds of childhood into an adult world of symbolic repetition of trauma to a space of healing where she can let the past go and be free. In Atom Egoyan's *Exotica*, transgression, the breaking of boundaries, is essential for the process of self-recovery. Everyone must break down in order to break through. The rite of passage is the journey away from denial, outward recognition and reconciliation.

5

Crooklyn

the denial of death

Hollywood is not into plain old sorrowful death. The death that captures public imagination in movies, the death that sells, is passionate, sexualized glamorized violent death. Films like *One False Move, True Romance, Reservoir Dogs, Menace to Society, A Perfect World* bring us the sensational heat of relentless dying. It's fierce—intense—and there is no time to mourn. Dying that makes audiences contemplative, sad, mindful of the transitory nature of human life has little appeal on the big screen. When portrayed in the contemporary Hollywood film, death is swift, romanticized by soft lighting and elegiac sound tracks. In the movies the sights and sounds of death do not linger long enough to disturb the senses, to remind us in any way that sorrow for the dying may be sustained and unrelenting. When Hollywood films depict sorrowful death, audiences come prepared to cry. Films like *Philadelphia* advertise the pathos so audiences can come prepared. Even before tickets are bought and seats are taken everyone knows that tears are in order, that the crying time will not last long.

The racial politics of Hollywood are such that there can be no serious representations of death and dying when the characters are African Americans. Sorrowful black death is not a hot ticket. In the incredibly financially successful film *The Bodyguard*, the sister of Rachel Marron (Whitney Houston) is accidentally assassinated by the killer she has hired to kill Rachel. There is no grief, no remembrance. In most Hollywood movies, black death is violent. It is often trivialized and mocked. As in that viciously homophobic moment in *Menace to Society* when a young black male crack addict holding a fast-food hamburger while seeking drugs tells the powerful drug dealer, "I'll suck your dick," only to be blown away for daring to suggest that the hard gangsta mack would be at all interested. Pleased with the killing, the dealer laughingly offers the hamburger to onlookers, a gesture that defines the value of black life. It's worth nothing. It's dead meat.

Even black children cannot be spared Hollywood's cruelty. Watching the film *Paris Trout*, audiences witness the prolonged brutal slaughter of a gifted southern black girl by a powerful sadistic racist white man. The black males who are her relatives are depicted as utterly indifferent. Too cowardly to save or avenge her life, for a few coins they willingly show the lawyer who will defend the killer the blood-stained places left by her dragging body, the endless bullet holes in the walls and furniture. Her life is worth nothing.

Audiences are so accustomed to representations that depict the brutal death of black folks in Hollywood films that no one is outraged when our bodies are violently slaughtered. I could find no Hollywood film where a white child is the object of a prolonged brutal murder by a powerful white male—no image comparable to the death depicted in *Paris Trout*. Yet no group in the United States has publicly protested this image—even though *Paris Trout* regularly shows on Home Box Office, reaching an audience far wider than an actual moviegoing public and finding its way into the intimate spaces of home life and the private world of family values. Apparently the representation of a prolonged graphic murder of a little black girl does not shock, engender grief or protest. There is collective cultural agreement that black death is inevitable, meaningless, not worth much. That there is nothing to mourn.

This is the movie culture Spike Lee confronts with his film *Crooklyn* which superficially represents issues of death and dying in black life as though our survival matters, as though our living bodies count, while in the final analysis reaffirming the usual Hollywood message about black death. Lee has made both a provocative and controversial film. To introduce that film to consumers who do not take black life seriously, advertisements give little indication of the actual content of the film. Huge ads tell consumers, "the smart choice is Spike Lee's hilarious *Crooklyn*," suggesting the film will be a comedy. The seriousness of its subject matter must be downplayed, ignored, denied. Expecting to see a comedy, moviegoers I talked with were not so much disappointed as puzzled by the fact that the comedic elements in the film were overshadowed by the serious representation of a family in crisis that culminates in the mother's death. When the movie ended, folks were standing around the theater in the Village where I first saw the film, mostly saying: "It wasn't what I expected. It wasn't like his other films." *Crooklyn* differs from Lee's previous work primarily because the major protagonist of this film is a ten-year-old girl Troy (Zelda Harris). Rarely do we see Hollywood films with black female stars, not to mention child stars. Positively radical in this regard, *Crooklyn* invites audiences to look at black experience through Troy's eyes, to enter the spaces of her emotional universe, the intimate world of family and friends that ground her being and give her life meaning.

Lee's magic as a filmmaker has been best expressed by his cinematic construction of an aesthetic space wherein decolonized images (i.e., representations of blackness that challenge and oppose racist stereotypes) are lovingly represented. However, this radical intervention occurs most often in a context where it is usually framed by a conventional mainstream narrative and structure of representations that forcibly reinscribe stereotypical norms. The laughing darky family portrait that advertises the movie is one example. Moviegoers want to see this image rather than images that challenge it. This contradictory stance tends to undermine Lee's ability to subvert and/or alter dominant, colonizing representations of blackness. His radical images are usually overshadowed by stock characterizations and can be easily overlooked, particularly by viewers who are more accustomed to looking for predictable stereotypes. Even progressive, aware viewers may be so taken with their own fascination with the funky, funny "Otherness" of black images typically seen in Spike Lee movies that they refuse to "see" any representations that challenge conventional ways of looking at blackness. J. Hoberman's review of *Crooklyn* in the *Village Voice* is a perfect example of the way in which standpoint can determine how we see what we see. Hoberman did not see a film highlighting issues of death and dying. To his mind's eye, "the grittier specifics of the Lee family drama" are exemplified by arguments at family dinners and witty disagreements about TV programs. Indeed, Hoberman saw the movie as having "no particular plot." Never mentioning the mother's death, he did not see the film as constructing a context wherein this event, more so than any other, leads to a ten-year-old black girl's coming of age. Hoberman is much more engaged with the comedic aspects of the film, especially those that center on the eldest child, Clinton (Carlton Williams), in this family of four boys and one girl, the character who most resembles Spike Lee. Not unlike the moviegoers I talked with, Hoberman seems much more fascinated with the antics of Spike Lee, controversial filmmaker, than with the content of this film. By deflecting attention from *Crooklyn*, and onto Spike Lee, neither Hoberman nor anyone else has to interrogate the film on its own terms. To do so would require coming to terms with *Crooklyn's* treatment of death and dying, as it is this aspect of the film that fails to excite and challenge our imaginations.

Crooklyn is most compelling in those moments wherein it offers fictive representations of black subjectivity rarely seen in mainstream cinema, images that both counter racist stereotypes as well as facile notions of positive images of "the black family." The property-owning, artistic, progressive black family portrayed in the film is unique. The Carmichaels in no way represent the conventional black bourgeoisie. They are not obsessed with upward mobility, with the material trappings of success. Counter-cultural—a mixture of the nationalist movement for racial uplift and a bohemian artistic subculture—they represent an alternative to the bourgeois norm. A 1970s black family that dares to be different. Woody (Delroy Lindo), the father, is an aspiring jazz musician and composer; the mother, Carolyn (Alfre Woodward), a nontraditional schoolteacher. Their five children are all encouraged by progressive hands-off parenting to be unique individuals, with their own particular interests, passions, obsessions. These are not your average kids; they take a democratic vote to see which television show will be watched. They are all made to participate equally in household chores. Though black-nationalist thinking shapes the family politics, the world the Carmichaels live in is multicultural and multiethnic. Italians, Latinos, gays and straights, young and old, the haves and the have-nots are part of the mix. This is the real world of cultural hybridity and border crossing extolled by contemporary progressive critics. Much of the film depicts that world "as is," as images that are artificially positive or unduly negative.

When the movie opens, we can revel in images that counter the prevailing one-dimensional cinematic portrayals of urban black life everyone is accustomed to seeing. Beginning in the style of fictive documentary (initially enhanced by the cinematography of Arthur Jaffa), Lee offers a panoramic body of visual images of black community that disrupts dominant representations. Highlighting scenes of play and pleasure, the beauty of black bodies, the faces of children and old men, bodies engaged in everyday life, the film offers us scenes of joy in living and not the usual stark images of racial dehumanization and deprivation. These scenes signal heightened creativity, an unbridled imagination that creates splendor in a world of lack, that makes elegance and grace so common a part of the everyday as to render them a not unusual expression of natural communion with the universe.

This opening sequence of images are moving pictures that function as a phototext, calling us to be resisting readers able to embrace a vision of blackness that subverts and challenges the normal way of seeing and looking. Lee engages a politics of representation which cultural critic Saidiya Hartman describes in an essay on black photography "Roots and Romance" as "a critical labor of reconstruction." She explains: "It is a resolutely counterhegemonic labor that has as its aim the establishment of other standards of aesthetic value and visual possibility. The intention of the work is corrective representation." At rare moments throughout *Crooklyn* this strategy is realized. It is marvelous to follow where the camera leads—to catch sight of such empowering images. Seduced by this initial moment of radical intervention, by the way it shifts paradigms and requires new ways of seeing, the enthralled viewer can sit in a daze of delight through the rest of the movie, failing to experience ways the cinematic direction and narrative structure which follows counteracts and undermines these initial subversive representations. A distinction must be made between oppositional representations and romantically glorifying and valorizing images of blackness which white supremacist thinking as it informs moviemaking may have rendered invisible. Visibility does not mean that certain images are inherently radical or progressive. Hartman urges cultural critics to rigorously interrogate this distinction, to ask necessary questions: "Simply put, how are redemptive narratives of blackness shaped and informed by romantic racialism, the pastoral and sentimental representation of black life? How is the discourse of black cultural authenticity and Afrocentrism shaped and informed by this construction of Africanism and do they too maintain and normalize white cultural hegemony?" *Crooklyn* is offered as a redemptive narrative.

The counterhegemonic images we see at the beginning serve to mask all that is "wrong" with this picture.

From the moment we encounter the Carmichaels at their dinner table, we are offered a noncritical representation of their normal family life. Shot like docudrama, these early scenes appear innocent and neutral. However, the ethnographic-documentary, day-in-a-life style of presentation demands that the viewer see nothing wrong with this picture. The camera aggressively normalizes. Didactic, these family scenes are presented unproblematically; hence they appear to be positive representations, and Lee fulfills his quest to bring to the big screen "authentic" black aesthetic subjects that are rarely seen.

Since Spike Lee's cinematic genius is best revealed during those moments when the filmmaker documents familiar aspects of a rich black cultural legacy wherein collective internal codes and references converge that may or may not be known to outsiders it is easy to overlook the fact that these counterhegemonic representations are constantly countered by stock stereotypical images. When these images are coupled with Lee's use of "animal house"-type humor appropriated from mainstream white culture a carnivalesque atmosphere emerges that seems much more directed toward mainstream, largely white viewers. This cultural borrowing, which gives the movie crossover appeal, is most evident in the scenes where Troy travels south to stay with relatives in a Virginia suburb. Though the cinematography didactically demands that the audience detach from any notion of the "real" and engage the "ridiculous and absurd," these scenes appear stupid, especially the mysterious, not really comical, death of the pet dog her aunt dotes on. Lee works overtime in these scenes to create a comedic atmosphere that will contrast with the seriousness of the Carmichael household but it simply does not work. The switch to an anamorphic lens confuses. No doubt that is why signs were placed at ticket booths telling viewers that this change did not indicate a problem with the projector. Fancy attempts at cover-up aside, in these scenes Lee mockingly caricatures in an uninteresting fashion the southern black middle class (who appear to be more like northerns in drag doing the classic Hollywood stand-up comedic rendition of southern life). Well Lee gives it to us in black face. It is predictable and you just can't wait to return home to the Carmichael family. However, it must be noted that while Lee strategically constructs images and scenes to normalize the dysfunctions in the Carmichael family, he insists on making this family pathological. This attempt at counterhegemonic representation fails.

From the start anyone who sees the Carmichael family without putting on the rose-colored glasses the film offers will see that they are seriously dysfunctional. Throughout the movie we see eating disorders (one of the children is coercively forced by verbal harassment to eat, so much so that on one occasion he vomits in his plate), an excessive addiction to sugar (dad's pouring half a bag of the white stuff into a pitcher of lemonade, his cake-and-ice-cream forays, his candy buying all hint that we may be addicted to more than sugar even though he is not overtly shown to be a drug user in the film) along with the lack of economic stability signified by the absence of money for variety in food choice, the shutting of electricity, as well as the dad's mismanagement of funds (the film never lets us know what he does with his money) are all indications that there are serious problems in the Carmichael household. By normalizing the family image, Lee takes a stance that does not engage the issue of psychological abuse. All interactions are made to appear natural, ordinary, comedic and not tragic. The autobiographical roots of *Crooklyn* may account for Lee's inability to take any stance other than that of "objective" reporter. Working with a screenplay collaboratively written with Joie, his sister, and Cinque, his brother, Spike Lee may have felt the need to distance himself from the material. Certainly emotional distance and detachment characterize the interactions between family members in the film.

To write the screenplay, Joie Lee relied on her family memories, stating that she "drew from the few memories I have of my mother," who died of cancer when she was fourteen. Yet the children in *Crooklyn* are much younger and are clearly deeply ambivalent about their mother. Portrayed as a modern-day Sapphire with direct lineage to the Amos 'n' Andy character, Carolyn, the mother, responds to the economic crisis in the family by constantly nagging, erupting into irrational states of anger and outrage that lead her to be mean and, at times, abusive. Even though the economic problems the family faces are caused by Woody's unemployment, his character is compassionately depicted. Seductively portrayed as an aspiring artist who just wants to be left alone to compose music, Woody is always laid-back and calm. Sexist/racist stereotypes about gender identity in black experience are evident in the construction of Carolyn and Woody as characters. Although Carolyn is glamorous, beautiful in her Afrocentric style, she is portrayed as a bitch goddess. Her physical allure seduces even as her unpredictable hostility and rage alienates and estranges. In keeping with sexist stereotypes of the emasculating black matriarch, Carolyn usurps her husband's parental authority by insisting that as the primary breadwinner, she is the sole authority figure with the right to dominate, shaming Woody in front of the children. These aspects of her personality encourage us to see her unsympathetically and to empathize with him. She is the bad guy and he is the good guy. His irresponsibility and misuse of resources are given legitimacy by the suggestion that his is an artistic, non-practical mindset. He cannot be held accountable. Since Carolyn's rage is often over-reactive, it is easy to forget that she has concrete reasons to be disappointed, annoyed, angry. Portrayed as vengeful, anti-pleasure, as dangerous and threatening, her moments of tenderness and sweetness are not sustained enough to counter the negatives. Even her sweetness is depicted as a manipulative gesture, whereas Woody's "sweet" demeanor is a mark of his artistic sensibility, one that enhances his value.

As an artist, Woody embodies the pleasure principle, the will to transgress. Always portrayed as gentle, his mild-mannered response to life that is infinitely more compelling than the work-hard-to-meet-your-responsibilities ethic Carolyn lives by. Being responsible seems to make her "crazy." In one scene the children are watching a basketball game when she encourages them to turn off the television to do schoolwork. They refuse to obey and she goes berserk. Woody intervenes not to offer support or reinforcement, but rather to take sides. Carolyn becomes the bad guy who wants to curtail the children's freedom to indulge in pleasure without responsibility. Woody responds to her rage by being physically coercive. Domestic violence in black life is sugar-coated—portraited as a family affair, one where there are no victims or abusers. In actuality, Carolyn has been humiliated and physically assaulted. Her demand that Woody leave makes him appear to be the victim and the children first attend to him, comforting and pleading with him not to go. Carolyn's pain goes unnoticed and unattended by her male children. It is Troy, who acts as caretaker, who assumes the traditional defined, desirable feminine role.

In sharp contrast to Carolyn, the ten-year-old Troy is concerned with femininity. Her mother expresses rage at not being able to "take a piss without six people hanging off my tits," repudiating conventional sexist thinking about woman's role. Troy is preoccupied with traditional notions of womanhood. Flirtatious, cute, she manipulates with practiced charm. It is she who advises her dad to take Carolyn on a date to make-up. Troy embodies all the desirable elements of sexist-defined femininity. Indeed, it is her capacity to escape into a world of romantic fantasy that makes her and everyone else ignore her internal anguish and torment. When she lies, steals, and cheats, her acts of defiance have no consequences. As the little princess of the household, she has privileges denied her brothers. When her mother is sick, it is only Troy who is sheltered from this painful reality—sent down South.

In the home of her Southern relatives, Troy meets a fair-skinned cousin who is portrayed as conventionally feminine in her concerns, though she is eager to bond with her guest. By contrast, Troy assumes a "bitchified role." She is hostile, suspicious, until charmed. Representing the light-skinned female as "good" and Troy as "bad," *Crooklyn*, like all Lee's films, perpetuates stereotypes that characterize darker-skinned females as "evil." While her cousin is loving, Troy is narcissistic and indifferent. When she decides to return home, it is her cousin who is sad that their time together is ending. She runs alongside the car that carries Troy away, tenderly waving. Troy appears unconcerned. This encounter prepares us for her transformation from girlhood princess to mini-matriarch.

Taken first to the hospital to see her mother when she arrives, Troy is given instructions as to how she must assume the caretaker role. Contemporary feminist thinkers are calling attention to girlhood as a time in female life when we have access to a greater sphere of power than that offered us in womanhood. No one in the film is concerned about the loss of Troy's girlhood. Yet the interruption of her girlhood stands in sharp contrast to her brothers' freedom to maintain their passions, their spirit of play. Clinton, the oldest boy, does not have to relinquish his passion for sports to become responsible because his mother is sick and dying. He can still be a child. Becoming a mini-matriarch requires of Troy that she relinquish all concern with pleasure and play, that she repress desire. Sexist/racist thinking about black female identity leads to cultural acceptance of the exploitation and denigration of black girlhood. Commenting on the way in which black girls are often forced to assume adult roles in her work *In the Company of My Sisters: Black Women and Self-Esteem*, Julia Boyd asserts: "Without fully understanding the adult tasks we were expected to perform, we filled shoes that were much too big for our small feet. Again, we did not have a choice and we weren't allowed to experience the full developmental process of girlhood." In keeping with the denigration of black girlhood in this society, Spike Lee romanticizes this violation by making it appear that it is a "natural "progression for Troy to become a matriarchal figure, that sexist gender politics are not coercively imposing this role via a process of socialization.

Carolyn did not make gender distinctions about household chores when she was well, and the movie fails to indicate why she has an unconvincing shift in attitude. As if to highlight patriarchal thinking that females are interchangeable, undifferentiated, and therefore one can replace another, the film in no way suggests there is anything wrong with a ten-year-old girl assuming an adult role in the household. This representation is affirmed. Indeed, the mother's dying is upstaged by the passing of the torch to Troy. The seriousness of Carolyn's illness is announced to the children by their father, who commands them to turn away from their gleeful watching of *Soul Train* to hear the news. Even in her absence, the mother/matriarch spoils their pleasure. Throughout *Crooklyn* Lee shows the importance of television in shaping their identities, their sense of self. While the boys panic emotionally when they hear the news, bursting into tears, Troy's feelings are hidden by a mask of indifference. The fact that the children obey the father in the mother's absence (not complaining in any way when he tells them to turn off the TV) suggests that he is better able to assume a responsible parental role when she is no longer present. Woody's transformation into a responsible adult with Carolyn's absence reinscribes sexist/racist thinking which suggests the presence of a "strong" black female necessarily emasculates the black male. When Carolyn dies her death is treated in a very matter-of-fact manner. We learn about it as the children casually discuss the funeral. We never see them grieve as a family. When Troy, who is emotionally numb, confronts the reality of this death, she does when jolted from sleep by what she imagines is the sound of the mother's angry raging voice. Bonding with the father in the kitchen, her suppressed grief does not unleash tears; instead, she vomits. This ritual cathartic cleansing is the rite of passage that signals her movement away from girlhood.

Taking her mother's place, Troy is no longer adventurous. She no longer roams the streets, exploring, discovering. She is bound to the house, to domestic life. We see her tending to the needs of her brothers, being the "little woman." Gone is the vulnerable, emotionally open girl who expressed a range of feelings, and in her place is a hard, impenetrable mask. Just as no one mourns the mother's death, no one mourns the loss of Troy's girlhood—the erasure of her adolescence. In their book *Failing at Fairness: How America's Schools Cheat Girls*, Myra and David Sadker document the pervasiveness of a "curricular sexism" that turns girls into "spectators instead of players." Troy, too, becomes a spectator, standing behind the gate looking out at life, a stern expression on her face.

Though dead, Carolyn reappears to reassure and affirm her daughter. This reappearance is yet another rejection of loss. The controlling, dominating mother remains present even when dead, visible only to her girl child. As a ghost, she becomes the guardian of patriarchy, who gives approval to Troy's submission and subjugation. While the male children and the grown-up dad continue to lead their autonomous lives, to express their creativity and will to explore, only Troy is confined, her creativity stifled. Since she is always and only a mother substitute, her power is more symbolic than real. Powerful black mothers, the film suggests, who work outside the home "fail" their families, as Carolyn does, by not fulfilling the sexist-defined feminine role. Their punishment is death. Yet even when she is dying of cancer and in serious pain, Carolyn takes the time to give lessons in sexism 101 to her daughter. While her career had ensured the family's economic survival, she does not encourage her daughter to think about a work future. The conventional sexism Carolyn expresses in these scenes runs counter to the values she has expressed throughout the movie. The Sadkers conclude their introductory chapter exposing the way sexist socialization robs girls of their potential with a section called "Silent Losses," which ends with this declaration: "If the cure for cancer is forming in the mind of one of our daughters, it is less likely to become a reality than if it is forming in the mind of one of our sons." Whereas *Crooklyn* attempts to counter racist assumptions about black identity, it completely valorizes and upholds sexist and misogynist thinking about gender roles. Order is restored in the Carmichael house when the dominating mother figure dies. The emergence of patriarchy is celebrated, marked by the subjugation of Troy. After the mother dies, all problems in the Carmichael household "magically" disappear. Life not only goes on without her, it is more harmonious.

Crooklyn constructs a redemptive fictive narrative for black life where the subjugation of the black female body is celebrated as that rite of passage which is restorative, which ensures family survival. Whether it is the grown woman's body erased in death or the little girl's body erased by the violent interruption of her girlhood, the sexist politics embedded in this film often go unnoticed by viewers whose attention is so riveted by the exploits of the male characters that they fail to either identify with the female characters or bring any critical perspective to these representations. In this way, audiences tacitly condone the patriarchal devaluation and erasure of rebellious black female subjectivity that this film depicts. Oppositional representations of blackness in the film deflect attention from the sexist politics that surface when race and gender converge. The naturalistic style of *Crooklyn* gives the viewer a sense of life "as is" rather than life as a fictive construction. Lee is indeed fictively re-imagining the seventies in this film and not merely providing a nostalgic portrait of the way things were. He constructs an ahistorical narrative wherein there is no meaningful convergence of black liberation and feminist politics. In actuality, black women active in national black-power groups were challenging sexism and insisting on a feminist agenda. In *Crooklyn* Lee's aggressively masculinist vision is diffused by excessive sentimentality, by the use of Troy as the central embodiment of the film's message. Writing about the dangers that rise when excessive emotionality is used as a cover-up for a different agenda, James Baldwin reminds us that "sentimentality is the ostentatious parading of excessive and spurious emotion. It is the mark of dishonesty, the inability to feel." Such emotional dishonesty emerges full force in *Crooklyn*. The focus on Troy's coming of age and her mother's death is really a nonthreatening cover for the more insidious anti-woman, anti-feminist vision of black family life that is the dominant theme of this film.

It is used to mask a repressive patriarchal valorization of black family life wherein the reinscription of sexist, idealized femininity symbolically rescues the family from dissolution. Death and dying are merely a subtext in *Crooklyn*, a diversionary ploy that creates a passive emotional backdrop onto which Lee imposes a vision of black family that is fundamentally conservative and that is in no way in opposition to the beliefs and values of white mainstream culture. The aspects of this film that are rooted in Lee's own life story are the most interesting; it is when he exploits those memories to create a counter worldview, one that will advance patriarchal thinking, that the narrative loses its appeal. Testifying that writing this script was cathartic, that it enabled her to confront the past, Joie Lee declares: "The emotional things that happen to you as a child, they're timeless, they stay with you until you deal with them. I definitely cleaned up some areas in my life that I hadn't dealt with before—like death." However, the film Spike Lee made does not confront death. In *Crooklyn* death and dying are realities males escape from. There is no redemptive healing of a gendered split between mind and body. Instead *Crooklyn* echoes the patriarchal vision celebrated in Norman O. Brown's *Life against Death*, where the hope is that "unrepressed man" would be rid of the nightmares ... haunting civilization" and that "freedom from those fantasies would also mean freedom from that disorder in the human body." The messiness of death is woman's work in *Crooklyn*. Expressing creativity, engaging pleasure and play is the way real men escape from the reality of death and dying. In the space of imaginative fantasy, Lee can resurrect the dead female mothering body and create a world where there is never any need to confront the limitations of the flesh, and therefore no place for loss and abandonment. In such a world there is no need for grief, since death has no meaning.

6

cool cynicism

Pulp Fiction

While all Quentin Tarantino's work so far plays around with the same themes (in regular Hollywood style), his stuff fascinates precisely because of the way each piece distinguishes itself, signifies on previous work—his or that of others. Cinematically, Tarantino is a master deconstructivist. No wonder then that everything he produces has such postmodern flavor and seduces both those who read and those who don't. When it comes to flavor he is definitely an equal opportunity employer. Unlike most contemporary border-crossing, "eat the other" culture bandits, he is not afraid to publicly pimp his wares.

Tarantino has the real nihilism of our times down. He represents the ultimate in "white cool": a hard-core cynical vision that would have everyone see racism, sexism, homophobia but behave as though none of that shit really matters, or if it does it means nothing 'cause none of it's gonna change, 'cause the real deal is that domination is here to stay—

going nowhere, and everybody is in on the act. Mind you, domination is always and only patriarchal—a dick thing.

In Tarantino's flicks women's liberation is just another scam, white women wanting to be let in on the deal even as they act just like that Enjoli commercial told us they would: they help "bring home the bacon, fry it up in the pan, and never let you forget" they're a w-o-m-a-n. Check out the white girls in *True Romance* (written by Tarantino) and *Pulp Fiction*. Even when they are absent à la *Reservoir Dogs*, that little opening dialogue about Madonna says it all—a piece of the action, their share of the cut. And black folks, personified simply and solely by black men, are just into a dick thing, wanting to be right there in the mix, doing the right thing in the dance hall of white supremacist capitalist patriarchy. Only the black woman who has no face—Jimmy's wife in *Pulp Fiction*, we see her only from the back—would raise any protest. The fun thing about Tarantino's films is that he makes that shit look so ridiculous you think everybody's gonna get it and see how absurd it all is. Well, that's when we enter the danger zone. Folks be laughing at the absurdity and clinging to it nevertheless. This happens first with *Reservoir Dogs*, which takes the hard-core white patriarchal dick thing and shows it for the vampire culture it really is. And when the white men have eaten each other up ('cause Tarantino would have us all know that when there are no white girls and niggers of all colors around, white boys are busy fucking each other over), it would be hard work for any viewer to see this film as a gleeful celebration of madness. *Reservoir Dogs* has a critical edge that is totally absent from *Pulp Fiction*, where everything is farce. Yeah, like it's really funny when Butch the hypermasculine phallic white boy—who has no name that means anything, who has no culture to be proud of, who comes straight out of childhood clinging to the anal-retentive timepiece of patriarchal imperialism—is exposed. Yet exposure does nothing to intervene on this evil, it merely graphically highlights it. As the work progresses, little Butch is still doing it or daddy— a real American hero.

Tarantino's films are the ultimate in sexy cover-ups of very unsexy mind-fuck. They titillate with subversive possibility (scenes that are so fine you are just blown away—like that wonderful moment when Vincent and Mia do the twist in *Pulp Fiction*), but then everything kinda comes right back to normal. And normal is finally a multicultural world with white supremacy intact. Note that even when the black male arrives at the top, as does Marcellus in *Pulp Fiction*—complete with a lying, cheating lapdog white child-woman wife—he is unmasked as only an imitation cowboy, not the real thing. And in case viewers haven't figured out that Marcellus ain't got what it takes, the film turns him into a welfare case—another needy victim who must ultimately rely on the kindness of strangers (i.e., Butch, the neoprimitive white colonizer, another modern-day Tarzan) to rescue him from the rape-in-progress that is his symbolic castration, his return to the jungle, to a lower rung on the food chain. No doubt had John Singleton, or any homeboy filmmaker, shot a scene as overtly gay-bashing as this one, progressive forces would have rallied en masse to condemn—to protest—to remind moviegoers that homophobia means genocide, that silence equals death. But it's fine to remain silent when the cool straight white boy from the wrong side of the tracks offers a movie that depicts the brutal slaughter and/or bashing of butt-fuckers and their playmates. If this isn't symbolic genocide of gay men, what is? Yet everyone has to pretend there's some hidden subversive message in the scenes. Hello! But that's the Tarantino message: everybody is in the corrupt jungle doing their own sweet version of the domination dance. This is multiculturalism with a chic neofascist twist.

Let's have a new world order in cinema: i.e., flashy flicks like Tarantino's, which kinda seem like the American version of Hanif Kureishi's stylish nihilism, so well done in *Sammy and Rosie Get Laid* and less well done in the rather tedious *London Kills Me*. Here most anybody can get a piece of the action, every ethnicity can be represented, can be fucked and fucked-over, 'cause in the end it's all shit. The real democracy, as *True Romance* tells us loud and clear, consists of a world where everyone has equal access to eating shit. Mind you, some folks come out of the shit smelling like roses, like our death-dealing white gender-equity couple in *True Romance*, who take their nuclear-family values to a warm place in the Third World and relax 'cause that's their way of getting away from it all. But when Jules (Samuel Jackson), our resident black male preacher-philosopher death-dealing mammified intellectual (he does pull out the tit and feed knowledge to everyone in *Pulp Fiction*:—magnificently, I might add—a stunning performance—particularly that closing monologue), decides *he* wants out of the rat race, he doesn't get to leave the plantation with riches in hand. John Travolta's Massa Junior makes it clear he must go his way destitute. 'Cause in the real plantation economy, no matter how many borders are crossed, no matter how many cultures are mixed and how much shit is appropriated (the everybody-is-a-nigger version of "We are the World"), when it comes right down to it Jules as our resident enlightened dharma bum has nowhere to go—no Third World playground he can retire to.

No doubt that retro hairdo he sports throughout the film keeps him from charting a new journey. It's his own signifying monkey. No matter how serious Jules's rap, that hair always intervenes to let the audience know not to take him too seriously. That hair is kinda like another character in the film. Talking back to Jules as he talks to us, it undermines his words every step of the way. 'Cause that hair is like a minstrel thing— telling the world that the black preacher-philosopher is ultimately just an intellectual arty white boy in drag, aping, imitating, and mouthing intellectual rhetoric that he can't quite use to help him make sense of his own life. Well, in steps the interpreter of dreams, Vincent "Lone Ranger" Vega, who has no trouble spelling out in plain speech to his beloved Tonto, alas Jules, that there will be no redemptive future for him—that if he leaves the white-boy setup and abandons his criminal destiny he will just be another homeless black man on the street, a bum. In the new world order Tarantino creates in *Pulp Fiction*, dead white-boy star-culture bandits live again and, like their ethnographic counterparts, know black folks better than we could ever know ourselves.

Well, as Tarantino's work lets us know, it's a sick, motherfucking world and we may as well get used to that fact, laugh at it, and go on our way, 'cause ain't nothing changing—and that's Hollywood, the place where white supremacist capitalist patriarchy can keep reinventing itself, no matter how many times the West is decentered. Hollywood is the new plantation, getting more chic with the times. That Tarantino can call it out, tell it like it is, give the ultimate "read," the on-the-down-low diss, is part of the magic. It's deconstruction at its finest—all dressed up with no place to go. That is, unless you, the viewer, got somewhere you wanna take it, 'cause this is the new crossover model—the new multicultural survival kit. It can be all things to all people. Like you can choose to come away from *Reservoir Dogs* thinking. Later for white supremacy, racism, and fascism, 'cause when that shit is on display anybody can see how funky it is. Or maybe you could even catch that moment in *Pulp Fiction* when Butch and Marcellus are boy-bonding, with the tie that binds being their shared fear of homosexual rape, and think, Doesn't Tarantino just name the homophobia of our times—calling out the way patriarchal homosocial bonding mediates racism? (I mean Burch and Marcellus, they end up like brothers.) But if you choose to look at it all from the right, that's okay too. 'Cause the shit smells the same whether you are liberal or conservative, on the right or the left. There is no way out.

If you don't get the picture, check out the fate of our cross-race boy-bonding team, Vincent and Jules. Throughout the movie we admire their cross-racial, funky solidarity, their shared cool, but this difference don't last: they don't end up as "brothers" 'cause they are both ultimately disloyal to the structure they should uphold (Vincent by taking a break and reading, i.e. sleeping on the job, Jules by wanting to retire into nothingness). The film takes no note of Vincent's death by showing Jules either grieving or seeking revenge. Like all the meaningful emotional ties in the film (Vincent and Mia) this one doesn't count for shit. In the end loyalty sucks. Betrayal delivers the goods.

Well, as the preacher man told us at the end of *Pulp Fiction*, the tyranny of evil does not disappear just because we change the channel. Tarantino shows us in his films that a good cynical read on life can be compelling, entertaining, and downright satisfying—so much so that everyone will come back for more. But as the poet Amiri Baraka reminds us, "Cynicism is not revolutionary."

7

mock feminism

Waiting to Exhale

In the past a black film was usually seen as a film by a black filmmaker focusing on some aspect of black life. More recently the "idea" of a "black film" has been appropriated as a way to market films that are basically written and produced by white people as though they in act represent and offer us—"authentic" blackness. It does not matter that progressive black filmmakers and critics challenge essentialist notions of black authenticity, even going so far as to rethink and interrogate the notion of black film. These groups do not have access to the levels of marketing and publicity that can repackage authentic blackness commodified and sell it as the "real" thing. This was certainly the case with the marketing and publicity for the film *Waiting to Exhale*.

When Kevin Costner produced and starred in the film *The Bodyguard* with Whitney Houston as co-star, the film focused on a black family. No one ever thought to market it as a black film. Indeed, many black people refused to see the film because they were so disgusted by this portrayal of interracial love. No one showed much curiosity about the racial identity of the screenwriters or for that matter, anybody behind the scenes of this film. It was not seen as having any importance, for black women by the white-dominated mass media. Yet *Waiting to Exhale*'s claim to blackness, and black authenticity, is almost as dubious as any such claim being made about *The Bodyguard*. However, that claim could be easily made because a black woman writer wrote the book on which the movie was based. The hiring of a fledgling black director received no critical comment. Everyone behaved as though it was just normal Hollywood practice to offer the directorship of a major big-budget Hollywood film to someone who might not know what they are doing.

The screenplay was written by a white man, but if we are to believe everything we read in newspapers and popular magazines, Terry McMillan assisted with the writing. Of course, having her name tacked onto the writing process was a great way to protect the film from the critique that its "authentic blackness" was somehow undermined by white-male interpretation. Alice Walker had no such luck when her book *The Color Purple* was made into a movie by Steven Spielberg. No one thought this was a black film. And very few viewers were surprised that what we saw on the screen had little relationship to Alice Walker's novel.

Careful publicity and marketing ensured that *Waiting to Exhale* would not be subjected to these critiques; all acts of appropriation were carefully hidden behind the labeling of this film as authentically a black woman's story. Before anyone could become upset that a black woman was not hired to direct the film, McMillan told the world in *Movieland* magazine that those experienced black women directors in Hollywood just were not capable of doing the job. She made the same critique of the black woman writer who was initially hired to write the screenplay. From all accounts (most of them given by the diva herself) it appears that Terry McMillan is the only competent black woman on the Hollywood scene and she just recently arrived.

It's difficult to know what is more disturbing: McMillan's complicity with the various acts of white supremacist capitalist patriarchal cultural appropriation that resulted in a film as lightweight and basically bad as *Waiting to Exhale*, or the public's passive celebratory consumption of this trash as giving the real scoop about black women's lives. Some bad films are at least entertaining. This was just an utterly boring show. That masses of black women could be cajoled by mass media coverage and successful seductive marketing (the primary ploy being that this is the first film ever that four black women have been the major stars of a Hollywood film) to embrace this cultural product was a primary indication that this is not a society where moviegoers are encouraged to think critically about what they see on the screen.

When a film that's basically about the trials and tribulations of four professional heterosexual black women who are willing to do anything to get and keep a man is offered as a "feminist" narrative, it's truly a testament to the power of the mainstream to co-opt progressive social movements and strip them of all political meaning through a series of contemptuous ridiculous representations. Terry McMillan's novel *Waiting to Exhale* was not a feminist book and it was not transformed into a feminist film. It did not even become a film that made use of any of the progressive politics around race and gender that was evoked however casually in the novel itself.

The film *Waiting to Exhale* took the novelistic images of professional black women concerned with issues of racial uplift and gender equality and turned them into a progression of racist, sexist stereotypes that features happy darkies who are all singing, dancing, fucking, and having a merry old time even in the midst of sad times and tragic moments. What we saw on the screen was not black women talking about love or the meaning of partnership and marriage in their lives. We saw four incredibly glamorous women obsessed with getting a man, with status, material success and petty competition with other women (especially white women). In the book one of the women, Gloria, owns a beauty parlor; she is always, always working, which is what happens when you run a small business. In the movie, girlfriend hardly ever works because she is too busy cooking tantalizing meals for the neighbor next door. In this movie food is on her mind and she forgets all about work, except for an occasional phone call to see how everything is going. Let's not forget the truly fictive utopian moment in this film that occurs when Bernie goes to court divorcing her husband and wins tons of money. This is so in the book as well. Funny though, the novel ends with her giving the money away, highlighting her generosity and her politics. McMillan writes: "She also wouldn't have to worry about selling the house now. But Bernadine wasn't taking that fucker off the market. She'd drop the price. And she'd send a nice check to the United Negro College Fund, something she'd always wanted to do. She'd help feed some of those kids in Africa she'd seen on TV at night ... Maybe she'd send some change to the Urban League and the NAACP and she'd definitely help out some of those programs that BWOTM [Black Women on the MOVE] had been trying to get off the ground for the last hundred years. At the rate she was going, Bernadine had already given away over a million dollars." Definitely not a "material girl." It would have taken only one less scene of pleasure fucking for audiences to have witnessed Bernie writing these checks with a nice voice-over. But, alas, such an image might have ruined the racist, sexist stereotype of black women being hard, angry, and just plain greedy. No doubt the writers of the screenplay felt these "familiar" stereotypes would guarantee the movie its crossover appeal.

Concurrently, no doubt it helps that crossover appeal to set up stereotypically racist, sexist conflicts between white women and black women (where if we are to believe the logic of the film, the white woman gets "her" black man in the end). Let's remember. In the novel the book is based on, only one black man declares his love for a white woman. The man Bernie meets, the lawyer James, is thinking of divorcing his white wife, who is dying of cancer, but he loyally stays with her until her death, even though he makes it very clear that the love has long since left their marriage. Declaring his undying love for Bernie, James moves across the country to join her, sets up a law practice, and gets involved with "a coalition to stop the liquor board from allowing so many liquor stores in the black community." Well, not in this movie! The screen character James declares undying love for his sick white wife. Check out the difference between the letter he writes in the novel. Here is an excerpt: "I know you probably thought that night was just something frivolous but like I told you before I left, it meant more to me than that. Much more. I buried my wife back in August, and for her sake, I'm glad she's not suffering anymore ... I want to see you again, Bernadine, and not for another one-nighter, either. If there's any truth to what's known as a 'soul mate,' then you're as close to it as I've ever come ... I'm not interested in playing games, or starting something I can't finish. I play for keeps, and I'm not some dude just out to have a good time ... I knew I was in love with you long before we ever turned the key to that hotel room." The image of black masculinity that comes through in this letter is that of a man of integrity who is compassionate, in touch with his feelings, and able to take responsibility for his actions.

In the movie version of *Waiting to Exhale*, no black man involved with a black woman possesses these qualities. In contrast to what happens in the book, in the film, James does not have a one-nighter with Bernie, because he is depicted as utterly devoted to his white wife. Here are relevant passages from the letter he writes to Bernie that audiences hear at the movie: "What I feel for you has never undercut the love I have for my wife. How is that possible? I watch her everyday. So beautiful and brave. I just want to give her everything I've got in me. Every moment. She's hanging on, fighting to be here for me. And when she sleeps, I cry. Over how amazing she is, and how lucky I've been to have her in my life." There may not have been any white women as central characters in this film, but this letter certainly places the dying white wife at the center of things. Completely rewriting the letter that appears in the novel, which only concerns James's love and devotion to Bernie, so that the white wife (dead in the book but brought back to life on-screen) is the recipient of James's love was no doubt another ploy to reach the crossover audience: the masses of white women consumers that might not have been interested in this film if it had really been about black women.

Ultimately, only white women have committed relationships with black men in the film. Not only do these screen images reinforce stereotypes, the screenplay was written in such a way as to actively perpetuate them. Catfights between women, both real and symbolic, were clearly seen by the screenwriters as likely to be more entertaining to moviegoing audiences than the portrayal of a divorced black woman unexpectedly meeting her true love—an honest, caring, responsible, mature, tender, and loving black man who delivers the goods. Black women are portrayed as so shrewish in this film that Lionel's betrayal of Bernie appears to be no more than an act of self-defense. The film suggests that Lionel is merely trying to get away from the black bitch who barges in on him at work and physically attacks his meek and loving white wife. To think that Terry McMillan was one of the screenwriters makes it all the more disheartening. Did she forget that she had written a far more emotionally complex and progressive vision of black female-male relationships in her novel?

While we may all know some over-thirty black women who are desperate to get a man by any means necessary and plenty of young black females who fear that they may never find a man and are willing to be downright foolish in their pursuit of one, the film was so simplistic and denigrating in its characterization of black womanhood that everyone should be outraged to be told that it is "for us." Or worse yet, as a reporter wrote in *Newsweek*, "This is our million man march." Whether you supported the march or not (and I did not, for many of the same reasons I find this film appalling), let's get this straight: We are being told, and are telling ourselves that black men need a political march and black women need a movie. Mind you—not a political film but one where the black female "stars" spend most of their time chainsmoking themselves to death (let's not forget that Gloria did not have enough breath to blow out her birthday candle) and drowning their sorrows in alcohol. No doubt McMillan's knowledge of how many black people die from lung cancer and alcoholism influenced her decision to write useful, unpreachy critiques of these addictions in her novel. In the novel the characters who smoke are trying to stop and Black Women on the Move are fighting to close down liquor stores. None of these actions fulfill racist fantasies. It's no accident that just the opposite images appear on the screen. Smoking is so omnipresent in every scene that many of us were waiting to see a promotional credit for the tobacco industry.

Perhaps the most twisted and perverse aspect of this film is the way it was marketed as being about girlfriend bonding. How about that scene where Robin shares her real-life trauma with Savannah, who is busy looking the other way and simply does not respond. Meaningful girl-friend bonding is not about the codependency that is imaged in this film. At its best *Waiting to Exhale* is a film about black women helping each other to stay stuck. Do we really believe that moment when Savannah rudely disses Kenneth (even though the film has in no way constructed him as a lying cheating dog) to be a moment of profound "feminist" awakening. Suddenly audiences are encouraged to believe that she realizes the dilem-mas of being involved with a married man, even one who has filed for a divorce. Why not depict a little mature communication between a black man and a black woman. No doubt that too would not have been enter-taining to crossover audiences. Better to give them what they are used to, stereotypical representations of black males as always and only lying, cheating dogs (that is, when they are involved with black women) and professional black women as wild, irrational, castrating bitch goddesses.

Nothing was more depressing than hearing individual black women offering personal testimony that these shallow screen images are "realis-tic portrayals" of their experience. If this is the world of black gender relations as they know it, no wonder black men and women are in seri-ous crisis. Obviously, it is difficult for many straight black women to find black male partners and/or husbands. Though it is hard to believe that black women as conventionally feminine, beautiful, glamorous, and just plain dumb as the girlfriends in this film can't get men (Bernie has an MBA, helped start the business, but is clueless about everything that concerns money; Robin is willing to have unsafe sex and celebrate an unplanned pregnancy with a partner who may be a drug addict; Gloria, who would rather cook food for her man any day than go to work;

Savannah has sex at the drop of a hat, even when she does not want to get involved). In the real world these are the women who have men standing in line.

However, if they and other black women internalize the messages in *Waiting to Exhale* they will come to their senses and see that, according to the film, black men are really undesirable mates for black women. Actually, lots of younger black women, and their over-thirty counterparts, go to see *Waiting to Exhale* to have their worst fears affirmed: that black men are irresponsible and uncaring; that black women, no matter how attractive, will still be hurt and abandoned, and that ultimately they will probably be alone and unloved. Perhaps it feels less like cultural genocide to have these messages of self-loathing and disempowerment brought to them by four beautiful black female "stars."

Black women seeking to learn anything about gender relationships from this film will be more empowered if we identify with the one black female character who rarely speaks. She is the graceful, attractive, brown-skinned lawyer with naturally braided hair who is a professional who knows her job and is also able to bond emotionally with her clients. Not only does she stand for gender justice (the one glimpse of empowering feminist womanhood we see in this film), she achieves that end without ever putting men down or competing with any woman. While we never see her with a male partner, she acts with confident self-esteem and shows fulfillment in a job well done.

The monetary success of a trashy film like *Waiting to Exhale*, with its heavy sentimentality and predicable melodrama shows that Hollywood recognizes that blackness as a commodity can be exploited to bring in the bucks. Dangerously, it also shows that the same old racist/sexist stereotypes can be appropriated and served up to the public in a new and more fashionable disguise. While it serves the financial interests of Hollywood and McMillan's own bank account for her to deflect away from critiques that examine the politics underlying these representations and their behind-the-scenes modes of production by ways of witty assertions that the novel and the film are "forms of entertainment, not anthropological studies," in actuality the creators of this film are as accountable for their work as their predecessors. Significantly, contemporary critiques of racial essentialism completely disrupt the notion that anything a black artist creates is inherently radical, progressive, or more likely to reflect a break with white supremacist representations. It has become most evident that as black artists seek a "crossover" success, the representations they create usually mirror dominant stereotypes. After a barrage of publicity and marketing that encouraged black people, and black women in particular, to see *Waiting to Exhale* as fictive ethnography, McMillan is being more than a bit disingenuous when she suggests that the film should not be seen this way. In her essay, "Who's Doin' the Twist: Notes Toward a Politics of Appropriation," cultural critic Coco Fusco reminds us that we must continually critique this genre in both its pure and impure forms. "Ethnographic cinema, in light of its historical connection to colonialist adventurism, and decades of debate about the ethics of representing documentary subjects, is a genre that demands a special degree of scrutiny." Just because writers and directors are black does not exempt them from scrutiny. The black female who wrote a letter to the *New York Times* calling attention to the way this film impedes the struggle to create new images of blackness on the screen was surely right when she insisted that had everyone involved in the production of this film been white and male, its blatantly racist and sexist standpoints would not have gone unchallenged.

8

Kids

transgressive subject matter—
reactionary film

Anyone seeing the previews for Larry Clark's *Kids* knows pretty much what the content of the film will be. Nothing will change when the movie begins, it will just be a more extended, more graphic account, both visual and verbal, of the short segments featured in the previews. Evidently, for a helluva lot of people this makes for exciting moviegoing. For some of us, having experienced most of what the movie had to offer in a few short moments, the actual watching of the film was boring. On one hand I had the sensation of wasting my time, being fucking bored out of my mind, on the other hand I struggled with blind rage, fierce anger at the way this film has been received and talked about. Not unlike the celebrated mystical book, *The Celestine Prophecy*, which chronicles the spiritual journey of a lone white man seeking truth and redemption in the Third World and which initially failed to convey in its advertising and promotional material that it was indeed a fiction and not a true story, *Kids* is presented and talked about as though it were a documentary ethnographic film sharing of the life of today's reckless teenagers. In actuality, it is a fiction, the product of Clark's imaginative obsession with adolescent hedonism. Speaking about the teenage actors in his review of the movie, a friend of the filmmaker Jim Lews writes that those actors tell a story in "performances so alive and on the money that one can easily forget that the film is fiction, and that every line is carefully scripted." Much of the hype around the film encourages forgetfulness. And often the film is presented as though it were Clark's documentary expose.

While it is really true that Clark hangs out with teenagers, he has the power to appropriate their narratives and render the private public through the filmmaking process in a way that they do not. Without naming any moral judgments about his being "in the scene," a phrase one of the teenagers used to describe his engagement with them prior to the making of the film, critics would be remiss not to raise questions about the myriad ways Clark appropriates the "true confessions" of his teenage cohorts, or the way he idealizes and glamorizes the harsh realities of their life in this film. Even though some folks have raised ethical questions about the fifty-two-year-old photographer-turned-filmmaker's interest in teenagers, they do not talk about the way in which the politics of age, race, sex, and class shape his vision. In an interview with *Spin* magazine Clark makes the declaration: "Sometimes you have to cut through the bullshit and tell the truth." The question of course is, Whose truth is the film telling?

Very few discussions of *Kids* talk about the actual content of the film. Clearly, Clark's fascination is not with the overall mindset of urban born-to-be-wild teenagers but more specifically with their attitudes toward sex and drugs. To be even more specific, he is not concerned with teenagers. This film could easily have been called "white kids." Indeed, the primary subjects of the film, the characters we hear the most from, are two white male teenagers, Telly and Casper, and a teenage white female, Jennie. Their favorite topic to discuss is fucking. When they are not fucking or talking about fucking, they are into scoring drugs, hanging out, getting high, and partying. Much of their language and manner of dress is appropriated from vernacular street culture, mostly the styles of black people and other people of color. Frankly, few people would find this film shocking or even mildly disturbing if its primary subjects were inner-city teenage black kids. That the "stars" of this show are white kids makes this film a hot topic. Many see it as documenting a crisis—the corruption of today's youth. The main agent of this corruption is never explicitly named in the film. Yet, since so much of the "style" of the white kids is based on the popular culture and mores of the on white poor, one more or less gets the idea that these influences are the corrupting ones. For example, rap music is always lurking in the background whenever negative shit is happening. The kids' appropriation of black street culture is mediated, however, by the heavy-handed racism expressed by the two "star" white boys.

"Nigger" is their favorite word to use when expressing contempt for black folks and just about everybody else they want to subordinate. Matter-of-fact white supremacy in this film takes a back seat only to the ruling ideology of sexism and misogyny. Now, there are two words that rarely come up in reviews of this film. Yet the spectacle of teenage sexuality that *Kids* exploits is one that is shaped and informed solely by patriarchal attitudes. The word "bitch" is the companion term to "nigger" in the film—used both to refer to all girls and to contemptuously put down any boy who is not toeing the macho line. From beginning to end the focus of *Kids* is on the two white boys. And this, despite parallel documentarylike scenes where we see first a group of teenage boys and then a group of girls talking about sex. As the film progresses, it is clear that though the girls can talk sex just as down and dirty, as rough and raw as the boys, it is only the girls who are getting fucked and fucked-over. In Telly and Casper's world, as in the real world these characters mirror, racism and sexism converge.

The racism of Telly and his buddy Casper is reflected in the casting choices and representations of the female characters, whose ethnic backgrounds are unclear. It is clear that the non-white-skinned females are cast (as is typical in Hollywood cinema) in ways that conform to racist, sexist stereotypes. They are the females who are depicted as sexually loose and wild. They are the freaks. The girls who have lots of unsafe sex, who suck dick, who take it in the ass, who do anything. Their fate is unimportant. The only girl the film highlights is the white-skinned Jennie, who, as the other, mostly nonwhite girls talk about their sexual experiences, confesses that she has had sex only once, with Telly. Even though she is no longer a virgin, against the backdrop of the other girls she appears to represent the world of innocence. Consequently, as is usually the case in racist, sexist iconography, she is the only girl who can be truly violated. Even though the thirteen-year-old, darker-skinned Darcy is targeted by Telly, who is HIV positive (though the film implies he has no awareness of this), and is seductively pressured into having unprotected sexual intercourse with him, she is never portrayed as a victim. Jennie is the only character sympathetically debited as a victim in this film. Even though she searches for Telly to confront him with the knowledge that he has transmitted the virus to her, when she enters the bedroom and finds him fucking Darcy (who is clearly experiencing pain, not pleasure), she simply closes the door and weeps. Drugged and practically comatose, she is then raped by Casper. At this point her body, indeed her very being, is subsumed by the dominating male body. We never see her face. We merely see Casper and hear the sounds of him raping her. Casper's rape of Jennie is parallel to Telly's seductive violation of Darcy. Yet in the end the camera will return to the bedroom and in soft lighting focus on the naked bodies of Telly and Darcy tenderly sleeping together. Suddenly, they are made to look like innocent children. This scene undermines the violence of their encounter by suggesting that bliss has been the outcome. Similarly, Casper's violent rape of Jennie is mediated by the presence of his voice and the absence of her own, of her living corporeality—Casper speaks to her as though they were sharing a moment of consensual pleasure. His voice distracts from the violence of his actions.

Cinematically, Jennie is represented as the only real casualty of teenage white male nihilistic hedonism. Her traumatic powerlessness lends the film its only pathos. All the other characters are presented as hardened. While the audience may see them as tragic, this is not the message the film conveys. Their complete lack of remorse after the brutal beating of an anonymous black male in the park provides another opportunity for the teenagers to register white supremacist patriarchal cool. The fact that the filmmaker throws a black male friend of Telly and Casper's into the mix serves to distract from the racism underlying the construction and shooting of this scene. Yet the way in which the camera fixates on his image, lingering, reveals the self-conscious awareness of this scene's artistic direction. Had there not been a dark-skinned black male in the mix, this scene would overtly announce its exploitation of racism. It's no accident that the only two prominent black male teenagers in this film are both dark-skinned. In this fictive New York City teenage transgressive utopia, no dark-skinned black girls exist. Violence toward aggressive black male strangers is acceptable to moviegoing audiences in a society that has become completely socialized by the mass media to see blackness as the sign of a threat.

Reviewers show no interest in commenting on this violence. They reserve their comments for Jennie. The trope of an innocent "white" virgin girl assaulted by dark evil forces is completely exploited in this film. Unlike the other kids in the film, Jennie always has money. She roams the city in taxis. While we know nothing of her class background, we do get a glimpse of Telly's home environment. He has a father that works, a mother who stays home looking after her baby. His home is patriarchal (we know this because the mother informs us that her husband has told her not to give Telly money). Of course, her refusal means nothing, for Telly is able to exploit her, stealing her hidden financial resources, just as he exploits the girls whose virginity he steals. Telly with his broken teeth and his not very expensive clothes does not represent the world of class privilege, though his best buddy, Casper, seems to. Casper's outfit is carefully chosen so that he can be in the groove. Though he looks like the idealized Hollywood glamour boy, Casper's apparent lack of interest in exploiting females throughout much of the film leads him to appear more innocent than Telly. In fact, the film suggests that the boys' homosocial bond masks Caper's envy of Telly, who is better at exploiting girls.

All the usual race, sex, and class hierarchies remain intact in the fictive teenage world Clark creates in *Kids*. Even when Ruby and Jennie are tested to see if they are HIV positive, the nurses are racially matched. Ruby has a dark-skinned nurse who is as nonchalant about the issue as is the teenager. Jennie has a white nurse who behaves as though she is both bored and indifferent. The only adults we see in this film are women. They are either hardened by experience (i.e., the nurses) or easily duped (i.e., Telly's mother). They are all ineffectual, unable to make a meaningful, constructive intervention in the lives of the teenagers they encounter.

Adults are not the enemy in this film. They are simply not on the scene. Many viewers will see their absence as the explanation for the corruption of these kids. This seems ironic, since these are not radical kids who have alternative values. The racist, sexist attitudes they exhibit, their addictions to substances are merely graphic, hyperbolic expressions of the attitudes and values that are the norm in this society. There are no subversive values in *Kids*, no radical political standpoints. All the forms of transgression the teenagers embrace are just violently exaggerated mirroring of the dominant conservative values of the culture. That so many viewers see this film as documenting a shocking hidden world of teenage transgression shows that most folks are in denial about the values they collectively uphold and perpetuate. Far from being a film that indicts teenagers, if there is any crime *Kids* exposes it is that this is the culture that white supremacist capitalist patriarchy produces. These kids are merely taking it to the extreme, acting out to the max. And here showing cannot be confused with critique. *Kids* lacks a critical edge. There is no resistance to domination in this film, merely a primitive embrace of ruling paradigms. The casualties are all the same as in the real world we live in, poor and working-class boys; people of color, especially black males; vulnerable colored girls; and good white girls who would be safe if they just stayed home.

It is no accident that most viewers are apparently unable to see that *Kids* merely mirrors the reactionary values that are the norm in our consumer culture (this is what makes the film boring to some of us, even as it simultaneously threatens). As Susan Bordo maintains in *Unbearable Weight: Feminism, Western Culture, and the Body*, advanced consumer capitalism tells us that as consumers "we must display a boundless capacity to capitulate to desire and indulge in impulse; we must hunger for constant and immediate satisfaction." Unlike most citizens in this nation, the fictive teenagers in *Kids* and their real-life counterparts are not responding effectively to societal attempts to regulate their desire. They are out of control. Much of the film's popularity rests on the voyeuristic pleasure that audiences, whose desires are rigidly regulated, experience as they watch a fictive world of adolescent nihilistic hedonism. Although they might not identify with the characters in the film, they nostalgically identify with the longing to act on impulse, with life-threatening narcissism.

To aid in this seductive process of identification, which deflects attention from *Kids'* primary emphasis on two teenage white males, the film relies on familiar strategies more commonly used in the construction of patriarchal pornography and erotica. Clark skillfully draws on his strengths as a photographer by using short splices of footage that give a still-photograph effect. Several shots of the young boys sleeping at the party illustrate this technique. In her book *The Imaginary Domain*, Drucilla Cornell defines pornography as "the explicit presentation and depiction of sexual organs and sexual acts with the aim of arousing sexual feeling through either (a) the portrayal of violence and coercion against women as the basis of heterosexual desire or (b) the graphic description of woman's body as dismembered by her being reduced to her sex and stripped completely of her personhood as she is portrayed in involvement in explicit sex acts." Using this definition, *Kids* can be seen as a film that makes use of the pornographic imagination. This is personified by intense cinematic focus on the phallic imaginary. From beginning to end

Kids is primarily about masculinity and masculine sexuality. Initially this focus is masked by the inclusion of female voices in a manner suggestive of gender parity. But as the action unfolds, it becomes evident that *Kids* is a film about the way white teenage male desire is organized around phallic power, around the power to dominate and penetrate. Telly's voice is there both at the beginning of the film and at the end at once announcing and glorifying this standpoint. It is Telly's pornographic imagination that shapes the narrative. His sexual fantasies dominate. Audiences are invited to be fantasized participants in the scenes presented to them. Whether we want to be or not, we become voyeurs in Telly's quest to find new virgins to penetrate, new bodies to conquer. And as Jennie confesses in the opening scenes of the film, the cause of the pain she feels is not that she has had her one and only act of sexual intercourse with Telly but that Telly no longer speaks to her. This is the ultimate moment of erasure. Since she desired to be with him, his triumph lies not in having possessed her sexually against her will but rather in rendering her solely a sexual object by refusing to acknowledge her presence, by refusing to establish and maintain ongoing contact.

The filmmaker's positioning of nonwhite females in sexually objectified roles is in keeping with traditions of pornographic representation and racial fascination that figure darker-skinned females as the ultimate "bad girls." In *Kids* the more sexually experienced nonwhite females are seen as too threatening and therefore not desirable. They cannot be controlled in the way inexperienced girls, virgins, can be manipulated and violated. Drucilla Cornell writes about the psychoanalytic understanding of the terror and fantasy of control that are central to the pornographic imagination, suggesting that "in this reductionist scene there are not women and men, but picks and holes." She contends: "It is this reduction to exaggerated gender identities as graphically depicted body parts that leads pornography to bolster and express what Louise Kaplan has called the 'perverse strategy.' For Kaplan, the perverse strategy is an over-investment in rigid gender identities as they are imagined in early childhood to be associated with the Big Others who have power." *Kids* celebrates patriarchal phallic agency. It in no way critiques. Merely showing that females are violated so that teenage boys can feel phallic potency in no way serves as a critique. Sub-textually the film in strategy and cinematography allies itself with phallocentrism and patriarchy. Even when two girls are kissing each other in one scene, their sexual agency is soon disrupted by male onlookers who insisted that they do it again for their voyeuristic pleasure. Even though the girls refuse, this is yet another scene that insists on the primacy of the patriarchal phallic standpoint.

There is nothing in *Kids* that indicates a concern with highlighting nonsexist perspectives. The coercion Cornell insists is central to the pornographic act remains the driving force of the film. Discussing the process of directing *Kids* with his colleague Jim Lewis, Clark states: "When I made the film I was still their friend, but I was also an authority figure. They were working. I was the boss; I was a dictator, I could be mean and yell at them, threaten them. It got pretty rough." In a perfect moment of heterosexist homosocial bonding, Jim Lewis adds his interpretation to Clark's statement: "Still, you can tell from the openness of the performances that the kids trust him completely, and you can tell from the film itself that they have no reason not to: All he wants is to show the disturbing beauty of their lives." Since the film reveals much that is tragic, one can only imagine that this 'beauty" can be evoked only by the imposition of an adult voyeuristic imagination that disidentifies with the actual experience of painful or traumatic adolescence, where the prevailing markers of abuse and abandonment must remain psychically buried if one is to project a fantasy of romanticized rebellion.

Given the reactionary vision that lies at the heart of *Kids*, it is not surprising that the movie is frequently talked about, by both the filmmaker and a host of individuals promoting it, as a useful intervention—a film parents should see with their kids. Of course, this group rarely talks about what "lessons" they hope will be learned from seeing the film. More conservative viewers urge teenagers to see it so that they will be so horrified they will not follow the path these fictive kids have taken. And of course young females are urged to see it by parents who want their daughters to understand not only that sex is bad but that their lives can be ruined forever by one night of unprotected intercourse. None of these lessons are progressive interventions.

Since the film in no way indicts patriarchal parenting, it can act in complicity with those cultural forces that view the dilemmas in teenage life as solely a function of the absence of coercive control and authority. Moreover, only individuals who have absolutely no awareness of the culture of inner-city poor and often homeless teenagers can be awed and shocked by this film. Given the persistence of class elitism, of racism and white supremacy, of fierce antifeminist backlash, and the desire on the part of the right to bring back rigid controls that will regulate desire, pleasure, sexuality, racial mixing, there is certainly a need for films that offer constructive insights, progressive alternatives. *Kids* is not that film.

The script is so narrowly focused on its concerns that it sheds no light on the complex reality of urban teenagers. Ironically, despite the film's transgressive allure, it will undoubtedly be used as evidence to support the notion that there must be greater repression, more surveillance, a return to benevolent, good old-fashioned white supremacist capitalist patriarchal values to keep teenagers on the "Right" path. Subversion does not happen simply because images are transgressive. *Kids* is the escapist fantasy of an adult imagination. The fact that the script was written by a young adult does not alter its standpoint or message. The playful and at times daring aspects of *Kids* that superficially appear to be subversive are not, precisely because Clark cleverly effaces the harsh social reality that is leading teenagers to nihilistic hedonism. Romanticizing this response is the way our culture continues its abuse and betrayal of kids in New York City, of kids everywhere. Like the sex and drugs in the film, such a response serves only to divert the focus from the real issues: patriarchal parenting, class exploitation, race and gender domination, exclusion and subordination.

9

artistic integrity:

race and accountability

Most filmmakers do not have to deal with the issue of race. When white males make films with all white subjects or with people of color, their "right" to do so is not questioned. No one asks a white filmmaker in the United States or Britain who makes a film with only white characters if he or she is a white supremacist. The assumption is that the art they create reflects the world as they know it, or certainly as it interests them. However, when a black filmmaker, or for that matter any filmmaker of color, makes a work that focuses solely on subjects exclusively black, or white, they are asked by critics and their audiences to justify their choices and to assume political accountability for the quality of their representations. Embedded in the body of ideas that ensure that some folks will be interrogated about their choices and others not is the both racist and sexist assumption that integrity of artistic vision matters more to the filmmaker who is white and male than to those who are nonwhite and/or female.

Ironically, more than any group white men are able to make films without being subjected to a constant demand that their work not perpetuate systems of domination based on race, class, and gender. As a consequence it is this work that is usually the most unthinking and careless in its depictions of groups that are marginalized by these institutionalized structures of exploitation and oppression. We might have witnessed a cultural revolution in the images of people of color and white women in cinema long ago had white male filmmakers been subjected to even a fraction of the critique that is directed at filmmakers from marginalized groups. Frankly, a little up-front interrogation can be useful. It can inspire any artist to be more vigilant. White male artists have not necessarily benefitted from the absence of certain pressures that would compel them to address their role in creating work that perpetuates domination. Filmmakers probably have more awareness than other people about the power of moving images in an age of ever-increasing illiteracy. Movies teach so much because the language of both images and words that they use is accessible. Luckily, individual white male filmmakers have begun to think critically some of the time about depictures of race, gender, or nationality. Certainly, it would benefit all filmmakers if this group would resist embracing the notion that they are more concerned with artistic vision than other groups.

Marginalized groups—white women, people of color, and/or gay artists, for example—all struggle with the question of aesthetic accountability, particularly in relation to the issue of perpetuating domination. Although this struggle is most often seen solely in a negative light, it enhances artistic integrity when it serves to help the artist clarify vision and purpose. A filmmaker like Derek Jarman was able to use the demand for accountability to strengthen his work. *Blue* is a powerful testament to the artistry of engaging overtly with the political and the metaphysical in such a way that neither is diminished and both illumined.

Stan Brakhage uses the phrase "aesthetic ecology" to articulate his belief that there must be a delicate balance between showing conscious concern for the political in artistic production and allowing an unfettered expression of artistry to emerge. He feels it is important that a filmmaker "be very careful not to allow social and political impulses to dominate" his or her work, because that would "falsify the balances that are intrinsic and necessary to make an aesthetic ecology." All too often filmmakers from marginalized groups struggle with the issue of entitlement that is necessary to maintain such a balance. Most black filmmakers raised in a white supremacist culture wherein the vast majority of cinematic images are constructed in ways that preserve and uphold this structure of domination feel compelled to assume responsibility for producing resisting images. In and of itself this desire does not undermine artistic integrity, but it has placed limitations on those artists who allow it to overdetermine everything, they do. It is this overdetermination that disrupts the possibility of an aesthetic ecology, for it upsets the balance.

To become filmmakers black artists globally start from the standpoint of resistance, no matter the culture they work in. That is why the term black filmmaker signifies something different from the simple word filmmaker. Speaking about the way in which this term can function to both close down and open up creative possibilities in an interview published in the magazine of culture studies, *Border Lines*, the black British filmmaker John Akomfrah explains: "I'm a black filmmaker—means that there are certain prescriptions that you're expected to take on board. I'm not particularly troubled by that because that is par for the course. What I am troubled by is the Kantian nature in which that prescription is placed on us as a separate categorical imperative—a black filmmaker has to do this. I think this is not just wrong because it's absurd, but it's also wrong because it forecloses questions we need to ask." In the United States it has been assumed both in the past and in the present that a black filmmaker will construct black images, will focus on narrative content that highlights black experience, and that the images he or she creates will necessarily work against the stereotypically negative ones represented in the white mainstream. This demand is imposed by both financial backers and audiences. No black filmmaker works with only white or other nonblack images. And while a wholly nonblack focus might not be desirable, the fact that it is not an acceptable choice just serves as a reminder of the limitations that are imposed on black filmmakers that are not imposed on everyone else.

For a long time in this culture it has been assumed that black filmmakers will make black films (i.e., will work with content and imagery that highlight black experience). Concurrently, given the dearth of compelling images of blackness in cinema, it is not surprising that so many black filmmakers choose to work within this visual terrain because it is a fertile frontier—so much had not been discovered or done. In this sense there is a freshness to working with black subject matter that you never really find when the focus is on whiteness. At some point in the way distant future blackness will also be overworked, overdone. Right now it is still being discovered by black and nonblack filmmakers alike. It is practically impossible to see any Hollywood film that is making use of transgressive subject matter that does not include black characters. For black images, absent for so long from mainstream cinema, allow for the creation of fresh perspectives and standpoints.

Enough work has been produced to ensure that black films will not cease to be made. It is now essential that black filmmakers not be locked into a position by financial bakers and funders where their focus must always and only be on blackness. While white critics will often praise black artists for not focusing on blackness, they do not urge white artists to cease their obsessional focus on whiteness. The critique of racial essentialism must work both ways. Just as it is important for us to see blackness from multiple standpoints—imaged by filmmakers who are not black—it's equally important that white and other nonblack experiences be imaged by black filmmakers. Asian filmmakers, both independent and mainstream, work with black subject matter but not vice versa. When black filmmakers are able to treat a range of subject matter, not just that which highlights blackness, then there is more freedom to resist the racial burden of representation.

Certainly the critique of racial essentialism has intensified awareness that the simple fact of their skin color does not ensure that black film-makers will create images that are radical or subversive. We now know, even if we are not willing to live the truth of this knowledge, that race is less the factor that determines the type of images created in a movie than the perspective of the filmmaker. When conservative black filmmakers make movies, the images of blackness they create are often in keeping with the status quo, as informed by internalized white supremacist aesthetics as images created by unenlightened white and other nonblack filmmakers. In the past it was just assumed that black filmmakers in the United States would create resisting images, that their work would offer a perspective challenging dominant stereotypes. Yet now that black film-makers make films that they hope will have mass appeal, they address the huge white moviegoing audience by providing them with familiar images of blackness. These images are usually stereotypical. Until both colonizer and colonized decolonize their minds, audiences in white supremacist cultures will have difficulty "seeing" and understanding images of black-ness that do not conform to the stereotype.

More than ever before, black filmmakers realize that it is not enough to create images from a decolonized perspective, there must also be a new aesthetics of looking taught to audiences so that such work can be appreciated. The process by which any of us alter the way we look at images is political. Until everyone can acknowledge that white supremacist aesthetics shape creativity in ways that disallow and discourage the production by any group of images that break with this aesthetic, audiences can falsely assume that images are politically neutral. In actuality unspoken restrictions govern the ways white artists produce images as much as they do other groups. Yet these restrictions can easily not be named when they are simply passively accepted. Or when conflicts about the politics of race and representation occur behind closed doors. When I interview Wayne Wang about his and Paul Auster's decision to make the thief a black male when they did the casting for *Smoke* (the racial identity of the thief was not given in the story), he did not really answer the question fully. By making the thief black, they were choosing to perpetuate racist stereotypes. Yet I am sure that the real reason for adding all the black characters to this story was to provide it with a different, to spice it up with racial contrast. There is an ethical dimension to aesthetic choices that no one wants to talk about. The decision to make this thief black was not an innocent one. Yet no one really wants to talk openly about the significance of this decision. And that includes many black actors who realize that lots of black people were cast once a black male was chosen as the thief. While they might not like the social and political implications of the film's narrative content, they want to work in Hollywood.

No Hollywood insider really wants to publicly disclose the role white supremacist thinking plays in casting. Or the degree to which it is simply easier for everyone to follow the continuum of a racist filmic legacy rather than challenge it. There has still been no collective political demand that Hollywood divest itself of white supremacy. Challenges are often made on the individual level, and they go unnoticed. Every now and then when a powerful white man in mainstream cinema chooses to act against white supremacist aesthetics, we are given a glimpse of the hostility whites subject themselves to when they defy the status quo. A good example is Kevin Costner's choice to make Whitney Houston the lead in *The Bodyguard*. This break with the conventional racism of mainstream cinema, with its insistence that black women leads just would not have mass appeal did not occur because of outspoken collective resistance to racism. It was merely the whim of an individual white male. And he has ceased to be the "golden white male" that he was before this production. Recently, Marlon Brando was forced to publicly apologize for denouncing the racism in Hollywood, and for suggesting that many Jews working in the business challenge the reproduction of racist stereotypes when the issue is Jewish representation even as they condone the creation of denigrating images of other groups, particularly non-whites. The ways in which white people are policed by other white people in the arena of cinematic cultural production receive little attention. This allows for the fiction to endure that there is more artistic freedom to create progressive representations of race than there actually is. And here, it is a matter of depicting not only black characters in a progressive manner but also white characters and everyone else.

Ironically, white directors now assume that simply putting black characters in their films means that they could not possibly be perpetuating racism by way of their work. When some critics referred to Quentin Tarantino's *Reservoir Dogs* as a real "white guy movie," they were articulating a concern about the way much of its intensity early on is attributable to racially and sexually charged comments. Of course, Tarantino has taken the lead role in putting down anyone who suggests that his use of racist or sexist epithets is not merely politically neutral or cool. Significantly, while he made a case for the repeated use of the word "nigger" in his films by suggesting that it is important to strip that word of its power, he makes no connection between that rationale and what would need to be done to strip whiteness of its power to dominate. In *Quentin Tarantino: The Cinema of Cool*, author Jeff Dawson declares: "the truth is, the casting of *Pulp Fiction* has well and truly dispelled any notion of racism." This declaration is indicative of our cultural failure to understand that merely putting black characters in a film does not assure that the work acts, whether covertly or overtly, to undermine racism. Those black characters can be constructed cinematically so that they become mouthpieces for racist assumptions and beliefs. Tarantino's "cinema of cool" has generated a backlash against the forces that demand artistic vigilance regarding the representation of race and gender. His movies make racism and sexism entertaining.

Mainstream cinema has so deeply invested in racist mythography as part of its narrative structures that it will take nothing short of a revolution (i.e., audiences simply refusing to pay money to see films that actively perpetuate systems of domination) to change this world. Right now audiences act in profound complicity with the status quo. When a film like *Corrina Corrina* shows audiences progressive images of a black woman character (giving Whoopi Goldberg a break from her usual racist, sexist role as mammy or ho), it is not a commercial success. White audiences are not the only ones that turn away from progressive images. Often unenlightened black and other nonwhite groups who, like many whites, have been socially conditioned to accept denigrating portraits of black people are dissatisfied when they do not see these familiar stereotypes on the screen. James Lull remind readers in *Media, Communication, Culture* that the system of white supremacist hegemony works because everyone is in on the act. "Dominant ideological streams must be subsequently reproduced in the activities of our most basic social units—families, workplace networks and friendship groups in the many sites and undertakings of everyday life.... Hegemony requires that ideological assertions become self-evident cultural assumptions. Its effectiveness depends on subordinated peoples accepting the dominant ideology as 'normal reality or common sense.'" Hence, even though in "real" life there is little evidence that young black males brutally slaughter Korean shopkeepers, when a film like *Menace to Society* depicts such a slaughter many young black folks insist that the dehumanized images of black masculinity are authentic, reflect reality. They both identify with and then seek to express culturally the identity the film gives them.

The culture most movies are making when it comes to race, both in mainstream cinema and independent work, is one that still upholds, either covertly or overtly, white supremacy. Independent films by self-identified progressive white women, straight and lesbian, still draw upon conventional, stereotypical ways of perceiving black womanhood to organize their narratives. This is true of both *Go Fish* and *The Incredible True Story of Two Girls in Love*. In the latter, the filmmaker casts a black woman as the homophobic, shrewish upper-class bitchy mother whose daughter has a lesbian fling. Even though the white filmmaker stated in interview after interview that she based this character on her mother, not a single reviewer asked her to discuss why she chose to cast this character as black. She could then have been asked whether or not such depictions perpetuate the notion that black women are more homophobic than white women, as they are in this film. Such interrogation does not take place because it is not seen as "cool." It's more hip to engage in an uncritical celebration of interracial same-sex desire. Black females are presented as shallow worshippers of Eurocentric culture in this film, and there is a link between these representations and those we see in *Waiting to Exhale*.

When it comes to the issue of race and representation, much of what we see on the screen paints a grim picture. As more nonwhite images appear on the screen, they at least promote public debate and discussion about the politics of representation. In the past everyone assumed racism and white supremacy would be challenged and changed in everyday life and that this would lead to a revolution in cinema. Reversing this process would pose a more strategic challenge to racism. Audiences have the power to shut down a movie. Picketing and boycotts are one of the cheapest and most effective ways to let the world know that the images we are being asked to consume are undesirable. Since movie culture is one of the primary sites for the reproduction and perpetuation of white supremacist aesthetics, demanding a change in what we see on the screen—demanding progressive images—is one way to transform the culture we live in. As long as no one makes this demand, we are not just helped captive by the imagistic hegemony of the collective white supremacist capitalist patriarchal imagination, we will not have eyes to see the liberatory visions progressive filmmakers offer us.

10

neo-colonial fantasies

of conquest

Hoop Dreams

Entering a movie theater packed tight with the bodies of white folks waiting to see *Hoop Dreams* I wanted to leave when it seemed that we (the two
black folks I had come with — one of my five sisters and my ex-boyfriend)
would not be able to sit together. Somehow I felt that I could not watch
this film in a sea of whiteness without there being some body of blackness to anchor me — to see with me — to be a witness to the way black life
was portrayed. Now, I have no problems with white filmmakers making
films that focus on black life: the issue is only one of vision — perspective.
Living in white supremacist culture no matter who is making a film
about people of color, the politics of location matters. In the United
States, white folks wanting to see and "enjoy" images of black folks on
the screen is often in no way related to a desire to know real black
people.

Sitting together in the packed crowd, every seat in the house taken, we joked about the atmosphere in the theater. It was charged with a sense of excitement, tension, and anticipation usually present at sports events. The focus on basketball playing may have allowed the audience to loosen up some but without knowing much about the content and direction of the film (whether it was serious or not) folks were clearly there to have fun. As the film began, a voyeuristic pleasure at being able to observe from a distance the lives of two black boys from working class and poor inner city backgrounds overcame the crowd. This lurid fascination with "watching" a documentary about two African-American teenagers striving to become NBA players was itself profound documentation of the extent to which blackness has become commodified in this society—the degree to which black life, particularly the lives of poor and underclass black people, can become cheap entertainment even if that it is not what the filmmakers intended.

Filmmakers Peter Gilbert, Fred Marx, and Steve James make it clear in interviews that they want audiences to see the exploitative aspects of the sports systems in America even as they also want to show the positives. Gilbert declares: "We would like to see these families going through some very rough times, overcoming a lot of obstacles, and rising above some of the typical media stereotypes that people have about inner-city families." Note the way in which Gilbert does not identify the race of this family. Yet it is precisely the fact of blackness that gives this documentary popular cultural appeal. The lure of *Hoop Dreams* is that it affirms that those on the bottom can rise in this society, even as it is critical of the manner in which they rise. This film tells the world that the American dream works. As the exploitative white coach at St. Joseph's high school puts it as he is verbally whipping these black boys into shape: "This is America. You can make something of your life."

Contrary to the rave reviews *Hoop Drams* has received, making it the first documentary film to be deemed by critics and moviegoers alike as worthy of an academy award for best motion picture, there is nothing spectacular or technically outstanding about this film. It is not an inventive piece of work. Indeed, it must take its place within the continuum of traditional anthropological and/or ethnographic documentary works that show us the "dark other" from the standpoint of whiteness. Inner city poor black communities seen as "jungles" by many Americans become in this film the boundary white filmmakers cross to document over a period of five years their subjects. To many progressive viewers, myself included, this film is moving because it acknowledges the positive aspects of black life that make survival possible. Even as I encouraged my family and everyone to see the film, I also encouraged us to look at it critically.

Contextualizing *Hoop Dreams* and evaluating it from a cinematic standpoint, is crucial to any understanding of its phenomenal success. The fact is it's not a great documentary. It is a compelling and moving real-life drama. Indeed, its appeal is a testimony to the culture's obsession with real life stories. In many ways the style of the film has much in common with those short documentary stories reported on the five o'clock news or on the more sensational programs like *Hard Copy*. In the United States, reviewers of the film, an overwhelming majority of whom are white, praised the work. Unlike many other films that examine the experience of black Americans (documentaries on Malcolm X, *Eyes on the Prize*, etc.), films that have overtly political content, that speak directly about issues of racism, the focus of this film was seen by many folks as more welcoming. It highlights an issue Americans of all races, but particularly white Americans, can easily identify with—the longing of young black males to become great basketball players. No doubt it is this standpoint that leads reviewers like David Denby in *New York* magazine to proclaim that *Hoop Dreams* is "an extraordinarily detailed and emotionally satisfying piece of work about American inner-city life, American hopes, American defeat." Such a comment seems highly ironic given the reality that it is precisely the way in which institutionalized racism and white supremacist attitudes in everyday American life actively prohibit black male participation in diverse cultural arenas and spheres of employment while presenting sports as the "one" location where recognition, success, and material reward can be attained. The desperate fear of not making it in American culture is the catalyst that drives the two young black males, Arthur Agee and William Gates, to dream of making a career as professional ballplayers. They, their family and friends, never imagine that they can be successful in any other way. Black and poor, they have no belief that they can attain wealth and power on any other playing field other than sports. Yet this spirit of defeat and hopelessness that informs their options in life and their life choices is not stressed in the film. Their longing to succeed as ballplayers is presented as though it is simply a positive American dream. The film suggests that it is only their potential to be exploited by adults who hope to benefit from their success (coaches, parents, siblings, lovers) that makes this dream a potential nightmare.

The most powerful moments in this film are those that subversively document the way in which these young black male bodies are callously objectified and dehumanized by the white male-dominated world of sports administration in America. *Hoop Dreams* shows audiences the way coaches and scouts searching to find the best ball players for their high school and college teams conduct themselves using an "auction block" mentality that to any aware viewer has to call to mind the history of slavery and the plantation economy that was built on the exploitation of young strong black male bodies. Just as the bodies of African-American slaves were expendable, the bodies of black male ballplayers cease to matter if they are not able to deliver the described product. Shrewdly, the filmmakers expose the ruthless agendas of grown-ups, particularly those paternalistic patriarchal white and black males, who are overinvested, whether emotionally or materially, in the two teenagers.

While the trials and tribulations Agee and Gates encounter on the playing field give *Hoop Dreams* momentum, it is their engagement with family and friends as well as their longing to be great ballplayers that provide the emotional pathos in this film. In particular, *Hoop Dreams* offers a different and rather unique portrayal of black mothers. Contrary to popular myths about matriarchal "hard" black women controlling their sons and emasculating them, the two mothers in this film offer their children necessary support and care. Clearly, it is Agee's mother Sheila who is exemplary in her efforts to be a loving parent, providing necessary discipline, support, and affirmation. Less charismatic, indeed she often appears to be trapped in a passive depressive stoicism, Gates' mother is kept in the background by the filmmakers. She is a single mother raising her children. The film does not show us how she provides economically.

Both Sheila and Arthur, Agee's mother and father, are articulate outspoken intelligent black folks. While the representation of their intelligence counters the stereotypes, the fact that they are not able to work together to keep the family healthy and free of major dysfunction reinforces other stereotypes. While the portrait of Sheila is positive, she is represented in the film as always more concerned with keeping the family together than the father. This is a traditional an often stereotypical way black women are represented in mass media, conveying the underlying racist and sexist assumption that they are somehow "better" than black men, more responsible, less lazy. Unfortunately, the news story reportorial style of the film precludes any complex investigation of Agee's father's drug addiction or the breakdown in their relationship. In keeping with stereotypical mass media portraits about poor black families, *Hoop Dreams* merely shows the failure of black male parents to sustain meaningful ties with their children. It does not critically interrogate the circumstances and conditions of that failure.

Even though one of the saddest moments in this film occurs as we witness Agee's loss of faith in his father, his mounting hostility and rage, he is never interrogated about the significance of this loss in the way he is questioned by the filmmakers about his attitudes towards basketball, education, etc. Concurrently, there is even less exploration of Gates' problematic relationship to his dad. Without any critical examination, these images of black father and son dynamics simply confirm negative stereotypes, compounding them by suggesting that even when black fathers are present in their children's lives they are such losers that they have no positive impact. In this way, the standpoint of the filmmakers creates a cinematic portrait that in no way illuminates the emotional complexity of black male life. Indeed, via a process of oversimplification the film makes it appear that the longing to play ball is the all-consuming desire in the lives of these young black men. That other longings they may have go unacknowledged and unfulfilled is not addressed by the filmmakers. Hence, there is no way to see how these states of deprivation and dissatisfaction intensify the obsession with succeeding in sports. Audiences are surprised when we suddenly see Gates with a pregnant girlfriend since until this scene appears the film has created a narrative that suggests basketball consumes all his energies.

This was obviously a strategic decision on the part of the filmmakers. For much of the dramatic momentum of *Hoop Dreams* is rooted in its evocation of competition dramatically evoked by the documentary footage of basketball games where audiences can cheer on the stars of the film, empathically identifying their success or failure, or via the competition the film constructs between Agee and Gates. Even though we see glimpses of camaraderie between the two black males, by constant comparing and contrasting their fate, the film creates a symbolic competition. The forces that oppose one another are the logic of racial assimilation which suggests that those black folks will be most successful who assume the values and attitudes of privileged whites and the logic of narrow nationalism which suggest that staying within one's own group is better because that is the only place where you can be safe, where you can survive. It is this latter vision that "wins" in the film. And it is perfectly in sync with the xenophobic nationalism that is gaining momentum among all groups in American culture.

Ultimately, *Hoop Dreams* offers a conservative vision of the conditions for "making it" in the United States. The context where one can make it is clearly within a nuclear family that prays together, that works hard, that completely and uncritically believes in the American dream. An almost religious belief in the power of competition to bring success permeates American life. The ethic of competition is passionately upheld and valued in Agee's family, so much so that it intensifies the schism between him and his dad. William Gates, who learns to critique the ethic of competition that he has been socialized to passively accept in white supremacist capitalist patriarchy, is portrayed as a victim. His longing to be a good parent, to not be obsessive with basketball, is not represented as a positive shift in thinking. After his health deteriorates, he is most often represented in the film as hopeless and defeated.

The triumphant individual in the film is Arthur Agee, who remains obsessed with the game. He continues to believe that he can win, that he can make it to the top. In her book *Memoir of a Race Traitor* the feminist writer Mab Segrest suggests that the ethic of competition undergirds the structure of racism and sexism in the United States, that to be "American" is to be seduced by the lure of domination, by conquest, by winning: "As a child of Europeans, a woman whose families have spent many generations on these shores, some of them in relative material privilege, my culture raised me to compete for grades, for jobs, for money, for self-esteem. As my lungs breathed in competition, they breathed out the stale air of individualism, delivering the toxic message; You are on your own." To be always in constant competition, hounded by the fear of failure, is the nature of the game in a culture of domination. A terrible loneliness shrouds Agee throughout *Hoop Dreams*. There is no escape. He has to keep playing the game. To escape is to fail. The subversive content of this film, its tragic messages, messages similar to those conveyed in other hot movies on the American scene (*Interview with a Vampire, Pulp Fiction, Natural Born Killers*), are subsumed by the spectacle of playing the game—by the thrill of victory. Deposit the costs, the American dream of conquest prevails, and nothing changes.

doing it for daddy:

black masculinity

in the mainstream

When feminist thinker Phyllis Chesler published *About Men*, she included a short narrative that has always lingered in my imagination. It concerns Charles Manson and the women who were sexual with him. The story is that one of the women was interviewed and asked to share what it was like to fuck him. She replied: "He said, 'Imagine I'm your father.' I did. I did. And it was very good." This is a story that I have told many times since first reading it. I have never returned to the book to find out if my memory is accurate. This story delighted me because it reveals quite innocently the extent to which patriarchy invites us all to learn how to "do it for daddy," and to find ultimate pleasure, satisfaction, and fulfill-ment in that act of performance and submission.

I thought of this story again recently when I was reading *USA Today*. In the section that brings us the top stories from around the nation was this report from Birmingham, Alabama: "The Jefferson County Commission voted not to remove a courthouse mural of a white female plantation owner, looming over black men picking cotton." No doubt the white woman in this mural is also "doing it for daddy," performing an act of domination that she hopes will win his approval and love.

In white supremacist capitalist patriarchy, black males and white females are uniquely positioned to compete with one another for the favors white "daddies" in power can extend to them. If the individuals from these groups should fail to understand either their connection to one another or their position in relation to white patriarchy, they are bombarded by mass-media images within the pedagogy of popular culture that consistently remind them that their chances of receiving rewards from the patriarchal mainstream and their hopes for salvation within the existing social structure are greatly enhanced when they learn how to "do it for daddy."

Thinking about the place of black men in the existing social hierarchy, I became fascinated by images of black males in popular culture that represent them as not only eager to "do it for daddy" but, even more, as individuals tortured by what I call "unrequited longing for white male love." For the most part, black males do not represent themselves in this manner. They are represented in this manner by white cultural productions, particularly in television, film and advertising. The colonizing culture's manipulation of representation is essential to the maintenance of white supremacist capitalist patriarchy. Representations that socialize black males to see themselves as always lacking, as always subordinated to more powerful white males whose approval they need to survive, matter in white patriarchy. Since competition between males is sanctioned within male-dominated society, from the standpoint of white patriarchy, black masculinity must be kept "in check." Black males must be made subordinate in as many cultural arenas as possible. Representations that socialize black males to embrace subordinate as "natural" tend to construct a worldview wherein white men are depicted as all-powerful. To become powerful, then, to occupy that omnipotent location, black males (and white females) must spend their lives striving to emulate white men. This striving is the breeding ground among black males for a politics of envy that reinforces the underlying sense that they lack worth unless they receive the affirmation of white males.

Two recent films that depict this structure of competition, envy, and black male desire for white male approval are *The Pelican Brief* (1993), directed by Alan J. Pakula, and *Philadelphia* (1993), directed by Jonathan Demme. In *The Pelican Brief*, Julia Roberts, one of Hollywood's leading white female sex symbols, shares top billing with Denzel Washington, "the" black male sex symbol. She plays a law student who, as one ad tells us, "writes a legal brief theorizing her ideas of who murdered two Supreme Court justices"; he plays a *Washington Post* reporter. Initially, the movie focuses on the relationship between Roberts's character and the white male she loves, her former law professor. Significantly, he is positioned as her superior. She admires him, and longs to save him from the alcoholism that is destroying his life. When, as the ad announces, 'Her brief hits the top levels of government, she must run for her life." Attempting to murder her, the powerful patriarchal white government officials kill her lover. Her mission then becomes twofold: she must expose those who murdered the Supreme Court justices and she must avenge the death of the "good" white patriarch.

Initially, the ads for this film showed a huge image of Julia Roberts's face with Denzel Washington's image in the background. Washington's public-relations agents threatened to withdraw him from the film if the publicity images were not reshot to portray the two stars on equal footing. Since the issue had not been raised by the backers, producers, or directors of *The Pelican Brief*, the need to distinguish the status of the two characters was, presumably, a concern of advertising. Ads are a primary vehicle for the dissemination and perpetuation of white-supremacist and patriarchal values. Think about how many ads you see in magazines or on television that depict a white, heterosexual couple engaged in some "fun" activity while a lone, black, male friend looks on with longing and envy. The message that the ad for *The Pelican Brief* intended to send was that the leading, white, woman star in this film would not be following the usual Hollywood romantic setup, and doing it with the leading man. To put it vulgarly: the pure white madonna would not be fucking the angry black beast. Even the reshot ad was constructed to make it clear that the two stars would not be a couple. And throughout the film, their bodies are carefully positioned to avoid any contact that could be seen as mutually erotic. Audiences can only wonder what went on behind the scenes during the shooting of this film. Did the director constantly remind the actors that the characters were just working together, that Denzel Washington's character should express a covert romantic interest but that the white female lead must always appear completely devoted to the patriarchal ghost of her white male lover? Both characters are depicted as completely allied with the existing social structure of white-supremacist capitalist patriarchy. They are in it together, to uphold law and order, to reinforce the values corrupted by evil, greedy, white patriarchs—they are on the side of the "good" white men, whom the system destroys. They vindicate daddy, without in any way questioning his right to remain superior, even in death.

While Roberts's character is initially surrounded by white friends and lovers, Washington's character is the lone, black, male body in a world that is all-white. He longs to succeed in that world, to be the best at this job, to excel. Portrayed as always pandering to the needs of his white male boss, pleading with him to trust him, Washington's character is a perfect image of the black male working overtime to assimilate into mainstream, white, male patriarchy. Of course, part of what makes his character "acceptable" is that he is not threatening to change the system; he is working hard to uphold the values of the existing social structure. There is an underlying insistence throughout the film that no other system could be as good. The film never makes explicit the reasons Washington's character is willing to risk his life to save both the white woman and the white, male-dominated system. The underlying assumption is that he commits to this because he worships, admires, and loves white patriarchal power. He longs both to occupy the power position and to possess the white goddess who is the prize. Significantly, Washington's character is the "good" black man. He not only accepts his subordinate status, he testifies on behalf of and exults in white male superiority. Since he is never portrayed as belonging to a "black" community, with family, friends, or lovers, his very existence depends on white affirmation. This imagery reproduces the narrative of colonialism. The servant/slave has eyes only for the "master." No doubt this is why Washington's character shows no romantic interest in the white female hero. He is merely protecting. To make it clear that these two are not together, the film ends with a caring farewell. After her value is affirmed by Washington's character, we see the white goddess resting triumphantly on her symbolic throne—a beach chair. Denzel's character, mind you, is still on the job, working hard to uphold the patriarchal status quo. But she is rewarded by leisure, by dominion over a little kingdom somewhere (could it possibly be in the Third World?), where she can reside in comfort, her needs taken care of by invisible others. Washington's character advances in his career. And Big Daddy, his boss, is pleased. Affirmed by the white patriarchal world, he is ready to work overtime once more to win daddy's love.

Sadly, this representation of black masculinity surfaces even when Hollywood shifts its usual white patriarchal focus and portrays a gay white male grappling with the issue of AIDS in the workplace. Until he becomes ill, the corporate lawyer that Tom Hanks plays in *Philadelphia* is in every way one of the white-supremacist capitalist patriarchal boys — seeking to rise in the hierarchy. Homosexuality, this film suggests, is not a stumbling block that will impeded his success; AIDS is the barrier the Big Daddy's of this film will not cross. Powerful, white patriarchal men are not presented as horribly homophobic in this film. The individual who most expresses antigay sentiment is the black lawyer, played by Denzel Washington. Yet somehow, when the sick, unemployed white male comes to his office demanding support, Washington is own over. His homophobia disappears. Just as *The Pelican Brief* depicted the benevolent white male patriarch as "tragic," *Philadelphia* depicts the corporate white gay male as vulnerable, as tortured by the system. He is made to appear more noble, more generous than other white men. A social liberal, he has a Hispanic lover, who is portrayed as living only to be the little mammy, taking care of the great white man. Both of these films represent black males and other men of color as acceptable, even lovable, only when they are willing to drop everything in their lives and care for the well-being of "superior" white men. Nothing in the script of *Philadelphia* even hints at what would lead Denzel Washington's character to divest himself of his homophobia and take time away from his wife and newborn baby girl to work overtime defending a gay white lawyer with AIDS. The implication is that "good" white males are inherently worthy, deserving of care, and, of course, always superior to black men in their values and actions, even when they are sick and dying.

Images representing black masculinity as based on an unrequited longing for white male love were the stock-in-trade of the television show *Tarzan.* As a child growing up in the segregated South, I would often overhear grown black men expressing their disgust with the *Tarzan* narratives and with the loving devotion the "primitive" black male gave the white male hero. This television show reminded its viewers that even in black nations, on alien soil, the white male colonizer had superior skills and knowledge that were immediately recognized and appreciated by the natives, who were eager to subordinate themselves to the white man. The "bad" black natives who refused to worship white masculinity were often in the roles of kings and queens. Of course, their leadership was corrupted by greed and lust for power, which they exercised with great cruelty and terrorism. Tarzan, the great white father, used his omnipotence to displace these "evil" rulers and protect the "good" docile natives.

Representations colonize the mind and the imagination. In his essay "White Utopias and Nightmare Realities," Henry Giroux discusses the distinction between the old racism, which relied on biology and science to reinforce white supremacist thinking, and the new racism, which suggests that racial difference should be overcome even as it reaffirms white power and domination. "Dominant groups are now driving very carefully over a cultural terrain in which whiteness can no longer remain invisible as a racial, political, and historical construction," he argues. "The privilege and practices of domination that underlie being white in America can no longer remain invisible through either an appeal to a universal norm or a refusal to explore how whiteness works to produce forms of 'friendly' colonialism." Representations of black males that portray them as successful yet happily subordinated to more powerful white females break with the old stereotypes of the lazy darky. The neocolonial black male is reenvisioned to produce a different stereotype: he works hard to be rewarded by the great white father within the existing system.

Another fine example of this politics of representation can be seen in the movie *Rising Sun* (1993), which stars Wesley Snipes and Sean Connery. Snipes's character is pupil to the powerful, patriarchal, white father, yet "outcast" from his own black peer group. In his secondary role, the subordinated black man not only happily does as the master orders him, always eager to please, he even falls in love with the Asian woman daddy has cast aside. Socializing, via images, by a pedagogy of white supremacy, young whites who see such "innocent" images of black males eagerly affirming white male superiority come to expect this behavior in real life. Black males who do not conform to the roles suggested in these films are deemed dangerous, bad, out of control—and, most importantly, white-hating. The message that black males receive is that, to succeed, one must be self-effacing and consumed by a politics of envy and longing for white male power. Usually black males are represented in ads and films in solitary roles, as though they lacked connection and identification with other black people. These images convey such racial estrangement as necessary for white acceptance. Even though some films, like *Lethal Weapon* (1987) and *Grand Canyon* (1991), portray the secondary black male hero as having a family and a community, all the black folks follow his patriarchal lead and worship at the throne of whiteness. More recent films like *Seven* and *The Shawshank Redemption* which represent lone male characters as embodying wisdom and moral integrity still subordinate them to white stars.

When images of homosocial bonding between white and black males converge with images of black male and white female competition for daddy's favor, a structure of representation remains in place that reinforces white supremacist patriarchal values. Two different images in recent issues of *Vogue* and *Us* share the convention of a staged competition between a white female and a black male. In an *Us* magazine cover story about Drew Barrymore (May 1994), one full-page photograph shows her naked to the waist, wearing only a dark bikini and a boxing belt and with boxing gloves covering her breasts. Behind her stands a dark-skinned black male boxer, whom she has presumably displaced, taking over his role and position in the arena. He stares off into space with a look that *Us* says conveys "attitude, displeasure, hardness." Both figures are looking off into the distance, their gaze focused on someone else. Traditionally, boxing was a sport wherein notions of racial superiority were played out in the physical realm, to see if white men were physically superior. Though established to reinforce white prowess, boxing became an arena in which black males triumphed over white patriarchy, using the same standards to measure superiority that the system had put in place.

Coincidentally, the June 1994 issue of *Vogue* magazine featured an advertisement that showed a tall, blonde white model punching a young black male boxer. The text alongside the ad offered this story line: "Going for the knockout punch in powerfully sexy gym wear." Like the image of Drew Barrymore, this ad suggests that black males must compete with white females for white patriarchal power and pleasure. And they both suggest that the white female has an edge on the black male because she can be sexually alluring; she can win, through "pussy power," in the heterosexual patriarchal arena. These images, and others like them, suggest that white females and black males should not be disturbed by racist, sexist hierarchies that pit them against one another but should rather enjoy playing the game, reaping the rewards. Both remain "objects" in relation to white male subjectivity. They share the politics of envy and longing for white male power. Represented as upholding the existing white supremacist capitalist patriarchy, they appear content and satisfied.

In most movies, the black male protagonist is clearly depicted as heterosexual. However, many ads that portray black males (particularly those that show them as the lone black male amid a group of white males engaged in homosocial bonding) leave ambivalent the issue of sexual practice and preference. Black, gay, male, cultural producers, both in film and photography, have been the group most willing to speak about the politics of envy and longing that characterizes some black male responses to white masculinity within the cultural context of white-supremacist capitalist patriarchy. Filmmaker Marton Riggs explored this issue in his documentary, *Tongues Untied* (1989), and Isaac Julien did the same in his short piece, *This Is Not An AIDS Advertisement, This is About Desire* (1992). Following their lead, Thomas Harris's video, *Heaven, Earth, and Hell* (1993), is an honest interrogation of the ways interracial sexual border crossing is informed by feelings of both black, male, racial inferiority and longing for white male affirmation and love. In his series *Confessions of a Snow Queen*, photographer Lyle Ashton Harris offers yet another critical look at that longing for white male affirmation and approval that emerges as an expression of the politics of white supremacy, and how those politics are played out in black life.

While these black gay males seek to interrogate, counter, and subvert conventionalized representations in mainstream mass media, black masculinity continues to be represented as unrequited longing for white male love. Since there is little public discussion about the way in which existing popular representations of black masculinity serve to reinforce and sustain existing structures of domination, these images are reproduced again and again. Countered primarily by mainstream constructions of the conventional racist/sexist stereotype of the black male as bestial primitive destroyer, these images work together to censor and suppress any complex representation of black masculinity. Until we start naming what we see, even if it is not a pretty picture, and following that articulation with strategies and practices for challenging and changing the image, we will be trapped in a scenario where we do it for daddy.

thinking through class:

paying attention to

The Attendant

Unlike many other black filmmakers Isaac Julien often takes the lead in situating his work theoretically. Often he does so in response to critiques of a particular film. He theorizes to explain, to talk back, to justify, and to interrogate. His comments on the short video film "Confessions of a Snow Queen: Notes on the Making of 'The Attendant'" make use of much recent diasporic queer theory to talk about how both the representations of sexuality in this film and the depiction of S/M iconography. While he critically reads the work in relation to the politics of sex and race, he does not take on the issue of class.

Without diminishing in any way the significance of the experimental fusing of various discourses of post-coloniality, race and sexuality, in this film (there is no spoken dialogue so we are all compelled to read these bodies) class relations are as significant in *The Attendant*. Yet it is the marker of class positionality that can remain unseen, go unnoticed eclipsed by our fascinations with sex and race. In her introduction to *Sadomasochism in Everyday Life*, Lynn Chancer reminds readers of the interplay between class and race: "The class division between proletariat and bourgeoisie central to Marx's conceptualization of capitalism is simultaneously an interpersonal relationship steeped in experiences of extreme dominance and subordination." The sexual sadomasochism in *The Attendant* is only one narrative of power and powerlessness depicted in the work. Present but not as graphically articulated is also a drama of class.

The museum in *The Attendant* is not just "constructed as the historical bastion" for the safekeeping of colonial artifacts, it embodies the contemporary expression of neocolonialism. Within this citadel of white culture there is a black presence because of the existence of imperialism in both the past and the present. The living bodies of the black uniformed male guard—the attendant and the black female conservator are markers of a cultural shift, they represent the space of cultural hybridity wherein "white" western civilization, defined by high culture, strives to affirm and reaffirm its dominance in the presence of those whose very existence is a testament to the decentering of the empire. As workers in this cultural sphere whose tasks are to guard and protect the labor of both the attendant and the conservator exemplify the way in which certain hierarchies of race and empire merely reinvent themselves in the present in different forms (black bodies no longer slaves are now servants). Their new location within the very heart of white supremacist mythmaking high art culture is simultaneously a site of subordination and a site of resistance. It is only by entering the center that they are able to survive the border crossing imperialism makes possible.

Their relationship to white Western civilization is interrogated by the ways their bodies are deployed to protect and guard that structure. As black workers/servants, their position is distinct from those real-life persons of color, Stuart Hall and Hanif Kureishi, whose unidentified cameo appearances remind viewers that class position is not determined solely by race. Although Hall and Kureishi are not white, they mingle as peers, as subjects in the same worlds. Like all the other visitors, they do not engage these workers. They are there as participants in the viewing relations dictated by the aesthetics of high culture. In fact, it is their presence (whether the audience knows who these actors are in real life or not) that disrupts the binary positioning that would place the nonwhite in the subordinate role and the white person in the dominant role.

Class mediates race. There are those individuals who have the leisure to look, to stroll, to let their gaze wander where it may. And there are the individuals whose positioning is static, who do not engage the gaze directly, who must stand in place or like robots perform their role as if they are not fully embodied humans. When there is a sustained direct gaze in the film, it is the unspoken covenant between the attendant and the conservator. Together class and race positionality unite them. The conservator appears to respect and enjoy the homosexuality of the attendant. She appears to understand that the space of transgressive desire is one location where historical relations of power and powerlessness are rendered less fixed and immutable. Desire disrupts conventional hierarchies. The conservator understands that no matter what form the sexual pleasure between the black attendant and the idealized white object of desire—the visitor who stays—takes, in the space of this pleasure there is always the possibility of subversion. While she listens with her ear to the wall, smiling, she sees that in the private space of desire all the neocolonial configurations of master and slave can be disrupted. Significantly, S/M sexual pleasure becomes the context for mutuality, where subject positions are fluid. One can play at being object, slave, the one who is beaten, and one can play at being subject, master, the one who beats. Pleasure is the space of utopian possibility. In the real work space where the attendant and the conservator must perform their job duties, class decorum, racial hierarchy, heterosexism prevail. Behind the scenes in utopian space all is possible.

The closeted queerness of the attendant is not solely a sign of heterosexism's repressive values. While I share with Julien the belief that "where there is a closet, there will always be bitterness and abjectness, due to the desires repressed by black conservative family values, which must produce silence at any cost," *The Attendant* does more than reveal this pain. It also lets us know that the need to be closeted carries with it the call to be inventive, creative when it comes to constructing a place where one's desires can speak. That the black worker fucks loudly in the pristine museum space where silence is the norm amplifies the sound of fulfilled desire. That sound permeates the rooms. It undoes the silence.

While Isaac Julien informs us in his comments about the making of his video/film that he sees the attendant as the conservator's husband, the images we see on the screen do not convey any such relationship. All too frequently the gaze of heterosexism imposes the reading that every bonding between a male and a female carries a sign of symbolic "marriage." To the eye that does not possess the knowledge the filmmaker holds, the guard and the conservator are not a husband and a wife but two workers bound together by both their tasks and their

relishing of secret pleasures. The conservator engages in no sexual relationship in this film. Yet the kiss she shares with the attendant solidifies
the pact, the covenant, between them. This kiss is not a sacramental
gesture affirming the guard's will to be closeted. For the camera has
already outted him. We know what he likes sexually. And she knows.
The kiss is an affirmation of that knowing—of the shared pleasure of
transgression.

The conservator's desire cannot speak its name because the world of
homosocial and homosexual bonding that takes center stage in the
video/film is one where the female body has no meaningful sexual presence. Within the context of *The Attendant*, and in the real patriarchal
world, there is no room for female desire. Ultimately that world silences
female pleasure. The conservator can be no more than a voyeur in the
culture of desire. Her sex has no house or home. Western patriarchal
civilization offers her not human contact but material artifacts. Her
desires must be displaced. The caress of the body given to an object, the
figure-heads of dead white kings as she dusts and cleans. Femininity is
here framed only by unrequited longing for the absent phallus. As
woman her desire in patriarchal culture can only and always be
voyeuristic.

The power she has that enables us to see her, in Julien's words, as "a
kind of dominatrix figure" is not defined by conventional heterosexuality.
It resides in that space of recognition in which she and the attendant
understand and appreciate the perverse. The power to look is not the
power to fuck. The pleasure of the gaze is not the same as the pleasure of
possessing. While the black attendant and the white visitor may "do the
wild thing," when they are not sexual they have no meaningful point of
contact. In one scene they stand side by side, unable, in psychoanalytic
terms, to give each other recognition that sustains. Their bonds are not
the bonds of love.

Such recognition can only emerge in the space where one is known.
It is the conservator who knows the attendant and not the white lover.
She knows him from the multiple standpoints of race, class, gender, and
nationality. Even though their bond is not a sexual one, they are united.
Julien sees their union as based on their shared investment in heterosex-
ism, but the video/film suggests that there are other ties that bind them.

An interpretation highlighting heterosexism as the point of bonding
between the attendant and the conservator works best if one ignores
class. When class is centralized, their union can be viewed differently. It
can be seen as a gesture of political solidarity. The two are both fighting

against the repressive nature of work. That the conservator colludes with the attendant, subverting the work place, making a space for the attendant's desire to speak, a private place not a closet, means that as co-conspirators that are able to alter the location where they are placed. There they reinvent themselves so that their identities are not fixed or static, no matter how visitors might see them. Their subordination as workers can never be the sole definition of who they are. This is the context of their shared understanding. Transgressive desire provides a site for this reimagining.

Another site to be taken over and reinvented is that of white Western classical music. Opera is an arena in Western culture where black bodies have little or no presence. In the operatic setting of *The Attendant* blackness is supreme. The guard and the conservator occupy this territory controlling both the theatrical space and the performance. In this space of ritual play they are transformed. The conservator emerges as a glamorous and mysterious audience member. The attendant is a passionate diva singing a mournful aria. In this arena of ritual play they do not need to react to the dynamic of white-and-black racial encounter. In their operatic space the attendant and the conservator can take center stage.

Even though the performance transposes Purcell's lament of Dido, who was abandoned by Aeneas, and gives it a new meaning, Julien is not staging a minstrel show in reversal. Instead the guard and the conservator have taken the white Western narrative and reimagined it. The call to be remembered is not just a longing on the part of the discarded, the disenfranchised, to be discovered again, it is a declaration of entitlement. When the attendant offers this heart-rending lament it does not simply address the power of whiteness to use and erase people of color, it speaks to all the locations where the powerless are forgotten by the powerful. The strength of this lament lies in the guard's courage to announce this mournful cry that he will not submit to erasure, that not even death will alter the significance of his presence.

Connections forged in suffering and pain cannot be easily forgotten. For it is not just the ties formed by a shared history of cultural domination but also those made by the fulfillment of desire, by shared ecstasy that must be remembered. As Ted Polhemus and Housk Randall state in their book *Rituals of Love*, "The enhanced physical and aural sensations of radical sex ritual allow for a transportation of self, or awareness of self, beyond normal everyday reference ... surrender is one of the most important and necessary elements ... a surrender of fear, inhibition, and ego to some deeper, unrecognized state within. Ecstatic revelation: this, by any other name is spiritual." It is only after he has surrendered to his passions, transgressed the boundaries, that the attendant regains his voice. Even though he is marked by Eurocentrism (the references to tragedy here are Greek), there is a universality in the quality of his mourning—a grief that transcends time and space. It is the collective mourning of the abandoned, of those who are rendered invisible by fate. "Remember me. When I am laid, I'm laid in earth."

Only the conservator is there to hear the guard's lament and to give recognition. When she applauds, the resounding clap of her hands "strike" like the whip that reminds us that here in this space of performance, where there are no other witnesses, she claims power. Masculine and feminine are inverted. Symbolically, the attendant plays the female Dido, and the conservator is the witness to his longing.

In solitary they have the opportunity to create an aesthetics of existence that will lead to the fulfillment of their collective longings. Jeffrey Weeks suggests in "Inventing Moralities" that the effectiveness of sexual stories "depends on an ability to tell them, and an audience to listen to them." Importantly he reminds us that "the task is not to order or legislate them away, but to interpret them and to explore ways of them speaking together, in a civilized conversation about the body and its sexualities." There are multiple narratives in *The Attendant*, to see them through the lens of queer essentialism ensures the erasure of all those sites where stories converge. Sexuality, yes; gay male desire, yes; but mixed in with class and race.

The points of convergence are the ones audiences have difficulty seeing. We are all so accustomed to looking solely from the standpoint of sex or race or class that the overlaps, the mergers, the place where nothing is as clear as it would seem are often ignored. Despite the interracial realm of sexual desire, the floating cupid who shoots an arrow with no regard for black or white or any other subject position, *The Attendant* demands that we see the ways bonds are forged from diverse subject positions. The inability to look from a wide angle, to let our gaze roam beyond the narrow scope of a Eurocentric vision is the limitation that makes audiences unable to see the whole picture when watching *The Attendant*. The images on the museum wall both past and present celebrate a narcissism that only lead to blind spots. If the "visitors" remain locked in the version of history these images tell them, narcissism becomes the defining trait of the culture of sadomasochism and all who fall for its lure will be perpetually blinded.

In the end *The Attendant* offers a way out. It is the open direct inviting gaze of the black Adonis moving toward us, walking it seems, right out of the camera and teasing us with the victory that comes from awareness. The eroticization of power is not the same as the eroticization of domination. When the visitor comes his desire is not for conquest but for satisfaction. Unlike the worker he seduces and pleasures, the anonymous white visitor exists with little "identity" markers. Leather is the sign we must read to follow his seduction. It is sexuality that is the central signifier of his being. The scenario the visitor and the attendant interact is not one of binary top and bottom. The two men take delight in the shifting of positions, in occupying multiple locations. Using pleasure to play with power, they divest themselves of the racialized hierarchies that shape white-and-black interactions in the non-utopian space.

It is the conservator in her spectacular S/M scenario who seeks an experience of the sublime solely through submission. She wants to be taken to a higher, purer plane of existence. That is why she is most fully "turned on" at the opera. She quests after the extrasexual. It is her strange mysterious passivity throughout *The Attendant* that is so alluring. She is totally without a story, completely abject, and yet at the same time radiating strength. Interpreting the way "the erotic submissive possesses the power to define power as an absurdity" Polhemus and Randall ask us to "consider the Bottom's unresponsive, unmovable demeanor—calmly complying with whatever the Top may demand but steadfastly refusing to react visibly to, or be fazed by, those demands. In the end, such passivity and unlimited compliance mocks rather than celebrates authority, for it denies it its raison d'etre." A hint of such mockery is there in the conservator's applause. The solitary audience, the sole listening ear, she refuses to lose herself in lament even as she accords it its place. After all, she has not abandoned the attendant.

Her unseen labor really begins when all the visitors leave. She understands the meaning of performance, the way unconventional desire enables transgression and transformation. After all, the conservator and the attendant have left work to make it to the theater—to be at the opera. There in that space of performance they can play. Fantasy is the space of release. It is this intimacy that binds them. The conservator will not abandon the attendant. The pleasure of work, and the work of pleasure, would not be the same without his presence.

13

back to the avant-garde:

the progressive vision

Whether or not progress has been made in representing race, sex, and class holistically in film can be gauged if we take a critical look at the ways black females are represented in both mainstream and independent cinema. Rarely do I see compelling representations of black females. Although there are films that represent black womanhood in ways that I enjoy and respect, constructing "positive" images, on a deeper level these images do not convey the complexity of black female experience that I hope one day to see interpreted on cinematic screens in the United States. It troubles me that for a long time I have had difficulty finding words to articulate what these images might be, ways I desire to see black females depicted. It troubles me that when I talk to other black women, I hear them speaking of the same wistful yearning and of the same difficulty naming what they want to see.

Certainly I want to see images that are more diverse and exploratory. I liked the representation of the black woman character in Woody Allen's *The Purple Rose of Cairo*. In the film within the film she plays the traditional part of the fat mammy-maid that was such a stock character in presixties Hollywood dramas. That moment when she walks off the screen to express her dissatisfaction with her job, with her dominating white mistress, and with her overall filmic role delighted me. It was a brief, pleasurable moment of cinematic resistance. Her few seconds of "talking back" to the screen required audiences to really take a good look at her—to stop rendering her image invisible by keeping their gaze always and only fixed on the white female star. Allen's subversive moment (an uncommon one in his films, which tend to give us witty versions of old racist, sexist stereotypes when representing black womanhood) felt like an experiment.

There are so few images of blackness that attempt in any way to be subversive that when I see one like this, I imagine all the myriad ways conventional representations of black people could be disrupted by experimentation. I am equally moved by that moment in Jim Jarmusch's *Mystery Train* when the young Japanese couple arrive in the train station in Memphis only to encounter what appears to be a homeless black man, a drifter, but who turns to them and speaks in Japanese. The interaction takes only a moment, but it deconstructs and expresses so much. It reminds us that appearances are deceiving. It made me think about black men as travelers, about black men who fight in armies around the world. This filmic moment challenges our perceptions of blackness by engaging in a process of defamiliarization (the taking of a familiar image and depicting it in such a way that we look at it and see it differently). Way before Tarantino was dabbling in "cool" images of blackness, Jarmusch had shown in *Down by Law* and other work that it was possible for a white-guy filmmaker to do progressive work around race and representation. And then there is that magic moment in Charles Burnett's film *Killer of Sheep* when the black heterosexual couple dances in their front room—no words, just the curious shadows their bodies make on the wall.

My passion for movies was not engendered by conventional cinema. I was obsessed with watching "foreign" films and drawn visually to avant-garde experimental work in the United States. Early on I developed a passion for Stan Brakhage's work that has been sustained. Coming to work by women filmmakers through explorations of feminist art practices, I was and continue to be fascinated by the work of filmmakers like Yvonne Rainer, Beth B., Leslie Thornton, Kathleen Collins, Julie Dash, and, of course the work of theorist and filmmaker Trinh T. Minh-ha, a longtime comrade and friend. Among this collective work, Minh-ha has centrally highlighted representations of blackness. At times she has been critiqued for this focus, interrogated about her choices. We have had long talks about the way in which white audiences and critics usually act as though an entire range of images constituted their purview but the moment an artist of color goes wherever their vision takes them, their right to such movement is questioned. In Minh-ha's case she was also often questioned by black people who were not "comfortable" with her work, with the images of Africa they saw in *Reassemblage* or *Naked Spaces*. Often these individuals approach her work from the standpoint of racial essentialism. Similar critiques about the construction of Africa etc. are rarely leveled at black filmmakers. The images I saw as a consumer of foreign films and experimental works in the United States shaped my visual expectations. Whenever I brought those expectations to bear on representations of blackness, I was sorely disappointed. I wanted a complexity that never was. Since feminist thinking informed my looking relations I was no more satisfied with what I saw in black films than the work of their white counterparts.

Indeed, patriarchal cinematic practices (ways narratives are constructed, images are shot) inform so much of what is identified as black film that it does not then become a location where blackness is represented in a liberatory manner, where we can see decolonized images. This is one of the dilemmas we face when our understanding of black experience is shaped solely by a focus on race, when the ways sex and class mediate racial identity are ignored. It has served the interests of contemporary black male filmmakers in the United States to look past the ways their relations are shaped by cinematic pedagogy in terms of both their technical training and what they are accustomed to seeing. Ironically, there are infinitely more transgressive visionary images of black femaleness in the work of a filmmaker like Oscar Micheaux than there are in that of most black male directors, precisely because Micheaux was not seeing through the lens of white longings and expectations. When contemporary black filmmakers, particularly males, offer audiences the same white supremacist aesthetics that we see in mainstream white cinema (making their lighter-skinned characters more feminine, more desirable; glorying in thin bodies; imaging black female sexuality as whorish), they are not making critical interventions. And very few critics, male or female, have wanted to openly interrogate why it was that films that were most talked about as breaking new ground for black cinema in the United States (*Sweet Sweetback's Baadasss Song* [1971], *Bush Mama* [1975], *Passing Through* [1977]), all made by black men at the onset of contemporary feminist movement, simply imposed on representations of black sexuality, and black female sexuality in particular, a pornographic, patriarchal frame. One film that was not usually talked about as much was progressive in the ways it depicted race, sex, and class—that film was Charles Burnett's *Killer of Sheep*. While every black person and his mother, too, knew about *Sweet Sweetback*, whether they were alive when the film first came out or not, few black audiences knew of Burnett's film. There is a continuum in the patriarchal imagination that informs these early works and the films made by black filmmakers today, whether independent or mainstream. This continued allegiance to patriarchy has made it easier for black male filmmakers who are in no way inventive when it comes to their construction of gender to make it in Hollywood.

While the making and production of Haile Gerima's film *Sankofa* was presented as an act of resistance, a challenge to Hollywood's white supremacist aesthetic practices, all the representations of black womanhood in the film were quite consistent with Hollywood narratives. In many talks Gerima proclaimed that the purpose of this film "was to disrupt Hollywood, ... to disrupt their sense of movies." Yet this film broke its pact with Hollywood only in the way it challenged audiences to see slavery from the standpoint of the pain and anguish of the enslaved. Overall, the filmic narrative valorized hierarchies—that of male over female particularly, more powerful male over less powerful male, positioned black women as positive mother figures or sexual victims redeemed only as they seek healing from the wise black male. The two leading black women "stars" in this movie appear in roles that are so in keeping with Hollywood narratives that it is mind-boggling. Mother Nunu's character was just a contemporary remake of Annie in *Imitation of Life*, only here her sacrifices and martyrdom are for her biracial son. The other female, Shola, is an African American model, who in the present has become a willing paid sex object for massa and in slavery is the victim of a brutal rape (surprise, surprise). If mainstream cinema's dominant representations of black women have been as "mammy or ho," the images in *Sankofa* follow this same continuum, only the end result is different. Shola changes her wicked wicked ways to affirm blackness. This depiction of the sexual black woman as a betrayer of blackness is common in the works of successful contemporary mainstream black filmmakers. It seems both white and black audiences are more comfortable watching black women when we are kept in our place by sexist, racist characterizations.

Filmmaker Haile Gerima states in an interview published in a newsletter entitled the *Gaither Reporter* that he "didn't think about male and female. I just thought about slavery and black people—African people. So I was not really into gender, women and men.... For me, all of them are supposed to come as human beings fighting to change a brutal circumstance." This comment seems completely disingenuous, since resisting representations of individual black men in *Sankofa* do indeed break with mainstream norms. Obviously the filmmaker thought about gender but not about the need to give audiences progressive, nonsexist images of black womanhood. Despite its positive construction of Africa as a common symbolic homeland for black people, *Sankofa* is conservative in its narrative, its construction of blackness, and its overall technique. Celebrated by black audiences from all classes, to some extent this film reinstitutionalizes an outmoded black aesthetic that sees black film as existing primarily as a tool in the liberation struggle. Gerima comments: "For me, film is not a playing toy. Film is used for social change. Film is not to duplicate our reality. Film is used to interpret our reality, to do something about our condition, to activate people, to even make people rise up against a system that is racist and make it change." Few black filmmakers would disagree with the idea that film can further liberation, but that cannot be its only purpose. Such a concept of the medium ignores the place of pleasure in relation to the visual and the need for diverse representations of our experience in the world, an experience that is defined by blackness even as it transcends it.

Focusing solely on representation and race tends to distort the perspective of black artists. Indeed, if more black male filmmakers were looking at the ways race, sex, and class converge, then their articulations of black experience might offer us more daring, complex interpretations—among them representations of black masculinity. Until black male artists challenge and change sexist thinking, their work will never have the power to engage black women and men fully in the work of liberation. The patriarchal cinema, whether black or white, is fundamentally distorted and can only give us incomplete images of males and females. If all sexist black male filmmakers (and their female counterparts) would abandon the patriarchal cinematic pedagogy, we would begin to see a visual revolution, for the images that would emerge from this new consciousness would necessarily be different.

Creating new and different representations of blackness should not be seen as the sole responsibility of black artists, however. Ostensibly, any artist whose politics lead him or her to oppose imperialism, colonialism, neocolonialism, white supremacy, and the everyday racism that abounds in all our lives would endeavor to create images that do not perpetuate and sustain domination and exploitation. The fact that progressive nonblack artists who make films, especially experimental work, challenge themselves around this issue is vital to the formation of a cultural climate in which different images can be introduced. Avant-garde/experimental work is central to the creation of alternative visions. Yet when black filmmakers embrace the realm of the experimental, they are often seen as practicing elitism, as turning their backs on the struggle to create liberatory visions.

In all areas of cultural production black artists confront barriers when we seek to do work that is not easily accessible, that does not have a plot or a linear narrative. My perspective on these issues has been informed by the dilemmas I have faced as a creative writer trying to gain acceptance for my own experimental work, which is not written in language that is as clear and plain as much of my critical writing. This creative writing is often poetic, abstract, nonlinear. In a similar vein, no matter how many essays I write that do not use abstract or heavily academic language, those few I choose to write using academic language tend to be harshly critiqued for not being clear enough. As a black artist who works with words and who makes visual art now and then, I am acutely aware of the way in which our longing to experiment, to create from a multiplicity of standpoints, meets with resistance from those whose interest in that work is primarily commercial, from audiences, and from critics. Whether we are talking about book production or the making of films, everyone wants more of what sells. Experimental work is always risky, all the more so in an area like film where the costs of production are so high. In his interview with *Border/Lines* filmmaker John Akomfrah shared his sense that "personal, reflective black cinema has been eclipsed in a way by a much more aggressive, marketed cinema."

Usually the relative dearth of experimental work in cinema by black artists in the United States is explained by the evocation of economic constraints. Filmmaker Julie Dash, who has made movies that mix the experimental and the conventional, says that the commercial "industry tells you there is no room for the avant-garde." In agreement with other black filmmakers I have spoken with, she reiterates that most people view the choice to be avant-garde as one that "ensures that you will be a struggling artist for the rest of your life." While it is obvious that economic constraints inform the artistic choices that black filmmakers make, that fact does not preclude an interrogation of the many other factors that inhibit and/or prohibit the creative expression of black artists.

Despite the differences between writing books and producing films, the fact that the incredible success of contemporary black writers has not created a climate in which more experimental writing by black artists can be published suggests that there is still an unwillingness on the part of producers and audiences to engage work by black artists that challenges conventional representations, whether in style or content, irrespective of the cost of production. Books are relatively cheap to produce, yet publishers still act as though there is no audience for unconventional work. The fact that publishing such work is not at all risky does not open up the cultural space for certain types of books to be mass-marketed, even as experimental writings by white authors garner acclaim. Actually, when a black writer gains widespread success with work that is conventional, it does not open spaces for a variety of standpoints and styles of writing to emerge. It usually happens that individual writers are encouraged to reproduce what already has been proven to sell. Hardly anybody talks about the significance of writing that has not been composed with the marketplace in mind. The few black writers I know who do experimental work have jobs that allow them to self-publish, or seek alternative publishing; they never intended to make money from this work. Despite the success of my critical essays, I still find that publishers and editors are reluctant to engage writing that is unconventional.

A culture that is not ready for black writers to experiment with the written word will be all the more closed to the idea of engaging experimental images. No matter what a filmmaker dreams of doing in his or her imagination, there has to be a reality base where those dreams are realized. It is hard for black filmmakers to let their imaginations soar when they face a culture that is still so closed. Many filmmakers feel they are still trying to convince mainstream culture that they can actually make standard films. Doing experimental work has little appeal. That is why director-cinematographer Arthur Jaffa raises the issue of "sacrifice" in relation to artistic vision. If there is not a growing body of black artists who are committed to exploring experimentally, then we will never really see truly revolutionary or even radical images of blackness on the screen.

To a grave extent the formation of a critical black cinema has been undermined by the cultural obsession with mainstream success that overdetermines the direction of artistic work, especially the work of black artists. Spike Lee's success in conventional cinema means that lots of young black filmmakers see no reason to engage independent filmmaking at all. They want to find the easiest route to the money and the fame. Many folks thought Julie Dash would have it made after the success of *Daughters of the Dust*, but of course she still has difficulty getting support for projects that are not conventional. The assumption that success in the mainstream makes it possible for other venues to emerge, for the unconventional to be affirmed is utterly false. In all areas of cultural production in this society those black artists who gain conventional success often act to censor and police art-making practices that they are not interested in. Until black artists and critics find ways to support and affirm the continual creation of experimental black cinema, visionary images will not emerge that will enable us to move to another level.

Black audiences have wrong-mindedly believed that the push for more "positive" images would necessarily lead to diverse representations of blackness. Yet the very insistence on positive images automatically acts to constrict and limit what can be created. The work of black artists in all arenas of cultural production in the United States is subject to heavy policing by consumers around whether or not that work is authentic, whether it is positive, and so on. All these efforts to impose a vision on the artist are restrictive. This is most evident in the filmmaking context.

Audiences who watched *Daughters of the Dust* (which merges the conventional and the unconventional) at an early screening witnessed resisting spectatorship. To a grave extent the film had to be positioned aesthetically before many viewers could see and appreciate it on its own terms. When viewers came looking for conventional cinema and did not find it, many were disappointed and enraged. The way in which black consumers hold black artists accountable for satisfying their conventional visual desire wrongly places incredible burdens on us. Again, this is especially true for filmmakers.

A vital dimension of critical black cinema will be lost if all black filmmakers abandon a passion for independent filmmaking to seek success in mainstream cinema. Until there are lots of black filmmakers who are willing to work as struggling artists to produce a variety of representations that emerge from unfettered imaginations, we will never really witness a cultural transformation of representations of blackness. The mainstream will never create images that perpetually intervene and subvert the stereotypes. While there are minor interventions here and there (and certainly Spike Lee has created some of those cinematic moments), they occur rarely, usually in only one scene, and thus are not apt to alter the visual impact of an entire picture.

One difficulty black artists encounter when they attempt to create unconventional films is that the more commonly accepted markers of avant-garde filmmaking may be too restrictive for work that endeavors to engage the politics of representation. Trinh T. Minh-ha found that the criteria conventionally used to determine whether work is avant-garde often do not conform to the strategies she deploys. To her a film might set itself apart "because it exposes its politics of representation instead of seeking to transcend representation in favor of visionary presence and spontaneity, which often constitute the prime criteria for what the avant-garde considers to be Art." Indeed, it is equally possible that a narrow vision of avant-garde practices leads black filmmakers to assume that they must conform to styles of working that disallow critical engagement with representations of blackness. If so, then another dimension of the work to be done involves expanding that vision. Audiences have been rigidly socialized to see cinema in fixed and narrow ways, especially when it comes to looking at representations of blackness. Again and again the persistent desire on the part of black audiences of all classes to see "realistic" and/or familiar images on the screen acts to curtail the imaginative scope of artists who do not wish to ignore those audiences or make films that they never engage. As a consequence, individual black filmmakers doing experimental work must join forces with critics to teach viewers a different aesthetic, to share new ways of looking.

At the same time, while it is crucial for black filmmakers to consider issues of accountability and the politics of representation, it is equally crucial that artists sustain the integrity of their vision. It should be seen as not only fine but essential to the assertion of liberated black subjectivity that there will indeed be black artists in all areas of cultural production who do work that will not be easily accessible. I long ago made a commitment to writing that would reach a larger audience, even as I continued to actively produce work that does not necessarily have wide appeal. Often black artists are encouraged to believe that the value of what we create is determined by audience acceptance. To expand the scope of creative possibility, we need to know that there is room for all types of cultural production, that artistic diversity is essential, and that some exceptional work will have mass appeal and some of it won't. To the extent that black audiences and black artists passively endorse the binary opposition between what sells big and what doesn't, the nature of artistic production will suffer. It should be possible for artists in every cultural sphere to do experimental work alongside conventional work if they choose, or to devote themselves to one or the other.

Overall, black artistic production will be severely damaged if the values of the marketplace overdetermine what we create. There are individual black filmmakers who have access to funds that would allow them to do short experimental works. Yet not enough folks are ready to take the leap. Calling attention to those artists who are fully self-determining with regard to their work is one way to show that it is possible to choose alternative strategies for artistic fulfillment and lead a satisfying life, even if there is not a lot of cash flow. Camille Billops has certainly created her own space in which to work. The rewards are different from those she would receive if she had chosen to focus on being commercially successful, but they are rewards nonetheless. Arthur Jaffa has been raising funds to make an independent experimental film. He does other work to make money. There is a growing number of independent black filmmakers charting different journeys. Only a few are seriously committed to experimental films, however.

If we long to transform the culture so that the conventional mass media are not the only force teaching people what to like and how to see, then we have to embrace the avant-garde/the experimental. Here is where we'll find radical possibility. We can deconstruct the images in the mainstream white supremacist capitalist patriarchal cinema for days and it will not lead to cultural revolution. For too long black people and everyone else in this culture have been socialized to see the avant-garde solely as a marginal place where art that only a few understand resides. The time has come to rethink our assumptions. When we embrace the avant-garde as a necessary matrix of critical possibility, acknowledging that it is a context for cultural revolution, new and exciting representations of blackness will emerge.

Imagine a film that dares to show us the naked black female form in a pro-sex narrative that does not begin with rape as the central metaphor of our existence and as the boundary of our sexual landscape. Or a film working with images of elderly black women. And how about a radical visual conceptualization of black heterosexual relationships? I dream of seeing a documentary film about a woman writer and the film-maker she loved that would use still images, a voice-over with love letters. No conventional story—a fragmented narrative, maybe a sound track with Celtic music or Coltrane or Sufi chants. When we are willing to dare, to risk, to stretch the bounds of the visual, moving our imaginations all over the place, all will be possible. There will be nothing that cannot be seen.

what's passion got to do with it

an interview with

Marie-France Alderman

All of bell hooks's essays include an unforgettable testimony, a personal story told with trust. Why people tend to remember hooks's words has to do with that trust—which is a leap of faith and which, in the face of what she chooses to talk about, remember, and imagine, makes her much more than "one of the foremost black intellectuals in America today." bell hooks has a way of offering herself up on the sacrificial altar of critical inquiry that involves my heart and mind: I am always left with the exhilarating insights only seasoned raconteurs can inspire. hooks is the personal is political thirty years later, flagrant proof that feminism engenders pleasure and hope and the renewed lives that come with them.

bell hooks's *Black Looks* established her reputation as an important film critic. Relentless in her conviction that "many audiences in the United States resist the idea that images have an ideological content," hooks goes about piercing "the wall of denial" with some of the fiercest and sexiest film analyses ever published. An essay hooks wrote for *Visions* about *The Crying Game* and *The Bodyguard* and an interview that took place in New York in September give us a glimpse into a mind for which intellectual pleasure, art, and political intervention are one and the same.

Marie-France Alderman

bell hooks: A friend from Ireland once said to me, "You know, you'll never make it in the United States because there's no place for passion"—not to mention for being a passionate woman. That's probably what feminism was initially about: How do we make room for self-determining, passionate women who will be able to just be? I am passionate about everything in my life—first and foremost, passionate about ideas. And that's a dangerous person to be in this society, not just because I'm a woman, but because it's such a fundamentally anti-intellectual, anti-critical thinking society. I don't think we can act like it's so great for men to be critical thinkers either. This society doesn't want anybody to be a critical thinker. What we as women need to ask ourselves is: "In what context within patriarchy do women create space where we can protect our genius?" It's a very, very difficult question. I think I most cultivated myself in the home space, yet that's the space that is most threatening: it is much harder to resist a mother who loves you and then shames you than it is an outside world that does the same. It's easier to say "no" to the outside world. When a lover tells you—as I've been told—"My next girlfriend will be dumb," I think, "What is that message about?" Female creativity will have difficulty making itself seen. And when you add to that being a black female or a colored female, it becomes even more difficult.

Marie-France Alderman: What about the representation of black female creativity in recent films?

bh: *What's Love Got to do with It*, *The Bodyguard*, and *Poetic Justice* involve passionate black women characters, but they all rely on this packaging of black women musical icons—Janet Jackson, Tina Turner, and Whitney Houston. No one says you have to see *The Bodyguard* because Whitney Houston is such a great actress, because we know she's not a great actress at all. We're going to see what this musical icon does in this movie. Is this Hollywood saying we still can't take black women seriously as actresses?

MFA: Perhaps only as entertainers —

bh: Why does the real Tina Turner have to come in at the end of *What's Love Got to Do with It?* It's like saying that Angela Bassett isn't a good enough actress—which I didn't think she was, by the way—and that's part of why, in a sense, it becomes Larry Fishburne's narrative of Ike, more so than the narrative of Tina Turner. It's a very tragic film, because you sit in the theater and you see people really identify with the character of Ike, not with the character of Tina Turner. In my essay "Selling Hot Pussy," in *Black Looks*, I talked about how Ike constructed the whole idea of Tina Turner's character from those television movies of *Sheena, Queen of the Jungle*.

MFA: And you talk about how she was, in fact, anything but a wild woman.

bh: *I, Tina*, Tina Turner's autobiography, is so much about her tragedy—the tragedy of being this incredibly talented woman in a family that didn't care for you. Then you meet this man who appears to really care for you, who exploits you, but at the same time, you're deeply tied to him. One of the things in the film that was so upsetting was when Tina Turner lost her hair. The filmmakers make that a funny moment. But can we really say that any woman losing her hair in this culture could be a funny moment? No one ever speculates that maybe Tina stayed with Ike because as a woman with no hair in this culture, she had no real value. That no amount of wigs ...

MFA: or great legs ...

bh: no amount of being this incredible star could make up for the fact that she had bald spots. I mean, think about the whole relationship—not only of women in general in this culture to hair, but of black women to hair. *What's Love* takes that incredibly tragic moment in a young female's life and turns it into laughter, into farce. What I kept thinking about was why this culture can't see a serious film that's not just about a black female tragedy but about a black female triumph. It's so interesting how the film stops with Ike's brutality, as though it is Tina Turner's life ending. Why is it that her success is less interesting than the period of her life when she's a victim?

MFA: Tina Turner lost control of her own story somewhere along the line.

bh: Part of what remains tragic about a figure like Tina Turner is that she's still a person who has to work through that image of her that Ike created. I don't know if this is true, but I heard that she sold her story to Hollywood but didn't ask to go over the script or for rights of approval. Obviously, she didn't. Otherwise how could it have become cinematically Ike's story? And why do we have to hear about Larry Fishburne not wanting to do this film unless there can be changes in Ike's character; unless that character can be softened, made to feel more human? I mean, Fuck Ike! That's how I feel. You know, all these black people—particularly black men—have been saying to me, "Ike couldn't have treated her that bad." Why don't they say, "Isn't it tragic that he did treat her so bad?" This just gets to show you how we, as black people in this country, remain sexist in our thinking of men and women. The farcical element of this film has to do not just with the producers thinking that white people won't take seriously a film about a black woman who's battered and abused but that black people won't either. So you have to make it funny. I was very frightened by the extent to which laughter circulated in that theater over stuff that wasn't funny. That scene with her hair is so utterly farcical. The fact is that no fucking woman—including Tina Turner—is beautiful in her body when she's being battered. The real Tina Turner was sick a lot. She had all kinds of health problems during her life with Ike. Yet the film shows us this person who is so incredibly beautiful and incredibly sexual. We don't see the kind of contrast Tina Turner actually sets up in her autobiography between "I looked like a wreck one minute, and then, I went on that stage and projected all this energy." The film should have given us the pathos of that, but it did not at all, because farce can't give you the pathos of that.

MFA: When you talk about Tina Turner going from a victimized, over-worked woman who is always sick to an entertainer who jumps to the stage—that's consistent with a conception of black life that goes from the cotton field to tap dancing.

bh: Absolutely.

MFA: Maybe we can't imagine anything about black lives beyond that.

bh: We can't imagine anything else as long as Hollywood and the structures of filmmaking keep these very "either-or" categories. *The Bodyguard* makes a significant break with the Hollywood construc-tion of female characters—not because Whitney Houston has sex with this white man, but because the white man, Frank Farmer, says that her life is valuable, that her life is worth saving. Tradition-ally, Hollywood has said, "Black women are backdrops; they're Dixie cups. You can use them and dispense them." Now, here's a whole film that's saying just the opposite. Whether it's a bad film is beside the point. The fact is, millions and millions of people around the world are looking at this film, which, at its core, chal-lenges all our perceptions of the value of not only black life but black female life. To say that a black single mother's life is valu-able is really a very revolutionary thing in a society where black women who are single parents are always constructed in the public imagination as unbeautiful, unsexy, unintelligent, deranged, what have you. At the same time, the film's overall mes-sage is paternalistic. I found it fascinating that we see Kevin Cost-ner's character related to God, nation, and country.

MFA: The same thing happened in *Dances with Wolves*.

bh: And in *The Crying Game*, where you have white men struggling with their identity. In *The Bodyguard*, we're dealing with a white boy who is the right, for God, for country but who somehow finds himself at a moment of crisis in his life—having sex, falling in love with this black woman. That's what he needs to get himself together, but once he's together, he has to go back. So we have the final shots in the film where he's back with God and nation. It's all white. It's all male, and of course, the film makes us feel that he's made the right choice. He didn't allow himself to be swept away by otherness and difference, yet the very reason this film can gross $138 million is that people are fascinated right now with questions of otherness and difference. Both Kevin Costner and Neil Jordan repeatedly said that their films had nothing to do with race. Kevin Costner said that "it would be a pity if people went to see *The Bodyguard* and thought it was about race." Well, why the fuck does he think millions of people want to see it? Nobody cares about white men fucking black women. People care about the idea of a rich white man—the fictional man, Frank Farmer, but also the real Kevin Costner—being fascinated by Whitney Houston. They want to see a film about love, not about fucking, because we can see any number of porno films where white men are fucking black women. *The Bodyguard* is about a love so powerful that it makes people transgress certain values. Think again about how it compares with *The Crying Game*, where, once again, we have this theme of desire and love so powerful that it allows one to transcend national identity, racial identity, and, finally, sexual identity. I find that to be the ultimate reactionary message in both of these films: We don't need politics. We don't need struggle. All we need is desire. It is desire that becomes the place of connection. This is a very postmodern vision of desire, as the new place of transgression that eliminates the need for radical politics.

MFA: In their introduction to *Angry Women*, Andrea Juno and V. Vale explained the current fascination with gender bending and sexual transgression as a reaction to overpopulation. In other words, humans know they've outgrown a certain system and "are starting to exercise their option to reinvent their biological destinies." Could that be why desire has become so important?

bh: That's a mythopoetic reading that I don't have problems with, but I think the interesting thing about it is that it returns us to a dream that I think is very deep in this society right now, which is a dream of transformation—of transforming a society—that doesn't have to engage in any kind of unpleasant, sacrificial, political action. You know a film I saw recently that was very moving to me—and I kept contrasting it to *Menace II Society*—was the film *Falling Down*. There is a way to talk about *Falling Down* as describing the end of Western civilization. Black philosopher Cornel West talks about the fact that part of the crisis we're in has to do with Western patriarchal biases no longer functioning, and there is a way in which *Falling Down* is about a white man who's saying, "I trusted in this system. I did exactly what the system told me to and it's not working for me. It's lied to me." That doesn't mean you have the right to be so angry that you can attack people of color or attack other marginal groups. In so many ways, though, that's exactly how a lot of white people feel. There's this sense that if this white supremacist capitalist patriarchy isn't working for white people—most especially for working-class white men, or middle-class white men—it's the fault of some others out there. It's in this way that the structure has fed on itself. The fact is, when you have something that gets as fierce as the kind of greed we have right now, then white men are going to have to suffer the fallout of that greed as well. That's one of the scary things about Bosnia and Croatia: we're not seeing the fallout played out on the field of the bodies of people of color—which is what America is used to seeing on its television. The dead bodies of color around the world symbolize a crisis in imperialism and the whole freaky thing of white supremacy. It's interesting that people don't talk about ethnic cleansing as tied to mythic notions of race purity and white supremacy, which are so much a part of what this country is struggling with. What South Africa is struggling with—that myth of white supremacy—is also being played out by black Americans when we overvalue those who are light-skinned and have straight hair while ignoring other black people. It all shows how deeply that myth has inserted itself in all our imaginations. *Falling Down* captures not only the horror of that but also the role that the mass media has played in that. In the one scene where the white man is trying to use that major weapon and the little black boy shows him how to, the man says to this little boy, "Well, how do you know how to use it?" The boy says, "I've seen it in the movies."

Menace II Society, which I thought was really just a reactionary
film on so many levels, offers itself to us as "black culture," yet
what the film actually interrogates within its own narrative is that
these black boys have learned how to do this shit not from black
culture but from watching white gangster movies. The film
points out that the whole myth of the gangster—as it is being
played out in rap and in movies—is not some Afrocentric or
black-defined myth, it's the public myth that's in all our imaginations from movies and television. There was the scene in
Menace II Society where we see them watching those white gangster movies and wanting to be like that, and that is the tragedy of
white supremacy and colonization. It's delivered to us in the
whole package of the film, as being about blackness, as being a
statement about black young people and where they are, but it is,
in truth, a statement about how white supremacy has shaped and
perverted the imagination of young black people. What the film
says is that these people have difficulty imagining any way out of
their lives, and the film doesn't really subvert that. It says to you
"When you finally decide to imagine a way out, that's when you
get blown away." The deeper message of the film is: "Don't imagine a way out," because the person who's still standing at the end
of the film has been the most brutal. But in *Falling Down* the white
man is not still standing. He hasn't conquered the turf. There's
this whole sense of "Yeah, you now see what everyone else has
been seeing, which is that the planet has been fucked up, and
you're going to be a victim of it too," as opposed to the way in
which *Menace II Society* suggests—mythically almost—that the
genocide we are being entertained by is not going to be
complete, that there are going to be the unique and special individuals who will survive the genocide but they're not the individuals who were dreaming of a way out. That's why these films are
antiutopian. They're antirevolution because they shut down the
imagination, and it's very, very frightening. In the same way, I
was disturbed lately by the film *Just Another Girl on the I.R.T.* Sub-
textually, it's a fucking antiabortion film. This woman who is
portrayed as so powerful and thoughtful, yet she can't make a
decision about what to do with her body. I teach young women at
a city college: these women would not be so confused when it
came to their bodies, but that's how people imagine lower-class
black women. I teach single mothers who have had the will and

the power to go forward with their lives while this society says to them, "How dare you think you can go forward with your life and fulfill your dreams?"

MFA: Camille Billops's film *Finding Christa* addresses that. Talk about revolutionary. A woman—Billops herself—does something for the sake of her art very few of us would ever *think* of doing: give her young daughter up for adoption. And then, twenty years later, far from denying anything, instead celebrates it all over again through the making of a film. *Finding Christa* is a very troubling and interesting film.

bh: I think it was disturbing on a number of levels. It's interesting that we can read about men who have turned their back on parenting to cultivate their creativity and their projects and no one ever thinks it's horrific, but a lot of us, including myself, were troubled by what we saw in Camille Billops's film. This woman went to such measures to ensure that she had the space to continue being who she wanted to be, and at the same time it felt very violent and very violating of the daughter. I've always liked Camille Billops's films. *Suzanne Suzanne* is one of my favorite films, because more than any other films by independent black filmmakers, she really compels people to think about the contradictions and complexities that beset people. We're not used to women artists of any race exerting that kind of relationship to art.

MFA: Billops did what *she* thought she had to do. You know, "A woman's gotta do what a woman's gotta do."

bh: It's funny. I was reading this interview with Susan Sarandon about *Thelma and Louise*, another very powerful film that turns into a farce.

MFA: *Thelma and Louise* is a reactionary film. The women might be feisty for a while but at the end they've got to off themselves. These women would have been heroic if they'd *refused* to disappear. Imagine the story of two males outlaws who, when the going gets tough decide to hold each other's hand and dive into oblivion. How cool is that? But somehow it is cool to think of women

disappearing, killing themselves. Maybe it's a collective unconscious wish.

bh: But there is this one scene at the beginning. When Susan Sarandon's character says, "When a woman is crying, she's not having a
good time." There is that sense that she doesn't shoot him
because of the attempted rape, she shoots him because of his
complete and utter fucking indifference. In that moment, a lot of
men saw how this indifference fucking hurts, but then, it's all
undermined by everything that happens after that scene. That's
the tragedy of *Thelma and Louise*: it doesn't offer empowerment by
the end, it's made feminism a joke, it's made rebellion a joke, and
in the traditional patriarchal manner, it's made death the punishment.

MFA: Yet many feminists—lesbian and straight—stood up and cheered
when the two protagonists decide to commit suicide.

bh: Filmmaker Monika Treut said something similar to what I'm
about to say, which is that if people are starving and you give
them a cracker they're not going to say, "Gee, this cracker is
limited. It's not what I deserve. I deserve a full meal." As a feminist, I think it's pathetic that people want to cheer *Thelma and Louise*,
a film so narrow in its vision, so limited. But I hear that from black
people about black films that I critique: "This is all we have." So
we've got to celebrate something magical and transformative in a
film and at the same time discuss it critically.

MFA: Artist Lawrence Weiner calls that flirting with madness.

bh: A lot of women have found themselves falling into madness
when the world does not recognize them and they cannot recognize themselves in the world. This is exemplified in the lives of
people like Sylvia Plath, Anne Sexton, Virgnia Woolf, and Zora
Neale Hurston. That's because there's a lot that happens to
women of all races—and black women in particular—who
become stars. There's envy. I was just home recently at a family
reunion, and people said such mean and brutal things to me that
I started to think, "What's going on here?" And my brother said
that a lot of what's going on here is envy. There's a part of me

that says, "I don't want to go further with my life, further with my creativity, because if people envy me, they'll torture me." It's not so much a sense of not being able to handle anything; it's a sense of not being able to handle torture. We hear all these statistics about how many women are raped and beaten every so many seconds, yet when we talk about having fear in patriarchy, we're made to feel that that's crazy. What incredible women today— especially those who are feminists—aren't talked about in many contexts as mad? We fall into periods of critical breakdown because we often feel there is no world that will embrace us.

MFA: When I think about madness, I am reminded of R.D. Laing, who said that one's self is an illusion, that we hallucinate the abyss, but that we can also make this leap of faith that the abyss is perfect freedom—that it won't lead to self-annihilation or destruction but the exact opposite.

bh: I think the reality is that the world exists only inasmuch as people like us make it. So I don't want to suggest that we can't have it. We have to make it. However, if a I am lured into thinking that because everyone's bought my books and I've got these reviews, there's already a place—that's where I could get really screwed. You can go crazy looking for these people who bought your books, wrote reviews, and said you were a great thinker or da-da-da-da-da. I think that's where envy comes in. That's why the movie *Amadeus* was so fascinating, because it says that sometimes people try to destroy you precisely because they recognize your power—not because they don't see it, but because they see it and they don't want it to exist. That's why Madonna, who is one of the most powerful, creative women in the United States today, has reinvented her public image to be that of the subordinate, victimized woman. In a sense, it allows her to exist without horror. What would really be going on for Madonna if she was putting forth an image that said, "I'm so powerful, I'm going to recover myself. I'm going to deal with the childhood abuse that happened in my life, and I'm going to continue to creatively imagine ways for women to be sexually free"? I think she would be a much more threatening image than she is in some little-girl pornographic shoot in *Vanity Fair*. Such images allow her to be bought and dismissed.

MFA: Perhaps it's a conscious strategy on her part: One soothing little girl photo session, then bam—she breaks or at least confronts a new taboo.

bh: Sandra Bernhard is another creative woman who has struggled with questions of transgression and has broken new ground. I just finished reading her book *Love, Love, Love*. There's something particularly exciting in the way she toys with the notion of difference, the way she problematizes black female and white female relations, and the way she talks about traditional seduction and gaslighting sexuality—capturing and conquest.

MFA: Which is a concept—to seduce and betray—that comes back a lot in your own work.

bh: I used to have this friend, we always wrote about movies in our journals—discussions of different movies. One of the things we wrote about was a discussion about gaslighting and how in the great gaslighting films of Hitchcock there was always some attempt at reconciliation, whereas now we get gaslighting films like *Jagged Edge* where no order is restored by the end of the film. There is no restoration of harmony that involves a union of male and female—some reconciliation of the act of betrayal. In real life—with friends, with lovers, with parents—we're always having to struggle to reconcile betrayal. We don't just drop everyone who betrays us and move on to better love. We are called upon by life to work through certain forms of betrayal.

MFA: To get to better love.

bh: Absolutely. Grappling with betrayal leads to an understanding of compassion, forgiveness, and acceptance that makes for a certain kind of powerful love. People get annoyed at me for this, but I liked Streisand's *Prince of Tides*. I thought that *Prince of Tides* was two films. One is about the issues of self-restoration in order to love, which is what the Nick Nolte character is all about. Then there's the bullshit film of Barbra Streisand wanting to seduce the WASP man. I recently looked at *Prince of Tides* fast-forwarding all the scenes of her sexual relationship with him and it became a very poignant film about male return to the possibility of love. The film does suggest to men that they're not going to be able to love and experience any kind of mature relationship and sustain a relationship of joy without some self-interrogation. A lot of white-male recovery films—*The Fisher King* and others—are trying to say just that: "White man, you're going to have to look at yourself with some degree of critical thought if you are to experience any love at all." But there don't seem to be any films that suggest to the black man that he needs to look at himself critically in order to know love.

MFA: What about Burnett's *To Sleep With Anger*?

bh: Charles Burnett is a powerful filmmaker, yet here's his weakest film, and that's the one that gets the most attention. The Danny Glover character is so powerful, yet we don't know why. Is he a symbol of creativity gone amok?

MFA: He's like the rainmaker—you know, Burt Lancaster's *Rainmaker*.

bh: Oh, absolutely. When he lies down on that kitchen floor, there's no capacity to utilize his magic and his creativity. He's just gone in terms of images of black men. I would just say that John Sayles's portrait of the black male character *Brother from Another Planet* is a transgressive moment. The love scene between that character and the women in *City of Hope* is an interesting representation of what allows males to enter the space of heterosexual intercourse in a way that is evocative of tenderness and mutual pleasure. However, I do think that John Sayles has a strange relationship with black women, because he always portrays us with these weird wigs—like the woman in *Brother from Another Planet* and the black woman in *Passion Fish*.

MFA: Let's talk about love and fear.

bh: *Sleepless in Seattle* is a very interesting movie about passion and love and fear. In both *Truly, Madly, Deeply* and *Sleepless in Seattle*, the fear is that you've lost a grand love and you'll never be able to experience it again. Passion and desire for love do have the potential to destroy people. It's like losing your sense of smell or taste. There is that intensity of passion in films like *Red Sorghum* and *Ju Dou*—that sense of being so deeply, spiritually, emotionally connected to another person. Tragically, there's so much weird focus on code-pendency in this culture—especially where women are concerned—that it has become very hard for women to articulate what it means to have that kind of life-transforming passion. I think that our culture doesn't recognize passion because real passion has the power to disrupt boundaries. I want there to be a place in the world where people can engage in one another's differences in a way that is redemptive, full of hope and possibil-ity. Not this "In order to love you, I must make you something else." That's what domination is all about, that in order to be close to you, I must possess you, remake and recast you. Redemptive love is what's hinted at in *The Bodyguard* and in *The Crying Game*. Then it goes away and we don't know where it's gone. Why did it go away?

MFA: For the same reason Thelma and Louise have to die.

bh: Absolutely. We have to go to films outside America to find any vision of redemptive love—whether it be heterosexual love or love in different sexual practices—because America is a culture of domination. Love mitigates against violation, yet our construction of desire in the context of domination is always, always about violation. There must be a tremendous hunger for this kind of hopeful love in our culture right now, because people are so drawn to films like *Raise the Red Lantern, Red Sorghum*, and *Like Water for Chocolate*. Pedro Almodóvar almost always explores this tension between our desire for recognition and love and our complete fear of abandonment. In *Tie Me Up! Tie Me Down!* we don't have this perfect middle-class vision of recovery. Many feminists hate it because the woman falls in love with her kidnapper, yet the fact is that in our real lives there are always contradictory circumstances that confront us. Out of that mess, we create possibilities of tran-scendence. I do feel that a certain kind of feminist discourse came to a compete and utter halt around the question of sexuality and power because people cannot reconcile the way in which desire can intervene in our political belief structure, our value systems, our claims of racial, ethnic, or even sexual purity. I don't think the average person in this culture knows what passion is, because daily TV and the mass media are saying, "It's best to live your life in certain forms of estrangement and addiction." We're seeing too many films that don't deliver the goods, that don't give us any world that calls us to feel again, and if we can't feel, then we don't have any hope of knowing love.

15

the cultural mix:

an interview with

Wayne Wang

The Buddhist concept of "maitri" is translated as loving kindness by many teachers here in the West. In *The Wisdom of No Escape*, Pema Chodron shares that we are here to study ourselves, to live in a spirit of wakefulness. To that end we need to be curious and inquisitive, alive and open, and it is that path that will lead us to "the fruition of maitri-playfulness." Her words resonate in my mind as I think about the unique magical aspects of Wayne Wang's work. All his early films—*Chan is Missing, Dim Sum*—and the more recent Hollywood films—*The Joy Luck Club, Smoke, Blue in the Face*—reveal a passion for ordinary detail, the dailiness of life. Wang's work is not documentary realism, instead he works to capture the meditative spirit of stillness and reflection that is often present in all our lives but goes unnoticed. He takes the fascination with small details, ordinary tasks that hint at a larger metaphysics. It is easy to see why the narrative of *Smoke* would intrigue him.

Working in enclosed space, without directing a great deal of attention to a large environmental context, *Smoke* reminds us of the way in which our lives are shaped and circumscribed by landscapes over which we have very little control. Wang juxtaposes those environments with the inner landscape—that place in the self where we can imagine and thus invent and reinvent ourselves. This spirit of tenderness is awesomely present in *Blue in the Face,* and is personified in the characters of Jimmy Rose (Jared Harris), who is a mixture of late bloomer, idiot savant, lovable "retard"; the Rapper (Malik Yoba) who is a combination scammer, street hustler, and philosopher; in the passionate and poetic longing of Violet (Mel Gorham), who desires fulfillment in love and cannot find it; and in Dot (a really powerful moving performance by Roseanne). In *Blue in the Face,* Wang teases out the complex inner layers of the psyche in a way that is marvelous.

This sense of magical complexity and the possibility of playful serendipity, of the beauty in the ordinary, is precisely what is not present in *Smoke.* When I first read the screenplay of *Smoke* I found it such a moving narrative. The story's insistence that we can never really "judge" another person because we do not know enough about the path that they have walked is a powerful intervention in a culture where we are socialized to judge by appearances. And Wang's decision to give racial diversity and identification to the characters, when this was not present in the original story, was all the more compelling. Evil cannot simply be designated as a characteristic of one group, and that which appears to be a lawless act might have a positive outcome. But when I saw *Smoke,* I was stunned by the way in which all the usual racial and sexual stereotypes are played out: the good guys are white, the bad guys black, loose women are working class or females of color, and on and on ... A screenplay that was skillfully deconstructive, challenging of the process by which we make superficial judgments, comes to the screen in a drama that not only does not allow us to really see the inner landscape of the characters but undermines this radical message.

Intrigued and enraged by *Smoke*, I longed to talk with Wayne Wang about his filmmaking process. And when I saw *Blue in the Face*, which really draws upon the themes and environment of *Smoke* and achieves a level of artistic enchantment, I was eager to talk with Wayne about the collaboration of characters and personalities that led to these films (there was a large crew of big-time actors and personalities in these works).

Seeing both these films sheds light on the process of art created in collaboration, when the mix of marketplace concerns and artistic visions converge and collide. It took four years for *Smoke* to emerge, and only a few short months for *Blue in the Face*. The end result reminds us that the act of creating work is always both a manifestation of the individual artistic vision and the way the work acquires a life of its own in the process. Making art, making a film, is still an act of creation that reminds us of the power of mystery, for the outcome is ultimately unpredictable.

bell hooks: You started with eclectic work like *Chan is Missing*, and you've gone on to move between different ethnicities and cultures. Could you talk a little bit about what has been the force behind that movement?

Wayne Wang: I guess it was growing up in Hong Kong, being Chinese, living under a British colony, watching Rock Hudson and Doris Day movies, listening to *The Eagles* ... (*laughter*) I've always been, in a sense, on the border, because my parents were always very Chinese. At the same time they wanted me to be more American, more, you know, "Western." I was exposed to movies, tv, music from everywhere—and I was always dreaming that I would be driving in California with *The Eagles* ... or surfing with Jan and Dean. (*laughter*) So I've really been sort of schizophrenic and torn as far back as I can remember.

bh: I dreamed I would be hanging out in New York City with Jack Kerouac, but I never realized that dream. It's fascinating to me that you were able to stay with yours.

WW: When I finished high school, my parents said, you ought to go to America and go to college. I knew that was, first of all, my chance to get away, and second, to realize that dream. It was literally a dream and a fantasy all along, and then I had the opportunity to make it real. So I took a boat, and I remember the trip was really long and boring. Finally we got to the Golden Gate Bridge (this is in 1967). I had a little transistor radio and I began to pick up the radio stations—there were like twenty, thirty rock stations. I was in heaven. There was only one english radio station in Hong Kong, so to have twenty of them all playing rock music ... The dream was coming true for me.

bh: Where did African American culture fit in? Was it in the picture yet?

WW: Not yet. When I first came, I had no contact with black culture or the black community. I had a lot of stereotypes about blacks, because the only exposure I had was really through movies, and most of the representations of black people in movies are really distorted. I went to a junior college in Los Altos, and it was almost completely white. I had very little exposure there, except in my second year I took this English course, and the teacher's main text for that class was *The Autobiography of Malcolm X*. I almost flunked that class because I had no idea what Malcolm X was talking about. It probably wasn't until I went to the California College of Arts and Crafts, when I started meeting a lot more black students, that things changed. As they began to explain things about them- selves, I began to understand what Malcolm X was all about, and what the African American community was about.

bh: It is interesting, because a lot of the writing I do is about what

kind of mindset we need to put ourselves in when we do representations of cultures in which we don't belong. It seems that,
much more than other filmmakers who cross that line in making
great independent films, and successful Hollywood films, you
think about the question of appropriation.

WW: The question of appropriation is pretty complicated. For myself, I
don't feel possessive of it, so to speak. I mean I don't agree with
people who say that you can only make films about blacks if
you're black, you can only make films about Chinese if you're
Chinese. The criteria for me is for the person to be open-minded,
and to do their homework on that culture, and whatever that
they're trying to portray. As long as there are also avenues and
opportunities for the minority cultures to represent themselves.
This is very important. Because otherwise, you don't have any so-
called true representation. For example, as long as Chinese Americans are able, and have the resources, to make films about
Chinese Americans, then I think it's fine for a white American
director to make a film about the Chinese American community,
because it's another perspective from the outside looking in.

bh: The filmmaker Trinh T. Minh-ha has done this. One of her early
films focused on African culture, and she was often questioned by
African Americans about how she positioned herself. There was
often a resentment behind those questions about what her place
was in this process. For me, it's a failure to understand subjectivity, and what freedom is, and to understand that part of our freedom is having our capacity to imagine with other cultures. But
the dilemma seems to be, as you touched on, the whole question
of when representations reproduce stereotypes. And I actually had
such a different sense of this in the two films you've done recently,
Smoke and *Blue in the Face*. *Smoke*, much more, seemed to run the
risk of working in very conventional Hollywood representations,
both in the representations of gendered relationships and in the
representations of ethnicities. I'm thinking of the Latina woman
character, Violet, and the character of Rashid, who is a very problematic character for me.

WW: How is he problematic?

bh: I felt that the script of *Smoke* was a very compelling story—an incredible screenplay. It was the type of story that had the potential magic of a film that is sentimental at heart, whose thrust from beginning to end is sentimental. But that doesn't mean that it doesn't have the potential for a powerful impact. The heart of it was questioning stereotypes, saying that the things that you imagine about where a person comes from, you may not actually know until you know their history. Actually this is one of the few films in which I felt the casting actually undermined what was the more subversive power of the screenplay itself.

WW: Are you just referring to Rashid?

bh: No, I thought the black actors in the film were weak.

WW: Including Forest Whitaker?

bh: Including Forest Whitaker, whom I'm a tremendous fan of.

WW: Weak in what ways?

bh: In that they seem to be caricatures, they seem to be parodied. You know it's difficult not to contrast *Smoke* with *Blue in the Face*, but *Blue in the Face* had this really laid-back quality, almost as if "We don't have to overplay, we can just be cool, and it's like, someone filming us right now, we can just be." But *Smoke*—I guess it's what happens when you cast incredibly famous people with people who have not yet made their careers. There seemed to be this overdoing that bordered on caricature and parody. The black characters were like soda that was flat.

WW: When we were auditioning, we saw a lot of good young black actors that were sodas with a lot of hot air. It was, like, gassed all over—they were really jivey and rappy, and very modern. I hated that, because you see that so often in Hollywood movies. The idea of Rashid was to portray a character who was from the projects, but his aunt brought him up differently. He had a great wit with his language that did not resort to "Hey man," "Fuck you, man," and "Shit, man." That was very important to me and Paul Auster. So we picked an actor who fit those characteristics. You may call it flat, but that's the character, and in that sense it goes against what I think is the worst stereotype of young blacks today.

bh: But he did not come across as a believable character. Something was missing. He lacked street savvy. And I was actually deeply fascinated by the film's whole context of undermining certain stereotypes. This is the hardest type of film to carry off, because there's not a lot of action.

WW: There's no action! (*laughter*)

bh: But *Blue in the Face* is just an exquisite example of how you can be deeply moved by very subtle things. Like that moment when Jimmy says, "Do you need a hug?" It's so perfect and there's nothing fake about it, you don't feel that it's corny. I wonder if it's the difference between independent filmmaking and when one is pitching to a larger, more diverse audience. How did you experience it as a filmmaker? You made a major Hollywood hit, do you feel like there's a difference?

WW: There's a lot of difference. It's very, very difficult for independent films in America to exist today. I believe that the truly independent films are *completely* financed outside of the studios. It is very hard to raise the money to make true independent films. The filmic representation has to be experimental and interesting rather than re-creating the Hollywood language. So the question is, How do you create, or re-create, the independent movie? In my mind, I don't even know what independent films are any more, if they exist at all.

bh: Do you feel like it would be hard for you today to make a *Chan is Missing*, because certainly *Chan is Missing* has a lot of those subversive qualities that you just descried.

WW: I think that I could still do it—but I would have to do it in video or something, because once I pick up a movie camera, unions are going to be on my back to say, you know, this's gotta be a union shoot, and all of a sudden it's a $5 million movie. So to be subversive and to do it the way I did *Chan Is Missing*, the only way I could probably do it is on the fly. That is the only way of doing it, and one that I'm still interested in. But whether it gets distributed or not is another story—I made a film called *Life is Cheap*, which I had to distribute myself. It was a very subversive, very interesting independent movie, but I could not get arrested for three years after that. (*laughter*)

bh: One of the things that's wonderful about your career is that one of the magical elements in *Chan is Missing* is the way you conceptualize space and detail. The cigar store becomes a world in and of itself. That quality of attention to not just space but the way details are focused on in space: the way we see the drawing in *Blue in the Face*, when Giancarlo Esposito's character's old college friend (Michael J. Fox's character) is chatting with him and we see by his doodling that he's not writing it down. That attention to detail affects how you respond to the scene and has nothing to do with language. Can you talk a little bit about that?

WW: A lot of people ask me why I'm so obsessed with the environment, with empty rooms, with inanimate objects. When I was growing up I spent a lot of time by myself at home. I had very little to play with, I didn't have many games, toys or guns or whatever. So I spent a lot of time sitting in empty rooms staring at the space and working my imagination. I would stare at the dining room where we ate and imagine dinner. So those rooms were what gave me my imagination and my fantasies. I invested them with real emotions and history too.

bh: It's also the experience of the postmodern, multicultural standpoint that we were describing earlier, and also the immigrant experience. Because I think that space for immigrants takes on different meanings, the details become crucial to your survival.

WW: And the details of how they organize that space are really, really important. A friend of mine used to do research on how the elderlies in Chinatown organized their space so that they could design spaces that would fit how the elderlies lived. And one of the things that they did was they put newspapers on the walls. They usually put their beds against the wall, the long side of it, and then they would put newspaper along the wall, because the newspaper would somehow cut the cold—"the yin chi"—that's coming off the wall. Eight out of ten of the rooms would have newspaper by the side of the bed—those little details of how they live and why they live that way are culturally very important to me. The other thing that is very important to me with spaces is when you first see a space, it's not loaded with meaning. You haven't seen people in it, nothing has happened in it. The first time you see an empty space, it is probably as pure as it can be. But as you see people interact in that space over time, it gains more meaning, and a different kind of meaning emerges from that image. So if you go back to the image of the empty shot of the room, that shot would have a different meaning because of what you have seen happen in it. It goes back to the whole theory of montage and the meaning of the image. That's something that I used a lot in *Dim Sum*: the dining room, the dining room with people, then the dining room with the whole family, and then each family member leaving until it's empty again.

bh: And we see that with William Hurt's character's apartment in *Smoke*. In all these films you see these fabulous apartments in New York City, even if the character is supposed to be working-class, the space is incredible. That's not how any of our spaces really are. And I think that was a really tender space for people, because it had a quality that was very real for many of us who are writers.

WW: A lot of credit goes to William Hurt. After they designed it, Bill went in for many days and tried to work in there, tried to sit in there, tried to throw things around, you know, so that it became a real, lived-in space. That's really the only way to do it. The other thing, also, in *Smoke* are the two shots of the Brooklyn trains: one leaving Manhattan going into Brooklyn at the beginning of the film and the other shot of that train snaking through Brooklyn at the end. Those were the only two shots of the environment in the film. Normally in a film you establish the place, you shoot the outside of the house, and then you go inside the house. In *Smoke*, I consciously stripped away all exteriors except for those two train shots, which, in a way, anchor the exterior world that the characters exist in.

bh: In *Blue in the Face* the exterior world is very much foregrounded, not so much by visual space, but by the way people talk about space. Like that moment when the elder black man talks about New York in an almost magical, surrealist, poetic way ... It was a very, very wonderful moment. In many ways *Blue in the Face* is a film which restores to dying American cities some of the integrity of human life in those cities. It seemed particularly poignant that it is New York City at this particular historical moment, when the very idea of the city is under attack—when so many people don't see the city as a place of magic, or a place of community only as this place of crime and stereotype. *Blue in the Face* was very coun- terhegemonic in its way of saying that the city still has its integrity and its force.

WW: Particularly Brooklyn. When we were location scouting for *Smoke*, I felt there was a strong sense of a city as a community in Brook- lyn. I mean New York City also has it, there are certain pockets of it, but Brooklyn has more of it. It's more neighborhood.

bh: But what's interesting is that you don't invoke the conventional, sort-of-white culture of Brooklyn that has come to stand in the public imagination for what real Brooklyn culture is. You see across so many ethnicities, and across so many immigrant groups, a consistent feeling of passion about the space, about the environ- ment, about Brooklyn. And I thought that was part of the film's magic as well. Where did the idea to do the documentary pieces come from?

WW: When we were scouting around Brooklyn for *Smoke*, I saw so much of this cross-cultural spirit of Brooklyn: the faces, the people, the mix of cultures, the crossing over of cultures, some- times not really getting along, sometimes sort of getting along. We just went out with a Hi 8 video camera and grabbed a lot of things on the fly. And when we started rehearsing for *Smoke*, the so-called OTB guys in the cigar store wanted to do some impro- visation so they could understand the relationship with each other in the store. And what they did was full of energy, very real, funny, and came from the gut. So I turned to Paul and said, "There's something very vital here—let's try to capture that." So that was really the origin of *Blue in the Face*. The actors and the place inspired us: let's make a movie in three days, let's not worry about the story, let's not worry about how it's going to end up. Let's just do it. So maybe that's a better way to make a film! (*laughter*)

bh: What makes *Blue in the Face* such a movie of the moment, of our historical moment right now, is that it does raise those questions of ethnicity and identity: Who is who; What does it mean to be black; or What does it mean to have a national identity? To me, these are very deep and profound political questions right now. In a very careful way, the film contests all sorts of constructions of pure identity, it reminds the viewer that so much is mixed, and that it's in the mixing and sharing that the magic arises. What was sort of tickling and funny about *Blue in the Face*, was that while it incorporates icons—Lou Reed, Jim Jarmusch, Roseanne, Madonna—it incorporates them in such a way as to deconstruct their iconic representations. They don't come across as stars playing characters. They actually come across as very believable characters, certainly Roseanne did as Dot. I felt sad for her, I wanted to jump in and say, "I'll drive you to Las Vegas!" (*laughter*) There was this tremendous pain there, about marriage, about desire ...

WW: Right before that she was going through the divorce with Tom Arnold, and she was full of conflicted feelings about marriage, about men. So we created the character from what was very immediate about her feelings, and what she came up with is, I think, a very real side of her at that time.

bh: That is true of the film as a whole. Jimmy's character, for example ... In *Smoke* he doesn't have much of a voice, he's more of a stock character who people respond to because he's supposed to be funny. But in *Blue in the Face* we see this character as incredibly tender. And he's not solely comic, although all the characters, I think, move, like we all do in real life, between moments of seriousness, and moments of comic.

WW: A lot of that had to do with the fact that we didn't try to make Lou Reed and Jim Jarmusch into characters; they were pretty much playing themselves. One of my biggest worries with *Smoke* is that we have a movie about very down-to-earth people and yet we've got big stars playing them. But my task was to strip away some of that persona, as much as I can. Sometimes that's pretty difficult.

bh: Harvey Keitel is still Harvey Keitel in *Blue in the Face*, that there is a way in which he blends more with the other characters in the film. I don't know if it's that the narrative of *Smoke* is, as you pointed out, a much more complex narrative than *Blue in the Face* is that it's more directly like written text ...

WW: They are written text—it's more like a play than anything else, and the whole first half of the film is shot with a proscenium around it. We didn't move in until later on because I wanted that artificiality as a framing device for the film.

bh: It reminded me of *Vanya on 42nd Street*, in that you had so much more materiality around you. So there's a tension between the part of your brain that's trying to process all the narrative and the part that's trying to process the images. In *Blue in the Face* there were these perfect moments when the characters were almost not moving—it was very uncharacteristic of American films in that it uses the pause in a very skillful way. There are moments of silence, in which you are actually able to reflect on what is happening. Most films are moving us forward, and you don't have that space. Was that accidental?

WW: In *Smoke* or *Blue in the Face?*

bh: *Blue in the Face.* There's that moment with Harvey Keitel's character, Auggie, when Dot's husband first comes in and says, "I'm thinking of selling the store." And there's this pause, like in real life when you hear something and you're trying to take it in. Not a lot of films give us that usually.

WW: It's probably somewhat instinctual and somewhat accidental.

bh: But *Chan is Missing* has a lot of those moments of perfect stillness in it.

bh: In *Smoke* the dynamic was much more in the narrative between Auggie and William Hurt's character. It had been more of that quality of passion. In the narratives between Auggie and Aunt Ethel, you see those moments of pauses and stillness. I was curious about the fact that in the Paul Auster story, the kid who's stealing is not racially identified.

WW: He is not racially identified—even the grandmother is not racially identified.

bh: Can you talk about this?

WW: I guess it was a presumption, but when I first read it I was imagining a black person. And then I went back and looked for something that would indicate that this person was black, and there was nothing. And then I called Paul and said, "Is this person black?" And he said, "Well, it's not specified, but he could be black." I guess the source for the inspiration came from when he was a census taker or something and he went around to the projects taking census, and this old woman thought he was someone else and he played along with it. And I like that idea. I'm interested in dealing with a culture that's different than mine and yet not so often represented on the screen. So now in the film itself when Auggie tells the story, there's also no specification that the character is black. And then at the end, when you see the story, it's actually through Paul's interpretation. And it's because of what he has gone through with Rashid that he decide to make him black in the Christmas story.

bh: I was very moved by the central metaphor of smoke, of tobacco. I grew up in a world of tobacco. My first memories as a girl in Kentucky and my family are tied to working both on the fields and the loosening floor where tobacco is cured. And I never thought of tobacco as evil, or associated with cigarettes. I know that some people are raising questions about that, which seems to be a good case of the madness of political correctness. One could say that smoke has all sorts of hazards, at the same time you could also talk about the traditions of smoking and around tobacco, particularly in indigenous cultures around the world, where it binds people and is part of an emotional and spiritual experience.

WW: In the culture I come from, at least in Hong Kong, people still smoke a lot. It's very much something that binds people together—it's ritualistic that after a meal you share a cigarette. Also, people, when they meet, after the present their card, they present a cigarette, as a gesture of friendship. Even tough they are now much more aware that it causes cancer, people take it as one of the factors, it's like driving on freeways or whatever. Here in the U.S., there's such a big thing made out of the political correctness of smoking or not smoking that it's just really stupid. There are even people who have written in to newspapers asking, How much did the tobacco companies give to finance this film?

bh: It seems to be a failure of our cultural imagination that people aren't able to identify with the idea of smoke as a metaphor. When Paul talks of smoke, he says, "It's something that's never fixed, constantly changing shape," in the same ways that the characters keep changing as their lives intersect. But what does it say about our imagination as a culture that we can only take things on one level, that things must exist on one plane only? It seems to be a real indictment that we don't have the capacity to imagine an experience that we might never have. Our capacity to understand the meaning of smoke in people's lives and the meaning of sharing tobacco doesn't have to go along with thinking tobacco is a great thing.

WW: Well, also in *Smoke*, after Auggie tells Paul the story, both of them naturally take out their cigarettes—it's after they've eaten, after they've exchanged the story. It's a ritualistic moment that they share, and to me it represents the friendship that they share with each other. It's not a lasting moment, it's like smoke—that ritual is the most lasting thing.

bh: *The Joy Luck Club* really was a woman's movie, and many people perceive it as a movie that conveys a very gendered reality, the reality of sisters and women together. Could you talk a little bit about that attempt to image women characters?

WW: Well, I try not to think about those things. I didn't go into *Joy Luck Club* thinking, This is a movie about mothers and daughters. It's the same way that I've talked about appropriation earlier: I'm trying to look into the world of mothers and daughters from my perspective. I was always conscious of the fact that because I'm a man I had to do a lot of homework, and really be open, and be sensitive to a lot of the issues surrounding it. When I went to my Chinese herbalist a few years ago, he told me that I had a female body—that all my symptoms of illness were very yin, that maybe in another lifetime I was a woman. I feel that there is a yin and yang in every person and that sometimes perhaps the yin is stronger in some people. In that sense, maybe that's why I work well with women.

bh: Many people criticize *Smoke* for being a boy-bonding movie. In *Smoke* we have much more conventional constructions of women as sex objects, both in the character of Auggie's ex-girlfriend, Ruby, and in the character of Violet. In *Blue in the Face*, when Violet is angry with Auggie for breaking the date, that is a rare passionate scene of a woman of color not seen much in American cinema. There's that wonderful monologue where she's facing the mirror. It's just an incredible scene, in one sense a balancing of the feminine energy, and at the same time you see that this is a strong woman who's not a victim, who's making choices. That does not come through in her characterization in *Smoke*.

WW: I agree. Because in *Smoke* she was only in one scene and she had practically nothing to do. It was difficult to give her any other sort of shading. So that's too bad.

bh: What I think you're pointing out, then, is one of the dangers, whether we talk about gender, race, or ethnicity, of not having space to develop certain characters. You run the risk of reproducing a flat or a stereotypical image.

WW: I agree.

bh: Because her image is such a wonderful image in *Blue in the Face*.

WW: I remember saying to Paul Auster, "You realize that this Violet character is dangerous, because she's in this one scene and she kind of represents some of the stereotypes of her culture." But in the end, I felt that there was so much energy and so much craziness in her that even though it was a little bit verging on stereotypical, I felt it was worth it to take a risk.

bh: A character like Ruby, who I thought was one of the excellent characters in *Smoke*, has this range of emotionality. And even though she had only a brief appearance in the film, it hit you; you see this whole childhood relationship, the loss of the father—and all of those things were tied up in a very short segment. I thought it was a very perfect monological moment.

WW: I felt that her character was so complex that you always questioned the reality of her life. You're never sure if what she's telling you is true or not true.

bh: Since we've spent so much of our time talking about border crossing, I think we should talk about the element of collaboration. Both of these films were, unlike your earlier work, not just the product of your single vision but the product of working together: yourself and Paul Auster and the larger collaboration with the collectivity of actors. Can you talk about that experience of working in collaboration—to what extent does it alter artistic vision, or does it illuminate one vision in particular ways?

WW: It illuminates my vision for sure. I'm not an auteur in the sense that I have a specific artistic vision and say, This has to be exactly this way. If I wanted to do that, I would go back to painting. That way I would be in a room by myself. My only relationship is to my canvas, and I could manipulate anything that I want, and I can do exactly what I want. Cinema is a collaborative thing. That's why, in a sense, *Blue in the Face* is so exciting for me, because there was no authorship, so to speak. As a director, more than anything else I feel like I'm always a facilitator. A traffic cop. I have a lot of experience which helps me organize and put into focus what I think should be the final product, but I don't try to make it only my vision. Maybe that's where my power lies as a director. I'm not a great theater director where I say, "I want you to read this line this way because this is what the subtext of it means, and this is where you should step over a quarter-inch," et cetera. I don't do that. I just help people do their best work by helping them focus and facilitating a prime working environment.

bh: It's really hard to frame certain questions without contrasting the two films, but *Blue in the Face* made me think of this R and B song "Second Chance on Love," where it's actually about going back to the person you've loved, that you lost contact with but you come to them again ... The films in many ways are both love affairs. It's the same love in a sense. There are lots of similar themes and issues. But the second film comes at them in different ways, comes at them with the experience of the first film, mingled in and converging.

WW: And that's why I think they should be seen as one film in a way. For all their different strengths and weaknesses, they belong together. They represent two different processes of working, of creating art. They do represent two different visions of Brooklyn. They do represent two different ways of telling stories about iden-tity, or crossing cultural identity. Why can't films be made twice that way? That's the question I keep asking myself. Why does it always have to be a finished script? You rehearse and you shoot it, and then you try to craft it as best as you can. Why can't you make a slightly different kind of film but also maybe about the same subject matter with the same sets and the same people and the same everything, but then it's completely different, and yet it's also similar? It's almost like when I was painting. I went through a stage where my painting was very realistic, almost photographic, and at the same time I was painting the same subject matter or emotion in abstract expressionism. *Smoke* is the realist painting, and *Blue in the Face* is, in my mind, an abstract-expressionistic painting.

confession—filming family:

an interview with

artist and filmmaker

Camille Billops

bell hooks: Camille Billops, when did documentary become important to you and why?

Camille Billops: It became important to me, at least subconsciously, observing my parents shooting home movies from the late forties into the seventies. When I began making documentary it was in the same context. I didn't know then that those projects would go on to be more than the home movies that my parents had produced.

bh: You have been more transgressive than any other straight black filmmaker I can name, in terms of using autobiographical material for your work. *Suzanne Suzanne* remains one of the most powerful documentaries of domestic life, of black middle-class life. Can you talk about what has allowed you to be so radically open.

CB: It is probably exhibitionism on my part. I don't know if I am that conscious of it, but some people say that our films have a tendency toward dirty laundry. The films say it like it is, rather than how people want it to be. Maybe it is my character that tends to want to do that, because I think the visual arts [artist?] in me wants to say the same kind of thing. So I don't know if I consciously did it; I think it is just my own spirit.

bh: How did you get your family members to agree to *Suzanne Suzanne*? To putting out the story of a daughter who is grappling with heroine addiction, who is in recovery, to putting out the story of domestic violence, of father-daughter physical violence, how did you get them to agree?

CB: They believe that I am their personal filmmaker. They come to me and they say, "Well, I didn't get my film." They want me to get the grants for them, these workers who work at General Motors. And they sign releases. When I did *Suzanne Suzanne*, I made my mother sign a release. You can't invest all that money and then have someone say, "Nah, you can't use my picture."

bh: We talked before about how several family members weren't prepared for what it would be like to have their life documented on the screen.

CB: That was my sister in *Suzanne*, my sister Billie. They liked the idea of being in front of the camera, but they didn't know what the results would be. There are parts where Suzanne is talking about being on the streets, and she had been out there. She did not want her son to know anything about this. I said to her, "For one, we are not going to interview you in your bathrobe. You have to get dressed, and your house has to look neat," because when we photograph people, we can exploit them through costume and background.

bh: This has been a way that black images have been exploited in photograph and in film.

CB: Yes, by staging the sleazy side.

bh: Part of what you show in the film is black people living in mater-
        ial comfort, surrounded, on the surface of their lives, by a veneer
        of Hollywood glamour. You show this in that incredible scene
        when Billie is getting dressed up. There is a strong sense of femi-
        ninity and glamour.

CB: And she is dressing Suzanne, putting the makeup on her. There
        were also the fashion shows. This was my mother's dream. When
        you leave South Carolina, then you leave nappy hair. You get a
        curl. You clean. You wear nice clothes. You are coming from a
        tradition where women freed themselves by being dressmakers.
        The fathers were cooks on railroads, so maybe in a sense that was
        the early setting for wanting to be bourgeois. You knew the dream;
        you just didn't have it. So you went north to get it. This is all
        shown in *Suzanne Suzanne*.

bh: *Suzanne Suzanne* shows what happens when the dream of marriage
        and privilege becomes a nightmare.

CB: Even when it appears to be okay, it's not. Brownie is not okay, and
        something is not okay with him. I do not want to demonize him.
        I would love to go and find his remaining relatives and find out
        what happened. How did he end up so violent, so injured by color
        and class? His father looked like an old white man, and he
        married a dark woman. That seemed to have been a problem in
        his family in Florida. When one marries dark, it is like white
        people talking about niggers, you have married *dark*. I do not know
        how he got injured. I just know that he was.

bh: What the film does through Suzanne's narrative is allow us a
        glimpse of this incredibly affable, interesting black man, but
        through her narrative we also see the terrorist, a cruel person who
        comes home in a rage, and makes everybody suffer.

CB: And it could happen at any time. She said she would just listen
        for the car door and feel the fear. I told you we recut the film,
        because initially we had cut the film in a way that depicted
        Brownie really harshly, and the kids were upset about it. We recut
        it to make him appear a little more caring, a little less violent.

Brownie's character almost tended to take over the film. We were trying to make a film about Suzanne, and it was fast becoming a film about Brownie.

bh: That is very interesting, because one of the complaints that I had about the movie *Once Were Warriors* was that by focusing so much on the male violence, it became less a film about the women. You became intrigued by these men, their bodies, the beauty of their muscles, by what was driving them, rather than the havoc that this violence had wreaked upon everyone. Part of the genius of *Suzanne Suzanne* is that it is taking place along before we have normalized public discourse on the dysfunctional family. You had the vision to represent how a family can unravel when the people are not in communication with one another.

CB: That's right. In those lower-middle-class families one did not have a shrink. One was not aware like that; you just shrugged and said, "Oh, well." That was the attitude I was moving against when I got pregnant with Christa. At that point in my life I had hung out with enough people who believed that you did not have to say, "Oh, well," like the women who stayed there in *Suzanne Suzanne*. You didn't leave a man or break up; you endured. You fought it out. You battled it out. When I got pregnant with Christa I didn't want to battle it out. I did not want to be a mother. I didn't want to be that; so I reversed it. This was the problem I had with "the family." I was to endure. Billie endured, and I said, "No, I don't want to do that. I want to go back to school." But Billie gets married at seventeen. She follows Mamma. She's a dressmaker. She's a first child, an adored, wonderful—

bh: Glamorous.

CB: Yes. They love her; she is fabulous. I used to hear them say, "Billie is so pretty, and Bootsie, you're nice. You're cute too." I always rebelled against this. When she started having children, I should say, "She's having babies like a cat." At this point I had joined the Catholic Church and I was Miss Imperious walking around the house. I didn't admire motherhood. That was not a road I wanted to go down even at ten. Billie had "family," and what you did with family was endure.

bh: There is the moment in the film when Suzanne interrogates Billie and wants to know why she hasn't left. This is part of what makes *Suzanne Suzanne* a really incredible feminist film. Billie has to answer her, and she has to answer her with the truth of her life. The replication of this old legacy is disrupted in that moment when the mother cannot keep the pretense of the fairy-tale existence in the face of the daughter's pain.

CB: Yes. She is also having a had time justifying why she did not take care of her daughter. Moms are supposed to protect. So what she does is say, "I was not protected myself." We are all watching this knowing the history of competition between Suzanne and Billie. Suzanne felt that she was always competing with the mother in the realm of beauty and glamour. When this happens there is the sense that Billie has upstaged her once again.

bh: You have talked about how that particular scene was not in the written script, that it was a spontaneous moment, a living-theater moment, when Suzanne confronts her.

CB: That was not in the script, it was utterly spontaneous—it was total exposure. I get the same dose in *Finding Christa*, but I say, "No, no, no. We're not going to have all this. I had enough guilt giving Christa up, we are not going to go through this *Suzanne Suzanne* moment." There are scenes in *Finding Christa* that threaten this, because Christa wants to do the same thing—to expose me—because of the anger of having been given up. She has the same rage Suzanne does against me because of the adoption. Adoptees have what they call "the great wound." Giving them away appears irrational, "not right." That becomes my *Suzanne Suzanne*, only I am saying that we are not going to go down the road of total exposure.

bh: When you were making *Suzanne Suzanne*, were you aware that you were making a "feminist film"?

CB: No. How would you know? Domestic violence was not talked about the way it is now.

bh: I have sat at film festivals and watched the whole room weep watching *Suzanne Suzanne*, because it gives you a very visceral way to understand the effect of violence upon self-identity. The fact that you link Suzanne's drug addiction to the physical abuse she suffered as a child was really very prophetic for its time.

CB: The liquor addiction also wreaks havoc. The two boys don't form a relationship. I used to go to Suzanne's house, and they never sat down to dinner. She had a partner who had been addicted too, and he was very nice, but there was no family. They would sit and eat the food out of the refrigerator.

bh: These are the stories of black family life, especially with the family life represented in *Suzanne Suzanne*, where people are not poor. This is not about people who don't have access to a certain way of life, but they are still wounded. You show those wounds.

CB: Yes, they are wounded, and this goes back to what I said earlier about my work in the visual arts and film. Their lives become my raw material to create stories that have been viewed as dirty laundry. They are willing subjects. I have little tapes of everyone. All of our plans are on these tapes. When we first find Christa, I am talking to Michael and I say, "Hey, Michael, we found Christa." He immediately says, "Hey, Bootsie, we're gon' go up there and we're gon' see her." All of that is my material. Now, with this last film I am bringing all of this back in.

bh: So what you have done is a family trilogy.

CB: It is all family, except *KKK Boutique*.

bh: This is incredibly transgressive. How many black people in America say anything revealing about their personal lives in the present? Whereas in *Finding Christa* and *Suzanne Suzanne* you do just that. This is the raw stuff of our lives. It has a strong impact. What has allowed you to break those barriers?

CB: It is the need to make sure that they are remembered.

bh: Absolutely. *Finding Christa* deals with issues of memory and reconciliation.

CB: That's right. It reminds us that their lives were here. I always tell people that if you are not on a piece of paper, then you don't exist. We don't know where the people are that built the pyramids. There are no monuments to them. They just died on the roadside. I always tell people the most revolutionary thing you can do is do a book about your life. Don't let anybody call it a vanity press. You just do this, this magnificent thing, and you put it on the best paper you can find. Put all your friends in it, everybody you loved, and do a lot of them so one day they will find you and know that you were all here together. That is why I gather up documentation of new relatives. We have a lot of the three-year-olds and five-year-olds on both sides of the family—the black, black, black ones and the light, light, light ones and all of that mix. For instance. I have carried little Michael on through the films and now he is twenty-three or twenty-four years old. They know me directly, and through Mamma and Mr. Dotson, as the one who shoots the film and does art.

bh: What were the circumstances after *Suzanne Suzanne* that led you to make *Finding Christa*? It is one thing to focus on other people's lives, but in *Finding Christa* you put the spotlight on you. Some critics, like Vincent Canby, have used words like "chilliness" to express the way they leave this film. What are they experiencing?

CB: It is cold. I appear as cold, very cold. I have asked people if it is because I don't cry, and they say, "Yes, you show no remorse."

bh: I think this is what makes it an incredibly radical feminist film, because you challenge all of the set assumptions about motherhood, about how a woman should feel about giving up a child. She should feel guilty. She should feel remorseful, and then we can understand. But, in fact, you make it clear that you still feel that this is the best choice you could have made under the circumstances.

CB: You are right. This as the best choice for both of us, because what appears to be well, as you see in *Suzanne Suzanne*, is only appearance. I did not think at that time that being an unwed mother was such a splendid role. You had to lie and play games. You had to do all kinds of things to protect your moral character. So I felt it was better to give her up to adoption. I was not a good mother. Christa did not stay with me. My sister kept her, and she came to me on the weekends. You see her in *Suzanne Suzanne*. The little baby in the beginning that Billie is running around with, that is Christa. All of the archival footage is from my mother's and step-father, Mr. Dotson's, home movies, and they are all in our films. That baby shower in *Finding Christa*, that was my mother there shooting the camera.

bh: That legacy of grappling with the visual is fantastic.

CB: It is. They gave our films history, their footage. Now I have all of their films. My mom is dead, and my stepfather, who is eighty-five, has given me all of the film. In *KKK Boutique* my cousin Carol, who is doing the "I'm the American dream" part, is at the zoo when she is three years old in Mamma's footage. This is stuff for them to use if they need it. We have said that when we drop dead, my husband, Jim Hatch, and myself, that wherever we leave the collection, it will be stipulated that all the film will be open to anyone who is perceived of as a family member, because it was their history. If we had this to go back to the time when my mother's great-grandmother was alive, what would I have? It would be incredible.

bh: I think this awareness of the need to document black life and not to let a sense of decorum hold one back is incredible. You talked about "how we don't want to show the dirty laundry," but there is a lot about our lives that we need to see so that we do not repeat.

CB: But, see, if you are black, you do not want to show dirty laundry, because it is too hard being black and having dirty laundry too. Owen Dodson talks about the doubled difficulties of being a black man and gay during the Harlem Renaissance, and why, because of this, they did not talk about it. It was too hard. Ulti-mately, those lies injure you.

bh: I feel that one of the most magical representations of black womanhood is in *Finding Christa*, and it was the representation of the black woman who adopts Christa.

CB: Margaret. Yes.

bh: We rarely see the heavyset, dark black woman imaged in any kind of film, by black filmmakers or anybody else, as tender, as loving, as open-hearted, but not in the traditional mammy way. We see her as an existentially self-reflective person, and we see her as a person who clearly is enormously philosophical in the way that she has thought about her relationship to you, her relationship to Christa, and her past. That was a real incredible thing you did as a filmmaker, being able to draw out those elements in Margaret, who adopts Christa, a person you both have a charged personal connection to but that you are also shooting as a filmmaker.

CB: I saw her as the little ship that helped me sail the dangerous night. I wanted to be free of motherhood. Margaret has a dream about a child that will replace the one that she had to give up, the child she was trying to adopt with her husband. But in making the film, we could clearly see that she would be seen as the "natural," the good mother who loves children.

bh: And you as "unnatural," because you gave your child away.

CB: I made a conscious choice to make Margaret who she is. It was my gift to her. Yet I am also blamed by people who see the film, who see Christa and Margaret as saints and think I'm a total bitch. I say, "I am not a bitch, and they are not saints. I *cut* the film." People believe film. It is scary when people say, "This is true," when you got a lot of truth down there on the floor, truth on the shelf, and lies in the film. Film is constructed. It documents reality; that's not the same as revealing truth.

bh: Audiences project that, because on the one hand we see Margaret as the Madonna figure, telling the narrative of adopting this cream child, but on the other hand we see her own children clearly suffering from a lack of attention. She seems to adore Christa, but that adoration is not there for the other children. If audiences idealize her as a saint, they're not taking the film on its own terms. The film did not portray her as a saint.

CB: They see her as such because they see me as so bad—a monster really. These are primarily males that see me as clearly a bad person. Lots of people felt I could be redeemed if I would only repent.

bh: But you don't. You refuse to judge yourself, and it is this absence of self-judgment that makes your commitment to pursuing your goal as a woman artist so threatening. This film challenged the notion that you can be *everything*, and this is what makes it subversive to feminism. Contemporary feminism has, in a sense, told a lie to women, all women, cross-race, cross-class. It has said, "You can have everything." What you brought back into the picture with this documentary is that you cannot be a woman committed to your artistic development and have *everything*.

CB: No.

bh: Especially if you are poor.

CB: Right, and you don't always want to be a mother. I did not want to be a mother. I know that is amazing to people. I think I did in the beginning, when I got pregnant with this romantic, gorgeous black male who was a lieutenant in the air force in California.

bh: You were how old?

CB: I was twenty-three. I got pregnant accidentally. I loved him, because he was fine. He was everything I wanted that thing to be. We were going to get married. I had five hundred wedding invitations printed. We had all that, and then I called that base and he was gone—discharged. He was gone. Gone. I found him in Baltimore and cussed him out, and that was the end of it. Then I called my friend Meboy, who was my brother-in-law's army buddy, and he had known me since I was ten years old. I said, "Oh, Meboy, he's gone." He said, "Well, fuck him. You gon' make it." With that I got on a bus and went out and bought myself a wedding ring. Another time I was in Hollywood, standing at the bus stop ninety-nine months pregnant, and a white woman, who I believe to have been an oracle, walked up to me, and she says, "You are going to have good luck," and walked way. And I had good luck. I had very good luck. I made it; I did it. Now I see I wasn't suppose to have him. I wasn't supposed to have any of that, and I am eternally grateful. I am not a victim. I don't feel like I missed him. I just wasn't supposed to have that.

bh: That feeling of rightness that you feel about the choices you have made, as an artist, that was a real challenge in the film. Here is a woman, and a black woman, who is saying, "I am willing to sacrifice a lot in pursuit of my self-actualization and my art."

CB: That's right. That's right.

bh: Men do that all the time and are valorized for it.

CB: Absolutely. They don't weep. They don't cry. They don't repent.

bh: And they don't look back; they disappear.

CB: Right, and it's no problem. And if you want to critique their failure to be responsible, everybody says, "Don't be so hard on the brother!"

bh: In both films, *Suzanne Suzanne* and *Finding Christa*, you urge women not to be so hard on ourselves. If we are always fearful of judgment, we can never take the risks that make it possible for us to be fully self-actualized. Here you are, Camille Billops, a black woman over sixty, young-looking, still creating, satisfied with the artist you have become. Satisfied with your work. Like the legacy of your mother's home movies, you are creating a continuum of work that can be passed on. You have created an alternative cultural space [the Hatch-Billops Archives], which you share with everybody. Your vision, your work is a necessary critical intervention. As an artist, you made hard and difficult choices. You sacrificed. And you are the witness who tells us it is worth it. The life you've made as an artist fulfills, satisfies, sustains.

17

a guiding light:

an interview with

Charles Burnett

bell hooks: Charles, you've been pretty consistently committed to creating serious drama, serious representations of black characters in
your films; we've talked about that.

Charles Burnett: I began making films wanting to tell a story about all the
people I knew and worked with, the problems that they're facing,
and how they were getting on. I wanted to depict that on screen as
well as what students were making films about. It's not that I set
out purposely to create an alternative cinema. I was just trying to
tell a decent story with real people. I think that if people are intelligent characters, that just makes the story more interesting.

bh: You just spoke with the kind of modesty of representation that
characterizes your personal energy. Clearly, your artistic

temperament is towards the serious, yet you are fascinated by complexity in everyday life—not the silly or the stupid.

CB: The serious interests me. And the silly too. The reason I care is because I depict the black community, and in any community there is a mix of these two things.

bh: In *Killer of Sheep* I am fascinated by scenes like the one at the table when the guy is saying that the heat from the coffee is like a moment in sex, and then the other guy makes the joke about malaria. That's a mixture of seriousness and humor and that intensifies the deeper metaphysical drama. It's metaphysical because we watch the characters develop their sense of being in the world. That's why your work is unique. It has always enchanted me, because you are so into an ontological under- standing of questions: how people come to see themselves in the world, how they construct a self, a worldview, an approach to life, and that is a fundamentally serious proposition that's always there in all your films—which is not to say that you don't use humor.

CB: Yeah, the underlying thing; I'd say yes to that, but I think most script pieces do that, even if it's comedy; whatever it is, it makes some comment about life.

bh: Commenting about life is different from an explanation of being. That's why *Killer of Sheep* remains an incredible piece. For years folks kept telling me to see the movie. I have become so depressed about black filmmakers and their work, and I thought, Yeah people are saying I should see this film, but when I do I'm gonna be heartbroken if the magic isn't there. Then I saw the film and I thought it was awesome—that your capacity as a filmmaker to give us images that depict the complex emotional universe within a class of people, the black working class and poor. Those of us from that background or living that life are made to feel that we don't have that deeper layer of being. The reality is that black working-class people are conventionally represented in a manner that says, "What you see, what you get." The magic of your artistry is the creation of visual images that compel people who see your films to see those deeper layers. Will you share what was going on for you when you were in the process of creating *Killer of Sheep?*

CB: It was a very difficult time for me. I was reacting to the life around me. There's a bar that I used to go to in Watts all the time, like a storefront. Mostly old men go there. I was going to UCLA at the time, and there was this program happening. It was a week or something to celebrate Paul Robeson's coming up. I just happened to bring up this issue with these guys, 'cause you know how you go to these barbershops and there's all this political talk. You know these guys get there and they comment on everything in life. And every time I hear that there's some discussion going on, I sorta add my two cents. I tried to champion this Paul Robeson event, and all of a sudden things stopped. All the elements of radicalism appeared to be there in this person, and we all were agreed that some change had begun. But then somebody started talking about his conservative stuff, and lots of blacks there were not into just celebrating. And there was a contradiction between what was happening in that bar and at UCLA, and I just wanted to show what it was like. And I wanted to do it without imposing the Charles Burnett way of life.

bh: Clearly, Charles, you have a distinct aesthetic vision. And I hear you saying that you're more interested in showing the diversity of the mix in black life than taking one standpoint, building a story around that standpoint, and drawing it to a conclusion. Your work shows all these different standpoints. That's the difficulty some viewers have had with *Killer of Sheep* and *To Sleep with Anger*, because they are not sure whom to identify with in the story. Your films don't dictate to the viewer, and that troubles them.

CB: People felt that because the film did not resolve everything happily that it was depressing. Whereas I thought, in the first film, why wasn't it significant, the fact that this person just struggled and survived? The only thing you can ask someone to do is to stay alive, to continue moving. It's hard, but as long as you keep your values in perspective, that's all you can ask of anybody. And that was what *Killer of Sheep* was showing, his values. He wasn't supposed to get anything—nothing. In most stories there's some object a person is after or a relationship or something that can be resolved in a conventional, expected way.

bh: A good example of that is the recent film *Just Another Girl on the I.R.T.*, a story of a girl who wants to go to medical school, but she's poor and everyone in her school is saying, "You can't do this," but you can follow that story up to its conclusion: she doesn't go to medical school in the end. And no one expects her to, because in our society we do not expect a young single black mother to fulfill her dreams. So people were happy with the ending; it was predictable. Even though they could see it as "sad," it was a familiar story. Most folks were unsettled by the ending of *To Sleep with Anger*. It didn't feel predictable in light of the things that had gone before.

CB: Why can't it be seen as a victory when folks survive potentially tragic events. It's like you weathered a storm.

bh: I watched *Killer of Sheep* with a young film student, a black woman who kept saying, "Is this the moment I should close my eyes?" She was certain that something dreadfully violent, really horrible was going to take place. She's young enough to be so influenced by a film culture in which most contemporary films, especially those made by black filmmakers, depict horrific violence. *Killer of Sheep* is so powerful because the most tragic moment in the film— that scene when the engine falls off the truck—is so ordinary; such a simple mistake. It's like when you go step out in everyday life to do something, a basic chore, but it matters so much to you; you put your energies into it, you put your heart and money on it, and it fails. This is so symbolic that this particular moment stands out. It evoked such a deep sense of failure—of not being able to beat the odds. It was fascinating that the young film student had the sense that horror registers itself in black life only through tragic, violent death, when it is actually so often registered in this mundane way. It's that sensitive cinematic exploration of this tragic quality in everyday life which makes your work problematic for Hollywood.

There is a big leap from *Killer of Sheep* to *To Sleep with Anger* for you as a counterhegemonic filmmaker. You try to take this serious drama that you've had in the independent film *Killer of Sheep* and bring it to Hollywood in *To Sleep With Anger*. Does it work?

CB: The moment you say "Hollywood," it's problematic; everyone panics. But when I was trying to get the funding for a film from alternative sources, it was much more difficult. Sometimes you can get a much better response in Hollywood as an independent. I didn't believe it, but it turned out to be true in a certain sense. Hollywood does so many films, and every now and then with some weird stuff, so in a way there are many more possibilities. When I did *Killer of Sheep* and *To Sleep with Anger*, I got a lot of criticism because they were both not like regular movies. I went on this tour once, and I was in Milwaukee, or someplace like that, at a Martin Luther King Center. *Killer of Sheep* was playing. There weren't too many people there, but there was a kid outside with his boom box and there was a "Freddie Kruger" movie playing, and that kid said, "Now that's a movie!" This is the way many people see films. And this documentary was showing and it was seen as really dry information. During the discussion, we began to have a battle about how our reality is reflected in films, about entertainment level and that kind of stuff. We debated the issue of making things accessible. But the moment we tried to talk about being relevant without any focus on being entertaining, we began to have a heated debate about the role of the filmmaker; whether one should be totally indulgent and say what you wanna do but still not be able to communicate, or whether to find ways to communicate in a language people can understand.

bh: Too much focus on accessibility limits creativity. I can watch *Killer of Sheep* with my family, with black people from all walks of life, poor and working-class black people, and they would identify with what they were seeing. And I think that is a different issue. It wouldn't be that it's not accessible to them; it's that it isn't entertainment. *Killer of Sheep* is not entertaining. The pathos of that film is deeply disturbing. It's very existential. It's really almost like a critically existential, reflective meditation on the pathos of working-class black life in a particular historical moment. Now the question comes whether black viewers of any class along with other viewers can bear that pathos. I think people find themselves, because it's not that the film is pessimistic but rather that it highlights and calls out a certain quality of anguish many of us live with day to day in our lives—and this anguish is unbearable. We don't usually see it at the movies. Your films foreground aspects of black pain that folks don't want to see. Audiences are not prepared to confront it—audiences of any race.

CB: It's a class thing too. When it screened at Howard University, folks weren't into it, because they want to see themselves on the screen. So they want you to do a film about the black middle class, like these films don't already exist. I wasn't as conscious of all this when I was doing *Killer of Sheep*. Over time it has become something that always troubles me as I work.

bh: How many films did you make between *Killer of Sheep* and *To Sleep with Anger*?

CB: I made *My Brother's Wedding* and I worked on another film.

bh: Clearly, audiences cause problems for independent filmmakers making serious drama. There are still so few films made by black filmmakers that the expectations people bring to their films are always so much greater than anything any one film could possibly satisfy. And if you choose to highlight the existential anguish of black people as you do in your work, you run the risk of people not being able to relate. Even though audiences were deeply moved by Julie Dash's film *Daughters of the Dust*, I was at one of the initial screenings where many black viewers did not respond favorably to the film because they didn't know what to do with this movie that didn't have the usual ingredients, a traditional resolution, a conventional Hollywood plot.

CB: Audience expectation is important. If an audience is receptive to a film, I think it generates more interest.

bh: It's much more difficult to make a film expressive of your own unique vision if you feel there is no audience ready to see that film. For example, there is a difference between the reception of a film like *Go Fish* and other contemporary independent films, because an audience of gay and straight consumers were eagerly anticipating this film. Here is a film made by very young white lesbian filmmakers that everyone compares to *She's Gotta Have It*, when it is much more similar to where Spike was with *Joe's Barbershop*. But there was an audience for *Go Fish*. In *Killer of Sheep* and in other films of yours, the camera often lingers at specific moments. There are long pauses—that wonderful scene, for example, when Stan and his wife are dancing in *Killer Sheep*; the scene in the car in *To Sleep with Anger*. Yet when your camera lingers, audiences think the film isn't moving fast enough. Now *Go Fish* can have similar moments, but it has an audience that is predisposed to respond to the artistry of that film. Independent filmmakers who are black who want to make work that is innovative and experimental need an audience to come to see their work—an audience that is not just concerned with context.

CB: The struggle to find support is continuous for independent black filmmakers.

bh: When filmmakers like Spike Lee and John Singleton first began to get so much play, I kept waiting for them to say, "Actually, black filmmaking isn't just beginning here with us; there's Charles Burnett, there's Kathleen Collins," but they didn't do that. It was good for their product to act as if they were unprecedented. And if you gathered all the early magazine articles on these two filmmakers, many of them structured their pieces like, "Spike Lee paved the way for Julie Dash." It's frightening that this ahistorical understanding of the work of black filmmakers is so pervasive, because we lose so much awareness of the process which leads from one film to another. And we then don't have public acknowledgement of the variety and diversity in black filmmaking. It's the experimental work that is often forgotten about. When Spike Lee or John Singleton are the beginning points, then audiences can't look at their work as referencing and signifying on the work of other black filmmakers. There are scenes in *Boyz in the Hood*, scenes in *Crooklyn*, scenes in *Straight out of Brooklyn*, that totally referenced *Killer of sheep* in terms of how they are shot, in terms even of location. But if people haven't seen *Killer of Sheep*, if they don't know the work of Charles Burnett, if they're not studying that in film school, they can't recognize a continuance of black filmmaking. They should be learning about the tradition of American filmmaking, contemporary American filmmaking, and black filmmaking at schools, but that knowledge isn't going to be there. That's why we need to focus on audiences—on how you construct an audience through time. It's very clear to me that an audience was constructed for *Daughters of the Dust*. Once it was clear that people couldn't bring their conventional ways of seeing to this film, people began to shift their paradigms and started coming to see the film knowing beforehand that they weren't gonna see something that they were used to seeing. So in a sense they were more prepared than those first audiences who came and expected action in the same old Hollywood manner and didn't get it. Haile Gerima says that counterhegemonic images will never be supported in Hollywood I don't think that's always true, because *To Sleep with Anger* had those images.

CB: I think it's very difficult; I think you'd find it difficult anywhere you go unless you just make entertaining films. No matter what you do Hollywood or anything. Haile had to suffer greatly to get his film made. He applied for so much funding that he did not get. And one of the problems was the absence of a conventional category to place the film in that funders could relate to.

bh: And when we compare the struggles of black filmmakers who want to defy categories with someone like Clint Eastwood, who has access to money, who can say in his lifetime that he wants to make lots of different kinds of films, we know it is really difficult for any black filmmaker to make films that are diverse in style and content. Black artists, irrespective of their medium, are made to feel that if we get one signature or one voice it has to be repeated. Audiences had trouble with Spike Lee's *Crooklyn* because they assumed it would be a comedy. It had funny moments, but it was not a comedy. Yet audiences just expect comedy from a Spike Lee film. In the United States, black artists must constantly resist the limits that culture wants to impose. It's just this continual battle to be able to assert an aesthetic vision that changes, that isn't the same. Your most recent film, *The Glass Shield*, certainly departs from the aesthetic vision in your early work. To me the change is disturbing, because you seem to have gone backwards rather than forwards.

CB: When I began *The Glass Shield* it was a different idea than what ended up on the screen. I felt that it was an important story about a man who had been on the "right side" of the law who wants to redeem himself. The film raises the issue of how you can be involved with something as innocently as possible, you think you're doing the right thing and then find out that you've made an awful mistake. But initially you had a dream about what life was supposed to be about. I like to do films about different aspects of people's experiences; films that explore what happens when you don't have a liberatory vision or plan, or a way of seeing the world. You just get swept away and bounce from one thing to another, and it's this tragicomic situation. Here's a story about a black male who works within the system as a cop, who has a decent job, who's just trying to make it in a world where night after night one dramatic thing after another is happening; and it's horrendous, folks are killing little kids, and the cop understands the circumstances but is really kind of caught in the middle. His job is to protect and enforce the law, even though he knows the law was not made to help the folks on the street. Whose side is he on? It's complicated. I wanted to show some of that in *The Glass Shield*.

bh: Charles, I can hear the pathos in what you are saying as you describe the idea behind *The Glass Shield*, but the film doesn't convey that. One of the difficulties I had with *The Glass Shield* is that I could not identify with the character of J. J. The actor didn't draw you into him enough so that you were seduced by his longing to assimilate and to go along with the program. He keeps repeating in the film that he's always wanted to be a cop and this is his dream, but there was something that wasn't compelling enough, so that I didn't give a fuck whether he fulfilled his dream or not. As a film critic, I think that the particular actor chosen weakened the film, because so much of the pathos centers around his struggle and he doesn't draw you in deeply enough. I felt like, here this film is technically obviously really good, but I felt it lacked pathos; it lacked the seriousness of your preceding work. I was disappointed watching this film and felt it lacked Charles Burnett's unique style. Do you experience it that way, or do you feel that Charles Burnett flavor coming through?

CB: Working in a group to make this film was difficult. Not all the choices were mine—especially when it came to casting.

bh: But isn't this the problem, then, when a visionary, gifted film-
        maker like yourself tries to make work in Hollywood and the film
        you wind up making is not necessarily going to be just the prod-
        uct of your vision but also of the collaboration that takes place on
        all levels, artistically and administratively? Do you feel there is
        enough room for the realization of your vision?

CB: That's the thing you fight for every moment. And it's a victory.
        I'm sort of happy about the film. In many ways there are some
        things I would certainly put back in and do differently, but, given
        the circumstances, I'm pleased. Knowing the circumstances—the
        way Hollywood works—I am always reluctant to speak about the
        work of my peers, because I know the wars and battles they've
        gone through. And even though the filmmaker is ultimately
        responsible, you can't really assess what has taken place if you
        were not on the set to see what went on. There is so much on the
        set; it's not just Hollywood. I've had so many problems working in
        other settings.

bh: Any time a black artist in white supremacist culture who's decol-
        onized his or her mind creates an artistic work, it's a struggle to
        market that work, whether it's a book or a film, when editors,
        public relations staffs, etcetera, are involved. It is harder to project
        what you may feel is your specific vision as a progressive, decolo-
        nized black person when you are also creating a commodity to be
        sold to mainstream white America, as well as everyone else.

CB: You have the same problem with black folks.

bh: That's why I used the term *decolonized*, because if you are trying to
        work with other black people who are just as mired in stereotypi-
        cal racist thinking ...

CB: It's really an issue of personal integrity. Each filmmaker writes his
        own script. If you give him a script, he is going to rewrite that
        script with all his references. You're really alone. You know you're
        going to have all these people who support you in many ways
        and stuff like that, but it's you who's gonna determine the work.
        So you need character and inner strength to hold the conviction
        that something can work. The point is not to be irrational,

because a film is one thing when it's a concept, when it's a script it's another thing, and when it's produced and shot it's another thing altogether. So you know you are at a different stage. Everyone looks at it and can't really see anything until it's done. As the filmmaker you have to weigh all that and then see what happens. Again, no matter where you go, no one can really understand your ideas but you. It's on you to communicate them. And when you have a unique experience, it's very difficult to get financing, because it's harder to share your idea with someone else. Most likely they will not understand it, 'cause you don't even really speak the same language.

bh: Yet when we are called upon as black artists not just to create but to have marketable persons, often those of us who are more serious don't get much play. All black cultural producers right now are almost always called on to make our persons part of the commodity part of the mix. I mean Spike Lee isn't where he is just because of his films. He's where he is because he was very good at marketing his person along with his films. When I meet a filmmaker like yourself—a very quiet, serious person who thinks before he speaks, not a flashy, glib guy, I think that this is an artist who projects a private aesthetic realm and vision. To what extent does that make it hard for one to succeed in a culture that places a particular demand on those of us from marginal groups to be like our product? If the product is glamorous, then we must be glamorous. I find that people are often disappointed when they meet me, because I am so soft-spoken, but my books have a very hard-hitting verbal edge. Then it's like folks want to drop me, like "she can't deliver," because my person doesn't deliver in the way my books do. Do you feel the same way as a filmmaker whose habits of being are not the kinds of habits that are easily commodified along with your product?

CB: You have to be able to act like a spy in order to survive in this business. It's not all about projecting that you know how to get a film done. It's about how well your film did at the box office the last time. To get backers you have to have the same interest in a certain sense, you have to be prepared to be on the team. Money and commercialism; that's what they identify with.

bh: What happens to someone like you then in that mix?

CB: Filmmakers like me fall by the wayside, into the cracks, and if we don't, it's an uphill battle.

bh: Charles, you have survived as a filmmaker. You have made compelling work. But is it satisfying?

CB: Well, not always. It's satisfying when you can make your own movies, and you can't in a certain sense unless you raise the money yourself and do it somehow or other. And when you make your own film, no matter how unlucky or successful with getting returns back, you're happy about that. But that's very rare. Julie Dash was able to do that and get a return. Making a film and getting it distributed is the thing that is key. You have all these people telling you how to sell the film. And you know you're talking about double consciousness and all that sort of thing. I'd like to do films about that—about the sort of schizophrenic way black folks live.

bh: If you could make independent serious films about subjects you want to make, why would you want to make a Hollywood film where there's even more constraints than if you were trying to make a small film with a small budget?

CB: What's a small film with a small budget if it doesn't exist? I mean if you make a film that costs $10,000, that's a hobby. When I was going to school that was fine, because I never thought we could make a living. But when you have a family, insurance, kids that go to school, that's a problem.

bh: We don't have a large enough African American audience that values independent films. And when that audience does promote an independent film, it will usually be one that is similar to Hollywood films—like Haile Gerima's film *Sankofa*. It's very Hollywood. Contentwise it may differ from Hollywood and in standpoint, but in the way it progresses as a story, in the way it highlights certain kinds of violence, particularly sexualized violence, it is very Hollywood. A distinction has to be made between a racist white public that might not want to support this film because of its standpoint—because they don't think it will sell—and the assumptions that radically parts in style and content from the norm.

CB: Well, no, it isn't so different in some ways. But within the limitations of the film, it makes progress—particularly in the way that it was funded. The content made the search for funding difficult. Haile has said, "That in itself was the threshold."

bh: Isn't it frustrating that within black culture, black folks who are wealthy have not created the foundations with funding where a young filmmaker who has great genius in making independent films of whatever kind could obtain the resources to make his or her work?

CB: I have a little bit of a problem with that suggestion, in a way, because one of the things about film is that there is always an audience problem and funding films is too expensive. I don't know if we could justify spending money on making films because of their limited effect on the public. There are so many other needs. There are always people who are having serious problems. You really have to justify doing a film anytime. That's the dilemma—I mean that's the dilemma we don't talk about enough. How much does it take to launch a book? For a film, you're talking real money.

bh: I know the crucial difference between the money it takes to produce films and books. It is because film is so expensive that we need new avenues and new sources of money. Let's face it, with the rise in black publishing in the United States, when a writer like Jill Nelson can't sell *Volunteer Slavery* to a white corporate press, she can go to a black press and have this major success. I'm just saying that it would be liberation for black filmmakers to have sources of money where there was the freedom to create whatever you wanted to create, whether it would draw a large audience or not. We are never going to be totally free as artists to realize our visions if we can't have a wide playing field. Why can't we have a film made by Charles Burnett that everybody in town is maybe gonna want to see and also have a film by Charles

Burnett that not everybody is going to be capable of seeing or approaching; in the same way that there are a whole lot of people who just couldn't hear that early Coltrane? Does that mean that it shouldn't exist?

CB: No, it doesn't, but I still think when I go back to sources and the audience, it seems to me the audience has to come first.

bh: It can't come first, Charles, not the audience, because audiences are made.

CB: They are, but I think that to generate the energy or money to do a film, there has to be a sense that someone out there is ready to receive it, to understand it, to respect it. Often you make the film and it just sits there, or when it is shown, the audience is not quite sure how to receive it because they have a whole different set of perceptions.

bh: Writing about film, I have to say that critics play a role in the creation of audience—in creating a visual aesthetic. I decided some time ago that I was not going to write another piece on a Spike Lee film. I'm over Spike. I'm over writing about this work. Yet when I saw *Crooklyn* and felt like I had read, you know, like ten fucking reviews by white people saying the film had no plot—that don't even mention the mother's death, and I think, What the fuck is going on here? As a critic you could say you didn't like the plot, but you can't say that that movie doesn't have one. I thought, Well, I'm really fascinated by the plot of this film—how Lee deals with representing death, and I'm going to write about it. But when I wrote about this film in a sophisticated way, when I take this film really seriously, giving it the respect it deserves, writing sixteen pages on it, a lot of hours go into that writing, and there is not going to be any economic reimbursement equal to the amount of hours it takes me to produce the critique. I do that work because it has the power to make people look at this film differently, look at it and see things of value happening in it, even as they read my criticisms—I didn't write a completely positive review. I felt the film was problematic. However, there are aspects of the film that are deeply compelling that people can easily miss because of the tendency not to "see" the complex shit that is really going on. Where, I ask you, were all of the incredible pieces of criticism on *Killer of Sheep*? If *Killer of Sheep* were a film that was being talked about in every film class in this country, if critics were writing about it, more people would see the film. The film would be referenced in certain kinds of ways. In the future, critics and black filmmakers need to be engaged more with one another. Look at the dearth of critical writing on works by African American filmmakers. If you teach a film class, you want to have this whole body of really sophisticated critical work to refer to because it doesn't exist yet. I think that these two facets must work together if we are to make new sites for black filmmakers to make whatever they want to. There has got to be a space where that work is given high-quality treatment. There have got to be more spaces where an audience can creatively approach the work. The public response to *Daughters of the Dust* showed us that you can create an audience, you can prepare an audience that has been addicted to seeing movies in certain ways by just letting them know that as they enter the theater to see this film they are going to have to suspend their traditional ways of looking and see differently. And they will go, and they will struggle with it, and they will try to appreciate what is happening in the film. That audience has to be made in the sense that viewers have to learn to see differently — if they don't, there will always be only a small, elite understanding and appreciation.

CB: The filmmakers already exist. There's a whole lot of work that's still on the shelf, that hasn't been shown, or scripts that go nowhere, because the first thing anyone approached to back a film, especially in Hollywood, wants to know is, If they put money in, how are they going to get the money back?

bh: Well, that's exactly why I raised the question of alternative sources — more radical forms of funding. Why is it unreasonable to expect that a rich black person in this society, who can drop millions on an institution (as you know black donors have dropped a few million on Harvard), can't support foundations in this culture to allow black filmmakers to create films without having to earn the money back? That's the only way that a decolonized people can have a liberatory cinema. As long as people have to prove that this film will sell, you always have to have a limited vision that comes out of the limited marketplace.

CB: Well, let me see, there was once a black cinema. Spencer Williams performed there and made relevant films. And there was an audience for that. Then somewhere along the line it sort of disappeared and black exploitation stuff emerged and set a whole new pattern. At that time folks like Kathleen Collins and Jackie Shearer and a whole bunch of them were making movies. It was a culture—film culture, black culture—where serious, relevant films were made. The issue of financing has become so complex—the question of whether black films or any film is worth financing is complicated. For example, if someone said they want to make this movie and it will take a million and a half dollars to do it and it's just for entertainment, would you finance that film?

bh: Yes, it's not an either-or question. We need a way to finance those films, but I'm more interested in unconventional work. If we cannot come up with untraditional ways of imagining stuff outside of the norm, we will always have a limited, narrow film-making process for African American people. As long as we try to work within the given structures, representations of black experience in film are never gonna change much beyond where we are now.

CB: Yeah, but my whole thing is that if there were more relevant films, they would attract audiences.

bh: If a black filmmaker wants to create a major entertaining film, they have a much better chance of working that film within the structures that already exist. It's precisely an incredibly filmmaker like yourself who wants to do more unconventional work that has difficulty. One of the tragic ironies of all spheres of critical production (not just filmmaking) in the United States is that as black people gain visibility, as we do more of everything, there's much more of a demand that everything we do be entertaining. On the one hand we're getting big bucks, more big bucks than ever before, as black individuals producing culture in American society. But if you start looking for cultural products that are deeply, existentially reflective, that have a certain kind of serious-ness, that have, God forbid, some kind of overt political radical-ism, you will not fund much. We don't see a great deal of change in this society when we look for diverse, complex visions of black life. We don't see a place for any of those products that are not simplistic. For example, black heterosexuality has not been really given much serious play in filmmaking, period. Even black film-makers like Spike Lee and John Singleton and other people who focus on love and romance create bullshit. There's a whole level of complexity in black love relationships that we simply don't see on the screen. One reason we don't see those images is that white crossover audiences are not interested in the depth of what black people do in their intimate life as we struggle to love and care for one another.

CB: Well, I think it's more than that. It's that for such a long time black films have offered images that suggest black people are first and foremost entertainers. I think we have to confess that black audiences feel that way too.

bh: Those perceptions of what black films should be like emerge in a consumer culture created by white supremacy. When I say that it is difficult to find concrete representations of black people in U.S. films by black or any filmmakers where the characters depicted are existentially self-reflective, I am saying we live in a culture where mass media and film particularly invest in the notion, rooted in racist assumptions, that there is no emotional complex-ity in black life—which means that we can see films about white people for days where they can reflect, sit and reflect, and do nothing; we can have *My Dinner with Andre, Swimming to Cambodia.* There can be no "real action" at all, but we don't yet live in a culture where black people can gain support for making such a film, or an audience where the work is supported.

CB: I know. That's the problem, and a lot of filmmakers are striving to try to change that and I think the critique of what audiences want has to come in to cause audiences to support the production of these different images. You say that you support that any black filmmaker should have a right to make whatever film they want to make, which is right; but at the same time, we don't support these guys that go out on a limb and try, even though we failed, it's like—

bh: You and I do.

CB: The fact is, most people don't.

bh: Then the question becomes, How can we widen the circle of people who support the recognition that black people will never be free until we can have a diversified expressive culture, which means to say that we need all kinds of films? I wanna live to see the day when a black person can make a film that doesn't have any black people in it if they don't want black people in it and it can be registered as something that's coming out of black expressive culture, and I think we're nowhere near that.

CB: Well, the fact is that we need space to discuss these issues, like "What is black?" We need to talk more about these issues which we seem to avoid.

bh: I hope that *The Glass Shield* does not represent your giving up a more contemplative aesthetic vision.

CB: No. I think one of the things that this film does do is allow me to get to the next step, so I can buy my own equipment to start doing what I wanna do. I don't feel bad about it. The themes in *The Glass Shield* are important. It makes a comment about society and racism. I think it's something you do to get it out of your system while you look for the next level. There's something in it that I tried to do, and I learn a great deal as I work in and out of the system. Working within the system, you're not going to make any major changes, but one of these days you're gonna get into a situation where you can get yourself an average system, get yourself a camera, and then you can just go off and, with a normal amount of money, make the kind of film you want. Maybe it will just end up on video, but then you have the film, you can use that and make money. I hope to do this someday.

18

critical contestations:

a conversation with

A.J. (Arthur Jaffa)

bell hooks: Do you think in terms of "black film" and "white film"?

Arthur Jaffa: In certain respects. I was just thinking about the issue of
criticism. I'm primarily a practitioner. And I feel that the whole
notion of criticism should follow the work in a way. As a consequence there's going to be some inherent limitations around the
"white critical vocabulary" with respect to talking about black
film, especially to the degree black film is trying to accomplish or
create an authentically black film, create form that expresses who
we are. Given the kinds of films that most black filmmakers are
making, we have not even begun to fully use the various critical
standpoints that might be used to talk about work like feminist
criticism. My whole sense of the relationship of criticism and the
work that's being done is somewhat problematic. As a practi-

tioner, I want critics to be able to read the larger picture and provide a larger view of what's happening. Because it's like being in a war, you know what I mean? You're in the trenches, and a lot of times you don't really have a big view of what you're trying to do. Critics should be able to bring that big view, be able to relate certain formal things and philosophical things to what filmmakers, who are on the ground in the running, are doing in the marketplace. Making films is expensive, and much of what any filmmaker does is determined by this. Generally, critical writing does not reflect this understanding, and much of it is just not insightful.

bh: Critical insights come from being passionately, as a critic, "into" film. One of the reasons I use terms like "black film" and "white film" cautiously is that many of the small number of individuals who are writing about film who are black often think they don't have to see any films that are not made by a larger group of filmmakers if they are writing about "black film." Or that they don't have to be familiar with diverse critical standpoints emerging from a world beyond black filmmaking. This leads to a ghettoization of so-called black film criticism, and often it means that no one expects writing about "black" films to be complex theoretically. Sometimes I feel discouraged as a black woman writing about film, but I feel compelled to write about work when I read what mass media has to say on the subject. When I decided to write a piece on *Crooklyn*, it was in part in response to the shallow treatment of the film in the mainstream press. All these white critics wrote about the film and said it didn't have a plot. And I was like, "Wow, wait a minute. The plot was so simplistic, how could you say it didn't have a plot? It had a plot, which was, 'Here's a family that has a lot if issues, and one of them is the mother gets sick and she passes away.'" It's like "That is a plot." So for me as a critic, I had to use feminist theory to think about, and psychoanalysis to think about, "Gee, how come white people don't see a black woman mother dying as a plot?" or does that just mean it doesn't interest them? And if they refuse to engage with the film on its own terms, then we have to hope that "aware" black critics will write about this work. Note that I emphasize "aware" to challenge racial essentialism. If you have a black critic that's no more aware than the white male critic

J. Hoberman writing in the *Village Voice* that the film didn't have a storyline, then you really don't have any more insight into what's happening in this film. A distinction must be made between critical writing on film that is just unenlightened and critical thinking that's visionary, that's on the edge. I feel like our difficulty is in producing both filmmakers who are black who are willing to go to the edge, go to the limit, and to then have a criticism that responds in the same way.

A.J.:   I read your piece on *Crooklyn* and you used psychoanalysis as a critical standpoint to begin talking about the film. I think that's great. Not because it's "psychoanalysis" but because underlying your use of this critical perspective was the desire to see the complexity of the work. When you come to black expression, there's a level of complexity that deserves a complex reading. It could be psychoanalysis, it could be a number of critical standpoints, structuralism, formalism, diverse standpoints. For example, if you consider the work of a filmmaker like Oscar Micheaux, who is the Louis Armstrong of black cinema, his work suffers from critical neglect. Often you can talk to someone who feels like they're very much engaged with the question of black aesthetics in film and they don't know Oscar Micheaux's work. When I studied at Howard University, his work was presented to me, initially, as all the things that you shouldn't do. You know what I mean? And there was a sense that if his work did something that was unorthodox, he was hardly ever given the benefit of the doubt that that lack of orthodoxy was a choice on his part, a choice that was reached for expressive reasons.

bh: That distinction is important. It's still rare that critics interested in black filmmaking will ever consider the influence of Oscar Micheaux. People who are only interested in black people making Hollywood films (and Hollywood is not a place where film is pressed to its limit from any category of people) are not going to talk about black filmmakers who were or are avant-garde, who are testing the limits. We have to talk about what it will mean for us to begin to conceptualize the critical significance of black filmmakers who are "making it," but not in relation to Hollywood. For many audiences black filmmaking begins and ends with Spike Lee. If I were to talk about excellence in black filmmaking, Spike would not be at the head of my list. I mean someone like Charles Burnett, Julie Dash, many more people might occupy that list. We miss so much complexity in the work of black filmmakers if Hollywood sets the standards.

A.J.:   Oh, yeah. Because what's really essential is values. When it comes to art it's always about interpretation and what you value versus what you don't value. In black film oftentimes we collapse financial market success into artistic or philosophical value, because we don't have sophisticated criteria to say that perhaps *Crooklyn* was a flop for Spike but could very well, at the same time, be his most significant film. Those two things don't necessarily go together. Or that we can point to a filmmaker who only made two films in his career and say, "Well that was a filmmaker who really mattered, not this person who made twenty films." You know what I mean? If we don't take some more compelling criteria for assessing value, then the meaning of our work will always be shaped by market forces. While we have to consider market forces if we reduce the relative success of a film to which film made the most money. Then in a sense, that's almost always gonna come down to which film people—white people (since there are more white people who are gonna attend black film)—see. It's like, Russell Simmons made this really interesting distinction, he was saying, at Def Jam they didn't make black music for black consumers, they made black music for consumers of black culture. When it comes to my work as a filmmaker, I strive to construct a complex model of black culture, which certainly takes into consideration market forces, but I understand the need for autonomous creative practices that are not just about following the money.

bh: That's an important distinction. The truth of white supremacy is that white people are not interested in radical black subjectivity for the most part, or I should say, "Racist white people are not, but our society is made up of racist white people for the most part." And let's go further and say, "Black people who have internalized white supremacist aesthetics are not interested in decolonizing black representation." For all the praise black people begin to give *Daughters of the Dust*, we were there at the opening night, where a lot of black people were saying, "What's going on in this film?" You know, black folks who would go to white foreign films and feel like, "Okay, this is something different," came to that film and still were expecting to see the same kinds of things they saw in Hollywood film. When they didn't, they were initially disappointed.

A.J.:   Absolutely. Says more about the ways we've internalized our own oppression.

bh: We've internalized a certain way of seeing. Representation is the "hot" issue right now because it's a major realm of power for any system of domination. We keep coming back to the question of representation because identity is always about representation. People forget that when they wanted white women to get into the workforce because of the world war, what did they start doing? They started having a lot of commercials, a lot of movies, a lot of things that were redoing the female image, saying, "Hey, you can work for the war, but you can still be feminine." So what we see is that the mass media, film, TV, all of these things, are powerful vehicles for maintaining the kinds of systems of domination we live under—imperialism, racism, sexism, etcetera. Often there's a denial of this and art is presented as politically neutral, as though it is not shaped by a reality of domination. And black people haven't engaged that discussion deep enough. We continue to stay on the surface, discussing whether images are negative or positive rather than raising more complex questions. Like "Why does a film like *Malcolm X* start off with Malcolm fucking some white woman?" Well, I totally relate that to the position of white women as consumers in this society and the fact that in any kind of activity, whether it's bookselling or filmgoing, white women are the top of the list for the consuming audience. So already you've got that audience hooked in, because they're seeing themselves. And they're seeing themselves at the very beginning, as though they are where this powerful black man's life begins. I see that as a marketing ploy, I don't see this and think, "Oh, Spike is just stupid and he, like, wanted to begin the film there, or that he's, like, thoughtless or he's not political." I think this is a filmmaker who's aware of consumers and of what hooks people in—interracial sex. I mean, look at this whole O.J. mess. Clearly, this culture is obsessed, to the bone, with he question of interracial sexuality. So by starting *Malcolm* at that point, there's already a "come-on," if you will, or an audience. Let's say the film started with a militant speech. How would this reshape the film?

A.J.:   Right. That's an issue that was raised when we did *Daughters*, and it is also very pertinent to what you're saying about *Malcolm X*. It's the whole issue of "Who gets to be at the center of these narratives?" And it's more complicated than that. The discourse is not just who this is about, but who is it directed at and what perspective is it coming from?

bh: And a lot of our film criticism doesn't consider these issues.

A.J.:   Absolutely, not at all. One of the most radical things that can happen in film is the foregrounding of black subjectivity. Because, essentially, black people always end up being backdrop, but very seldom are we in the subject position. I remember giving a talk at the New School about *Daughters*, and a woman stood up and said, "When I see this film, I don't see a black family, I see that grandmother as my grandmother, as universal," and all this kind of stuff. And I replied, "Great, I'm glad you see it like that, that's a good place to start, but why is it mutually exclusive that the family would be a black family and still be universal?" It really has a lot to do with the kind of egocentrism white supremacy produces. It comes down to "If I got to see a text, even about black people, I wanna see a text about what black people think about white people." It really can never *really* be about black people. It's like, early on in Spike's career one of the things that he was constantly asked was, "When are you going to get some white characters in your films?"

bh: As though their presence immediately means a more expansive vision.

A.J.:   Absolutely, absolutely. Because white supremacist thought dichotomizes the universe. If you see a film like *Bladerunner*, there's not a single white critic or audience person I've ever heard in my life say, "There are no black people in *Bladerunner*" or "There are no black people in *2001: A Space Odyssey.*" The implication of that, if we take that logic to its fullest extent, is that black people have no relation to a concept of the future. Or to New York, Woody Allen's New York. You know what I mean?

bh: Or for that matter there's this new film being made about bicycle messengers by a white woman director, and there are no black people at all in the film. And when she was asked, "Why aren't there any black people?" she was like, "Oh, well, you know … " It's like, come *on*. When I think of bicycle messengers in New York, I think of black men, but she denies this reality so that she does not have to voice her belief that she doesn't perceive her audience to be interested in black men. So she can have this eighty-year-old white man as a bicycle messenger, but only because she feels like that is a storyline that's gonna interest white consumers. How many eighty-year-old white men have we seen bringing messages? And it seems to me that this is the tremendous burden black artists in every arena suffer under, which is: "How can we produce, how can we take our work to the creative edge if we're always working within the limits defined by white supremacy?" And as long as everyone creates as though it is only the desires of white consumers that matter, then white supremacy will continue to shape all cultural production. The logic of white supremacy suggests that audiences, especially crossover audiences, are never going to be interested in depictions of radical black subjectivity. That's why so many audiences had to be educated to appreciate what *Daughters of the Dust* had to offer. They had to be told, "This is not a Hollywood film, but this is a powerful film that is about us, that you must see." Audiences also felt like they had to approach Haile Gerima's *Sankofa* in a different way. Before any of us saw it, it was positioned as a film white people don't want to see. And if films must struggle to find an audience, what about critical writing? I think it's just really hard, because how do you function within that? How do we function? I don't feel that any magazine on film would have taken my piece on *Crooklyn*. The first thing I wanted to do was to situate that film in relation to Hollywood. I wanted to say, "Spike's work is not a counter to Hollywood narratives. Most of the time, Spike's work functions within the paradigms that Hollywood sets out," which raises again the issue of racial essentialism. It isn't enough just to be black. There are black images in work by white filmmakers like

Jim Jarmusch and John Sayles that are more radical than black images in Spike's work. But that's largely because when they use a black subject, they're not called upon to be funny. One of the major problems Spike Lee has had as a filmmaker is the demand by white producers and white viewers to put humor at the center of anything he does.

A.J.:   And the demand for humor is not really even about Spike. What that humor is about is putting them at ease with black subjectivity. Here's my example. As a black man, if I go into a predominantly white social gathering and I don't say anything, and I'm just quiet, it puts everybody on edge. It has nothing to do with the way that I look. White people become uneasy when I'm not constantly externalizing my subjectivity in the way that they're comfortable with, which is what entertaining and making people laugh is about. It's like saying, "Be at ease." But when I am reserved, I am suspect. People assume I'm angry.

bh: I wouldn't even say it's about seeing you as angry. It's about demanding that you not be complex or mysterious. We don't associate blackness with mysteriousness.

A.J.:   We don't associate black Americans with mysteriousness, because the social structure has always demanded that we put white people at ease. And if we don't put white people at ease, they don't know how to deal with us. It's like the dark, silent Negro is the most frightening thing, because he must be the one who's plotting the slave revolt, though that might be the farthest thing from that person's mind.

bh: That was one of the points made by *The Spook Who Sat by the Door*. This way of thinking is the reason work like Charles Burnett's films or a film like *Losing Ground* by Kathleen Collins doesn't get the critical attention it deserves, not even in film magazines. Often white film critics who write about black cinema don't necessarily think that they need to place a film within a context of other films. They can talk about the individual films as though they exist in isolation. When we look at *To Sleep with Anger*, we do see elements of subtlety and mystery, and that's why so many audiences had difficulty with the film.

A.J.:   My comments about externalization of black subjectivity were meant to emphasize that it is always about settling white anxiety in the face of what's going on in black people's minds. Essentially, they police our bodies.

bh: But isn't it black anxiety too? Because, don't you think that black audiences also desire "flat" images?

A.J.:   The basis of that black anxiety was different when *Superfly* came out. A certain section of the black community was in an uproar, and they complained about the whole trend of drug dealers as heroes. Was it really that we thought that all of a sudden this film was gonna actually make black people go out and wear big white hats with big feathers and, you know, shoes that didn't make any sense, that weren't logical? Was that really the basis of the anxiety of that section of the black community? I really don't think this kind of negative image is actually converting black youth into being drug dealers. Their anxiety was about the recognition of their powerlessness to control the perception of the black community. If you're in a society where you're a minority and you have no control over your own representation, and you know, too, that it's a segregated society where most white people do not have intimate relationships with black people, whether it comes from white filmmakers or black filmmakers, they will take what they see as truth. There's a certain part of the community that's anxiety-ridden about this. They don't want to just admit that, essentially, there's a certain way in which blacks, the black community and black people in general, always get stomped on around white presumptions about who black people are. It's like, their lack of information becomes the starting point for the production of black representation. That interpolation really crushes black people. When it comes to a film like *Daughters*, or *To Sleep with Anger*, one of the most radical aspects of the work, and one of the most difficult aspects to talk about, is not what the film does but what the film refuses to do.

bh: Take a film like *She's Gotta Have It* and think about how people talked about it. And this film *was* talked about in mainstream white film cinema. No one talks about the character of the cello player. How often do we see black women depicted with a classical Western musical instrument, dedicated to her work? Yet no people who wrote about the film mentioned that. So what that means in terms of criticism is, even when that unusual or subversive image is there, or when there's a variety of images, those images get effaced and erased in the critical act. For example, I went to see *Go Fish* and I was pissed off that critics, white critics, were comparing it to *She's Gotta Have It*. *She's Gotta Have It* is ten times more sophisticated than *Go Fish*. But because they're both about sexuality and they're both, in some ways, about a sexuality that hasn't been allowed to speak its name, people can see them as the same. However, aspects of *She's Gotta Have It* never got noticed by white critics in any way—the camera work that was interesting, the use of different formats, the documentary format. *Go Fish* is pretty much straight ahead, the camera work amateurish.

A.J.:   One of the specific reasons that white critics might have difficulty seeing the differences between a film like *She's Gotta Have It* and *Go Fish* is that, essentially, all they can see in *She's Gotta Have It* are the things which they have collapsed into stereotypes. But, as you were saying, the black woman who's a cello player is essentially invisible. So they have equated the invisibility, their incapacity to see all this range, this diverse range of black representations, with what in *Go Fish* is a lack of sophisticated representations; they literally aren't there.

bh: No, it's a narrative about sexuality for the most part.

A.J.:   Absolutely. Reggie Hudlin always said something I thought was really interesting. He suggests that one of the reasons *She's Gotta Have It* was so successful was that it had diverse representations of blackness. He took this to be a paradigm for what commercially viable and sophisticated black cinema should do, that it should have a range of representations. In *She's Gotta Have It*, you get a B-boy, you get a middle-class black man, and then you get an upwardly mobile black man. You have this range of characters. And then you get Nola Darling, you get the lesbian character— even though she's a caricature, she's there. You get the Joie character with the cello.

bh: Who's very mysterious.

A.J.:   Incredibly mysterious, you don't know anything about her. You
        know that she had a boyfriend. I was always more transfixed by
        her character than any other character in the film. I was like,
        "Well, why didn't they just make it her?" You know, why didn't
        they make the film about her? But, then, that raises the question
        "Who would want to see a film about her?"

bh: I think a lot about the representation of black sexuality and black
        heterosexuality in a film, and I remember my extreme disappoint-
        ment when I saw *Poetic Justice*. I thought, "here we are in the 1990s
        and this is what gets projected." Instead of seeing a certain kind of
        love story between a black man an a black woman, it is adoles-
        cence. It's like black heterosexuality stopped at thirteen or some-
        thing, in terms of how it's imaged. And then I thought,
        partially—again—once you have a crossover market, you've gotta
        give a representation of black sexuality that can cross boundaries.
        And what if, in fact, in codes of intimacy, as black people, we actu-
        ally speak differently, act differently from familiar codes that white
        culture has for us? I know, for example, as a Southerner (and you
        and I are both Southerners), I find, particularly when I'm encour-
        aged in some kind of sexual activity, I much more rely on vernacu-
        lar speech, my own Southern speech, 'cause I think it's the speech
        of intimacy for me. But again, who do we have a cinema that can
        actually have that vocal range for black characters? One of the
        things that I think we saw with *Paris is Burning* is that a lot of the
        times when something that's specific to a cultural code that white
        people may not understand is shown, that critical moment is dis-
        rupted by laughter that is inappropriate, or by some other kind of
        response that is about their announcing, by the response, "We
        don't really understand what's going on, we feel left out, so we're
        going to take the moment back from the film with our disruptive
        response." I think that happens often.

A.J.:   Yes, that happens a lot. A friend of mine, this really, really attrac-
        tive young lady with dark skin and a beautiful smile, worked with
        me on *Daughters*, and I remember, at the beginning of each day I
        would see her, and I was, you know, chipper, and I would say,
        "Hey, that's the smile that conjured the minstrel syndrome." And

the thing that was so strange about what happened over the course of a week or two is that she ceased to smile. And I said, "Well, why did you stop smiling?" and she said to me, "I was really disturbed by what you said." And I said, "I meant that as a compliment." I meant that, basically, what happens is black people can generate (especially a dark-skinned black person with very white teeth) a smile that very few white people can do, just for the physical reason of the contrast. And that when white people are confronted with things that black people can do and this can't be denied on some level, those characteristics are undermined by pathologizing them. If you can't stop it from being, then we can control how you perceive it to be.

bh: Or we can, in a sense, restructure that look where it then becomes something that you feel bad about rather than that you claim as "This is what announces my difference from you."

A.J.:   Absolutely, and it's not even because it's about difference. That's what I mean about pathologizing something. Making something that's inherent to who you are become something that you should be embarrassed about.

bh: I keep mentioning Charles Burnett as an exemplar of black filmmaking. I know that you are really into his work and have been influenced by it. He gives us such a range of images in *Killer of Sheep* and other work of his.

A.J.:   Once I did an informed survey whereby I wanted black independent filmmakers to make lists of their favorite films. And I would always ask them to make two lists. One would be their top ten films of all time. The other one would be their top ten films by black filmmakers.

bh: Yeah, I can remember us sitting around doing that.

A.J.:   And the reason I had people make two lists is because it was always interesting for me to see if there was any overlap; like, how many films from people's top-ten list of all time, how many of the black films would also be on that list? Charles Burnett's *Killer of Sheep* was the consensus among most filmmakers. Everyone agreed that this was a significant piece of work. I have my own ideas about why it's significant. It's a very emotional film. It's a sublime film. It's one of the few films that posits black complexity at the same time that it shows how black folks can be trapped inside a structure. A lot of films can't negotiate these two spaces. Either black people are being moved by social structures where they're types or just statistics, or they're just individuals who seem to be completely free of larger social structures. And *Killer of Sheep* does this incredible depiction of this family, and it's a very specific family. And you never lose the sense of the specificity of who they are, where they come from, what their particular dynamics are, but at the same time you never lose the sense of these black people as being representative of black people in a certain circumstance. Another interesting aspect of this film is its narrative structure. It's often called episodic. So, if you say it's episodic, so what does that mean? It's like saying a person isn't straight. What does that make them? It can't make 'em a lotta other things. No one really talks about "oral logic" in *Killer of Sheep* as a way of structuring the film narratively. When I talk to my mom on the phone, I tape the conversations if I can, because it is really fascinating to look at how she structures events and sequences, the internal logic. She'll start of talking about somebody's birthday, and then she'll go to talking about the sale, you know, the sale that was on at the grocery store, and then she'll be talking about my aunt who just died. And if I just put it down literally, it would be as avant-garde as anything James Joyce ever did. It's very much a vernacular way of structuring events. Charles's film conveys this. It has the sense and sensibility of *Jet* magazine. In *Killer of Sheep* the climatic scene with the car engine captures that existential quality of black life in the vernacular. When one of the guys says—I remember the line, he says something like "Ain't nothing we can do to fix it ..." This is a really, really sad scene. Music comes in and makes you really feel bad. On one hand, you wanna laugh at 'em, 'cause it seems so idiotic, what they did, but you can understand, you know, the whole context that would generate that particular kind of moment. It's such a profoundly bittersweet moment.

bh: That scene is an existential metaphor for the black exilic experience, which is that you are struggling within bizarre limitations that the culture puts forth for you. You work hard, and then fate, unforeseen circumstance, a gap in one's understanding produces this tragedy. It's both a tragedy felt in the realm of the mundane, a larger, more universal tragedy of dashed hopes and broken dreams. I am not a big fan of *To Sleep with Anger*, but in certain shots we see the way Charles is able to take that space of the everyday and bring to it a quality present in Greek tragedy.

A.J.:   In Charles's films, he takes black people's complexity as a given, and he starts from there. He's not trying to explain black people. He's really interested in observing black people. What do they do? Why did they do it? *To Sleep With Anger* was problematical for some audiences because he didn't explain everything. The inherent contradiction of trying to make a sophisticated black work, as a black artist in a white supremacist society, is that this society is always questioning any representation that does not conform to the stereotype.

bh: One of the most moving scenes in *House Party* is when the dad comes upstairs at the end and gives that beating; that was an incredible, surreal use of everyday life. It was a beautiful scene. That spoke to me and other black people, because we got those beatings, and we recognized that this was an aspect of black life that we hadn't seen imaged on the screen. I looked at it as "Damn, this movie just, like, brought the brutality out there ... "'Cause for me, it was brutal. But, once again, when the film is written about, this last part of the film isn't talked about at all. The fact that they must suffer for the pleasure that they have had should alter the way we understand the film. It should make critics think about pleasure and punishment in the Foucauldian sense. It should make us all think about sexuality and intimacy on a more sophisticated level. And black critics don't discuss this any more than white critics.

A.J.:   There are very few people who have enough sophistication and cultural confidence to say, "Look, if I recognize this thing in this film as something of my life as a black person reimagined on screen, then that's enough." People who saw *Crooklyn* and did not like it complained that the family was always yelling, you know, they were always fighting, and that this was abnormal. And I don't understand my particular family situation as being abnormal, but that's what it was like growing up in our house.

bh: Oh, yeah, that's what it's like when I go home today.

A.J.:   Yeah, you know what I'm saying, fighting and everything. And it's not to say that's not a dysfunctional family kinda vibe; that was just the whole reality of looking at cartoons, fighting, pushing people out of the bed, arguing all the time. I can't remember how many times my father would say, "Dang niggers, if y'all would fight the world the way you all fight each other, you know, maybe you'd be gettin' somewhere." You know what I mean? The fear a film like *Crooklyn* generates emerges because people see it as an unapologetic and unflattering portrait of the black family. In that sense, representations in the film are radical.

bh: In my review I talked about the power of this counterhegemonic imagery. It said, "This is not a *Spanky and Our Gang* notion of togetherness. This is a different sense of black bonding." It's not buffoonery. It's not the sitcom black family. This is a black family where we see textures and layers. There's wit, there's humor, and there's this tragic element of dysfunctionality which coincides with a world of care and seriousness. That was really particularly fascinating about *Crooklyn*. Unfortunately, the film doesn't keep that momentum. Ultimately, it does fall into the stereotypes, the buffoonery that the dominant culture needs to be hooked. Clearly, if the dominant cultures's best white critics could not engage the seriousness of the loss of a black mother, then how can we expect that the average viewer who goes to this film can actually say "*Crooklyn* really made me think about the death of a parent"? An understanding that both sees the universality in that structure at the same time that it sees the specificity. And it doesn't happen.

A.J.:   Racism and white supremacy create this blind spot. If you think of Nazi Germany, it's pretty straightforward. What happens is at the point that they said the Jewish community is a problem, the first thing that they did was try to reshape the Jewish community in the image that they needed to justify genocide. If I was trying to treat a human being like a bug, if I wanted to step on that person like a bug, the first thing that I would have to do is reduce that person's humanity. If I allowed them their humanity and then treated them as if they weren't human, then that would create conflict. In this society, in American cinema, it's important to keep images of black people one-dimensional.

bh: It's that black people are socialized to believe this one-dimensional subjectivity is who we are. I have talked about the scene in *Jungle Fever* where Spike positions the black man in relationship to his work as an architect and having sex with the white woman. In that scene where he's having sex on the desk, a stereotype about black males is reproduced. He's more interested in fucking than in doing his job. We have to critically interrogate this image. Why has Spike given us that kind of image? Why is he not capable of envisioning this guy as saying, "Work matters to me in such a way that I can value it and at the same time long for some white pussy, if that's what I'm longing for. If that's the experimental moment that I wanna have"?

A.J.:   When I saw the film I remember having much more empathy for the white woman.

bh: She was a much more complex character—her family too.

A.J.:   I remember seeing her on the *Tonight Show*, and she was saying, "Well, you know, Spike was constantly just sayin' it was about boning, that it was just about a jungle-fever thing." But she was saying, "No, I refuse that, because my experience as a human being is telling me that it's always more complex than just being about sex, even though that might be a significant component in it." In other words, she refused Spike's simplistic characterization of her character, his imposition of it. And I saw him on TVB saying, "We didn't get along, because, basically, she had different ideas about why the character was doing what it was doing." In the film you see this woman bring more complex dimensions to her character. I came away more sympathetic towards her than to him, especially because of her background and the class dynamic of their relationship.

bh: Absolutely. We see her in the family. We see her through the lens of both gender and class. As an actress, she changes the dynamic of the script. That white family scene is complex. The scene that I most remember is the sexism in this white working-class family where she is treated like nothing. And these scenes are more poignant than any scene with the black family.

A.J.:   Because you feel, "Who's sacrificing the most?" You really feel she's sacrificing the most. She's going to be disowned by her family. She's a secretary. He's an architect. He just moves out and opens a new law firm. The implication is that he has quite a bit of money. And even though I think one of the most mundane levels a film can function on is around "Who do you identify with?" it's striking to me that in black films that come out of Hollywood, in general, there are usually more complex portrayals of white people than of black people in those spaces.

bh: That's because a black filmmaker has to prove to a white audience, via characterization, that their humanity has been acknowledged. Then the filmmaker is vigilant. No such standards are brought to bear on the image of the father in *Jungle Fever*, on the black male drug addict. That's another powerful scene. This character is played by Sam Jackson. I'm struck by the fact that in Spike's films, as in other black films, the guy who's a failure is often the thinker, the critical mind. It's the Sam Jackson character who thinks deeply about class, about the politics of interracial desire who runs it down to us in terms of serious critique of pleasure and danger and allegiance and solidarity, etcetera. Yet these characters are depicted solely as failures. Whether we're talking about *Menace II Society* or a host of other black films, again, you have the sense that the black person who's the thinker will have a tragic fate.

A.J.:   Or is dead, literally. Quite literally. He speaks from the dead, that's the only place to speak from.

bh: That is such a tragic thought. The challenge for both filmmakers and critics is to construct cinematically counterhegemonic images. But how can this happen if we start off caught in the binds white supremacist patriarchy creates?

A.J.:   With any kind of bind, the first challenge is to unravel it. We can always try just to function inside of the bind. We have to look at the components that make this binding dynamic continue.

bh: Right. Because Foucault would say, within the binding structure you have some degree of freedom, and that your power comes in isolating that freedom. One way to break the hold is to get more attention, to actively seek a larger audience.

A.J.:   When you're talking about independent films where you don't have "stars," then it behooves us, as filmmakers, to understand that we have an obligation to push the work. When *To Sleep with Anger* came out, the first critique I made of it was that it said, "Danny Glover—*To Sleep With Anger*." And I couldn't understand why Charles's name, for better or worse, wouldn't be posted all over the film, so that at the very least the people who saw *To Sleep With Anger* would know who Charles Burnett was after that, so he wouldn't have to start at the same place with the next project. It would be, "Oh, Charles Burnett. Oh, that's the brother that did ..."

That is one of the things that Spike has demonstrated so effectively. He has constructed himself—Spike Lee, the entity—as a filmmaker, first an foremost as his handle to sell the thing. You know what I mean? He is his own marketing angle. Because, short of *Malcolm X*, I think, Spike has never even really worked what you would call a box office draw. I remember when *Mo' Better Blues* was first happening, there was a lot of debate going around about who was going to star in it. At one point they were actually saying that it as gonna be Denzel and that Gregory Hines was gonna play the Shadow (the countercharacter). And then at a certain point it didn't work out, and I remember telling someone, "Well, Spike, he doesn't need anyone else if he's got Denzel as a 'star attraction,' because he also has himself." Spike's name has marquee value. Those things have to be actively constructed, and we have to be vigilant about them. It took me a while to work through my whole issue around ego, to understand the need to make one's name heard, recognized so that folks can, and will, associate it with a body of work.

bh: Living in a culture that seeks to erase our subjectivity, we have to have concrete practices that say, "I'm not going to allow you to erase my subjectivity." We haven't even talked about how white filmmakers draw on what they see in black cinema to go back to the films they make and create scenes with black characters.

A.J.:   And black actors.

bh: And in a sense that appropriation can take place often without anyone recognizing that they have learned from black filmmakers. Someone can write about John Sayles in *City of Hope* and not say that he uses the same kind of camera angle or shot that was so successful in *Boyz In the Hood*, or any other kind of urban drama, so that there's always that risk that we will fall in the gap of erasure. Even though *Daughters of the Dust* is popular, there's still that risk that five years from now people won't know Julie Dash's name as a filmmaker. And people can still talk about Spike as though Spike sprang out of the —

A.J.:   the head of Zeus.

bh: Right, by himself. No other black filmmakers present. With John Singleton close behind. Can we talk more about why a film like *Poetic Justice* doesn't work? *Poetic Justice* was an exciting concept. Lots of viewers were totally wanting to see a black love story. What makes a film like that fail? We make these constant comparisons between where black people have gone in terms of music, other forms, certainly in terms of jazz—why is it that we seem to be so stuck in film? And are unable to imagine black heterosexuality as transgressive, or interesting, in any film we could name? And that includes *Sankofa*. The more interesting romance in *Daughters* is between Iona and St. Julien Last Child, the Native American character.

A.J.:   There are some obvious structural limitations. As you said earlier, Hollywood is not conducive to any kind of exploration of human interrelationships with any kind of sophistication. It's just exacerbated when they feel like there's not even a market for those explorations. Now, I think market forces become one of the most important things. The other thing is, quite frankly, John Singleton is a very, very, very young man who's trying to accomplish some things that he hasn't had the life experiences to do yet.

bh: I felt that very strongly.

A.J.:   That was pretty obvious. I mean it was obvious that *Boyz in the Hood* came from a more familiar place.

bh: But, this says to me, "Then why doesn't this young man say, 'Here's an area where I'm weak. I need to hire some consultants' or 'I need to hire people who can help me because they have been in the business longer.'"

A.J.:   It's the immaturity of the filmmaker. Don't think that's an accident, on a certain level. *Boyz In the Hood* is clearly coming out of some familiar lived experience, whereas when you go to *Poetic Justice*, you definitely feel it's conjecture. That wasn't as apparent in *Boyz In the Hood*. That's not an accident. There is a relationship between Spike and John Singleton, just like there's a relationship between John Singleton and Jackie Robinson. When the major-league baseball teams decided that they were going to integrate the all-white major league, they didn't go to the Negro baseball league and get Satchel Paige or Josh Gibson or somebody like that who was a proven, at this point, a proven producer of runs and this and all these kinds of things, because in the summer what would happen was Babe Ruth and all these guys in the major leagues would go down to Cuba to compete against, like, Satchel Paige, because they wanted to test themselves against who they thought was the best pitcher in the world bar none, right? Now, when they get ready to integrate the major-league baseball team, who do they go get? They go get Jackie Robinson. You know? And this is not a critique of Jackie Robinson's skills as an athlete, because obviously he was a superstar, and he turned out to be a great, great choice, but one of the reasons that they chose him had absolutely nothing to do with skills, which, to a large degree, weren't tested. It had to do with the degree to which they could control Jackie Robinson as a young man who had had very limited experience in terms of the world at large, you know what I mean? They could bring him in and basically create him in their own image, in a sense or contain him in a way where he, essentially, wouldn't have as many options as a Satchel Paige would have. 'Cause Jackie Robinson, once he was brought into major-league baseball to start off, wasn't gonna go as readily to the Negro baseball leagues.

bh: And that's why Forest Whitaker was chosen to direct *Waiting to Exhale*. White supremacy creates a situation where white people worship at the throne of black mediocrity. And that means it will always seek to nurture that which is half-formed in the black expressive culture over that which does demonstrate some quality of vision, illumination, what have you. Isn't it fascinating to you — I know we've talked about it at different times — that music is a terrain where black people in fact do push to the limit, do always go everywhere there is to go and beyond that? Why is that not something that enters into the filmmaking culture and the film-making process?

A.J.:   The obvious thing to me again is structure, but there is also a psychological dimension. Film is incredibly capital-oriented, which means that just to get in the game, even to get in the game and do a bad job of it, is very, very significantly different from getting in the game of music. One of the things that you see with hip-hop as the dominant postsoul musical form to be invented by black Americans is that what makes hip-hop possible, what made it possible to come into being was the advent of certain types of technology that made production easier. The development of hip-hop coincides with the basic destruction or the degeneration of the music education in the public schools, so that you had a whole generation of kids who don't learn to play instruments in school. Whereas jazz people and musicians before learned how to play an instrument in marching bands and things like that. You didn't have that any longer. So the only way the people had to entertain themselves was to play records. You know, in the summer. And they just took the structure that was designed to reproduce and turned it into producing structure. With film the capacity to make those kind of interventions is much, much more difficult because of the capital-intensive nature of making film.

bh: I agree with you. But let's take a work like *Crooklyn*. One of the arguments I've made about *Crooklyn* is that people came to see what Spike Lee's latest film was going to be. They were going to come no matter what. You know? Then that means, to me, that Spike can go further if he wanted to. Is it a question of vision? Is it a question of needing better scriptwriters? You can't say he has no control over the product. You were there. You shot the film. Certainly we have a better sound track for *Crooklyn* than in some of the other films. Do you think that there's this whole ego thing that gets in the way of black filmmakers seeing areas where there needs to be growth and change? Better editing, let's say, both in independent films and in feature films?

A.J.:   I wouldn't try to diminish the psychological dimensions of that, but a lot of that can come down to capital, in the sense that when you're talking about black film culture, you're talking about a film culture that is incredibly underdeveloped. That means that one of the things that's happened in the last couple of years, and it hasn't really been pointed out in print, is that hip-hop has provided the basis for the whole development of a whole generation of black technicians, just through the music videos that they've done. Even in terms of organizing production companies and stuff, nothing like that was in place when I first got into film. The terrain was so radically different, as you know. To envision being an independent filmmaker then was much different than it is now. In the sense that I became a "cinematographer" because I always felt black independent films failed because they didn't look good. I always assumed that I was going to have to shoot my own film, because I didn't assume there were any technicians that would be able to do the work. It's completely different now. We are seeing some advances.

bh: We know hip-hop culture comes out of a deeply male, deeply homosocial bonding culture. Sharing of resources. Does that happen in filmmaking?

A.J.:   It's a different kind of sharing of resources. What's so revolutionary about hip-hop is, the means of production are accessible to individuals in a way that there's no equivalent in terms of film. Absolutely not. Film is not only collaborative in terms of individuals, but a vertically integrated structure has to be in place to even get a film made. Forget getting it made with any kind of quality. I'm talking just to get it made, you gotta deal with labs, you gotta deal with film stock, you gotta deal with exposure. It takes so many different things.

bh: I feel that videomaking is connected to filmmaking, and it is a
        successful medium, but we're not seeing this huge group of young
        black visual artists saying, "Okay, we don't have the structure to
        make certain kinds of film, but we 'can make' great ideas." I'm
        interested in the issue of vision.

A.J.:   Vision and desire. They're intricately linked. The vision part is
        about one's capacity to see what's needed. The desire part is one's
        capacity to pursue what one wants. In a lot of ways, the underde-
        velopment of black film culture is also about a lack of construc-
        tive desire. We haven't really found our pleasure. Music is one of
        those arenas where black people have so much cultural confi-
        dence and there is a vision. Even though it is driven by the market
        and making money (everybody wants to get paid). There's a level
        of inherent pleasure in the process of making black music for the
        musicians. While I don't want to diminish the importance of
        making a living, I don't think that black people have transformed
        cinema as a form, or mastered the given even, in terms of
        methodology and procedure and stuff enough where the process
        is pleasurable. I really don't feel like it. Actually, in my experi-
        ence, it hasn't been a pleasurable process. We have to figure out
        how to make the making of film something that you would do
        even if you weren't getting paid.

bh: The same is true of writing film criticism.

A.J.:   Oh, absolutely.

bh: Because partially, let's face it, no piece that I write about film is
        going to bring any large sum of money. Writing one of the little
        Essence "Back Talk" pages will get five times as much money as
        writing that particular sixteen-page piece on *Crooklyn*.

A.J.:   Ultimately, although I don't want to sound too utopian, it's gotta
        be about elevating our gains. When I go out and invest energy in
        doing something where there's not gonna be a direct financial
        recoupment on my part, it's really about a more communal sense
        of elevating the gain. When I criticize Spike's films, or even Julie
        Dash's films, whatever films I've been involved with, or films I
        haven't it's really not about trying to knock 'em down, like a lot

of people think criticizing things is about knocking things down. It's about saying that at a certain point, if we all don't realize that we play the game of "The Emperor's New Clothes," because it's a commodity market and we're doing what we have to do and become more sophisticated as filmmakers, that's fine. But we have to know the difference, in our head, between being butt naked and having clothes on, or else we will never be able to go to clothing ourselves effectively. We will never be able to create black film that is deserving of a notion of a new black film renaissance. By misreading the sophistication, we're actually actively preventing our development. You have to call it like you see it.

bh: By overemphasizing celebration we forget that it's important to challenge and interrogate.

A.J.:   Like most black artists, I continue to see music, especially jazz, as the height of black expressive culture. We're constantly trying to catch up if we're in other mediums. We always use that music as a model of what's possible on the level of moving people, but, by the same token people who just say it's jazz as opposed to it's jazz and blues and the whole history of black people expressing themselves in sound in America refuse to see the continuity, to look at the music wholeheartedly.

bh: If we look at the life of an Ornette Coleman, if we look at the life of a John Coltrane, it's not something inherent in the music-making process that creates cultural revolutions in the work. It's that these people are going through incredible psychic transformations in their lives. They are going all around the world and learning different instruments. They are not just sitting in the corner doing some essential, inherent music making. We have to take risks—creative risks. Which goes back then to what you said about the Singleton film, which is that there has to be some maturation in the visionary process of the artist if there's going to be a complex cultural product and an ever-changing cultural product. If we look at John Coltrane at the beginning of his career and John Coltrane at the time of his death, if we look at a Cecil Taylor at the beginning of his career, Julius Hemphill, so many other people we could name, we see this development, but it's a development that's going on in their lives on a psychic level.

People don't know, necessarily, that people like Cecil and John Coltrane were readers that got into all kinds of metaphysical thinking, and Sun Ra ... Spike Lee never addresses his engagement with a realm of thought that is outside of cinema. We won't hear about how Spike is getting into the Dali Lama and reading about Tibetan Buddhism. So many of the jazz musicians that we can talk about take it to another level—Alice Coltrane, her whole engagement with Hatha Yoga. We can see people getting into experiences that transform them, hence their vision is transformed and the work is transformed. You're one of the first filmmakers, and Kathleen Collins was for me as well, that talked about having a broad range of knowledge as a base. Seeing your own development as a thinker alters what you produce as a filmmaker.

A.J.: I took music as a jump-off point for what was possible just in terms of the most basic level of moving black people. I feel like two things have to happen in film. One is, we have to have a message to communicate. So that's about my ongoing struggles to understand the world in a more complex fashion. But we also have to master the form so that we can communicate what we want to say as beautifully as possible. You can look at hip-hop on one hand and see almost a certain theorem in process that says, "He or she who rules the beats rules the streets." So it's something like that that you can see if you go out to a dance of black people. I had this amazing experience at the premiere of *Crooklyn*. I was dancing, I'm happy, I finished *Crooklyn*, whatever, you know, and I'm with my friends, and we're celebrating the completing of the film, it's out with. And people are dancing, and Snoop Doggy Dogg's jamming, and Juice comes on. Now, when Juice comes on, it's like a great cook comes in and goes, like, "Heeeyyy!" So however many people were there on the dance floor doubles in that one instance. And people are dancing, you know, and Snoop is singing the song, and then there's this part of the song, and he says, you know, whatever, "We don't love them hos." And it was really weird, because the deejay was spinnin' the record, and then he cut it out, he did a dropout, and everybody in the whole facility said, "We don't love them hos!" They all shouted together, like the chorus, now, 'cause that's a great line in the film. I was dancing and thinking. Now, to me, I'm dancing, and I go, "Oh, shit, this is very weird," because it wasn't just guys, say, for example, who yelled it out. Now, to me, that was one of the most primal demonstrations I've ever had of the power of the beat, because Snoopy has achieved musical mastery such that he would have people who own ... let's even be conservative. I will at least assume some of the women don't believe that sentiment, "We don't love those hos." And I also would have to assume some of the brothers aren't that for it too, but everybody screamed it out. Now, my whole thing is this, is that if we achieve that kind of mastery in terms of making films, then we would have a certain power. I think that it behooves black filmmakers to approach the question of mastering the medium with that in mind. We aren't going to be able to make a lot of films for quite some time, so what we have to figure out is how to make films that have more power to transfix our people, so that we can then bring them in sync with some sentiments that are going to be conservative towards them reaching a new level of development.

bh: Maybe there has to be more of a collaborative motion of creative expression, so that "A Love Supreme" that John Coltrane arrives at really is where we start thinking from about black filmmaking processes. Not going back to some beginning like where jazz began, but starting with that level of excellence that is being called for and evoked in that particular musical performance.

A.J.:   Absolutely. And when you talk about going back—going back to black music is about acknowledging my love of black people's expression. On the most basic level, I have a real, pure love for what black people do expressively. Sometimes it can be some-thing on the side of the road, somebody scratched it, and I could just say, "Wow, that shit is so bad," or remember growing up in Mississippi. I would see those Day-Glo kind of posters for Bobby Blue Bland, and they would staple them to the telephone poles, but after you had a spot where they stapled fifty different posters over a two-year period, all those staples would rust and become like the nails in those African fetishes. I was able to see this and have enough of a cultural frame to be able to appreciate it, not just as junk, but as some sort of manifestation of cultural tradi-tions. If you can see that, you can bring to bear that same sensi-bility on film. It's as simple as looking at home movies by black people and trying to figure out, Is there anything inherently that black people are doing that could be utilized, used as a basis for understanding what the black cinematic vision could be?

bh: Hopefully, more black films will splice in those home movies, giving us a lot of different ways of seeing ourselves, whether documentary footage or other kinds of stuff. We have that experimentation in black film that we often just don't see.

A.J.:   We need the experimentation, because we need to be able to create contexts where we can play. Again, that's where that whole market thing comes in. The more money is involved, the less free you are to play. You look at the development of black musical forms in America, there always is the context where it's about play. It's not about entertaining white people, it's not even really about entertaining black people.

bh: As somebody who engages in a kind of critical writing that is a form of play, that is a form of "*jouissance*," I need to remind you, there's a level of sacrifice that you make to have that play.

A.J.:   Oh, absolutely.

bh: You sacrifice certain kinds of monetary reward, a certain kind of flashiness, because that kind of seriousness, even if it's about a context in which we have ecstasy—you know, like the scenes that you shot at the beginning of *Crooklyn* where we see black people in the ordinariness of their lives but with a quality of integrity of being that takes us beyond colonization and subjugation—that is not the big-money-making work. We can't have that if we're not willing to sacrifice for that moment.

A.J.:   I agree with you. We often sacrifice pleasure—absolutely. Black musicians have created environments where black people played for themselves, for their own pleasure. And creating those environments where we can do that, and then bring those things to bear back to the marketplace, things that we've discovered while we've been playing, is very crucial to move our creative visions forward.

the oppositional gaze:
black female spectators

When thinking about black female spectators, I remember being punished as a child for staring, for those hard, intense, direct looks children would give grown-ups, looks that were seen as confrontational, as gestures of resistance, challenges to authority. The "gaze" has always been political in my life. Imagine the terror felt by the child who has come to understand through repeated punishments that one's gaze can be dangerous. The child who has learned so well to look the other way when necessary. Yet, when punished, the child is told by parents, "Look at me when I talk to you." Only, the child is afraid to look. Afraid to look, but fascinated by the gaze. There is power in looking.

Amazed the first time I read in history classes that white slave-owners (men, women, and children) punished enslaved black people for looking, I wondered how this traumatic relationship to the gaze had informed black parenting and black spectatorship. The politics of slavery, of racialized power relations, were such that the slaves were denied their right to gaze. Connecting this strategy of domination to that used by grown folks in Southern black rural communities where I grew up, I was pained to think that there was no absolute difference between whites who had oppressed black people and ourselves. Years later, reading Michel Foucault, I thought again about these connections, about the ways power as domination reproduces itself in different locations employing similar apparatuses, strategies, and mechanisms of control. Since I knew as a child that the dominating power adults exercised over me and over my gaze was never so absolute that I did not dare to look, to sneak a peep, to stare dangerously, I knew that the slaves had looked. That all attempts to repress our/black people's right to gaze had produced in us an overwhelming longing to look, a rebellious desire, an oppositional gaze. By courageously looking, we defiantly declared: "Not only will I stare. I want my look to change reality." Even in the worst circumstances of domination, the ability to manipulate one's gaze in the face of structures of domination that would contain it opens up the possibility of agency. In much of his work, Michel Foucault insists on describing domination in terms of "relations of power," as part of an effort to challenge the assumption that "power is a system of domination which controls everything and which leaves no room for freedom." Emphatically stating that in all relations of power "there is necessarily the possibility of resistance," he invites the critical thinker to search those margins, gaps, and locations on and through the body where agency can be found.

Stuart Hall calls for recognition of our agency as black spectators in his essay "Cultural Identity and Cinematic Representation." Speaking against the construction of white representations of blackness as totalizing, Hall says of white presence: "The error is not to conceptualize this 'presence' in terms of power, but to locate that power as wholly external to us—as extrinsic force, whose influence can be thrown off like the serpent sheds its skin. What Franz Fanon reminds us, in *Black Skin, White Masks*, is how power is inside as well as outside:

> The movements, the attitudes, the glances of the Other fixed me there, in the sense in which a chemical solution is fixed by a dye. I was indignant; I demanded an explanation. Nothing happened. I burst apart. Now the fragments have been put together again by another self. This "look," from—so to speak—the place of the Other, fixes us, not only in its violence, hostility and aggression, but in the ambivalence of its desire.

Spaces of agency exist for black people, wherein we can both interrogate the gaze of the Other but also look back, and at one another, naming what we see. The "gaze" has been and is a site of resistance for colonized black people globally. Subordinates in relations of power learn experientially that there is a critical gaze, one that "looks" to document, one that is oppositional. In resistance struggle the power of the dominated to assert agency by claiming and cultivating "awareness" politicizes "looking" relations—one learns to look a certain way in order to resist.

When most black people in the United States first had the opportunity to look at film and television, they did so fully aware that the mass media was a system of knowledge and power reproducing and maintaining white supremacy. To stare at the television, or mainstream movies, to engage its images was to engage its negation of black representation. It was the oppositional black gaze that responded to these looking relations by developing an independent black cinema. Black viewers of mainstream cinema and television could chart the progress of political movements for racial equality via the construction of images, and did so. Within my family's Southern black working-class home, located in a racially segregated neighborhood, watching television was one way to develop critical spectatorship. Unless you went to work in the white world, across the tracks, you learned to look at white people by staring at them on the screen. Black looks, as they were constituted in the context of social movements for racial uplift, were interrogating gazes. We laughed at television shows like *Our Gang* and *Amos 'n' Andy* at these white representations of blackness, but we also looked at them critically. Before racial integration, black reviewers of movies and television experienced visual pleasure in a context where looking was also about contestation and confrontation.

Writing about black looking relations in "Black British Cinema: Spectatorship and Identity Formation in Territories," Manthia Diawara identifies the power of the spectator: "Every narration places the spectator in a position of agency; and race, class and sexual relations influence the way in which this subjecthood is filled by the spectator." Of particular concern for him are moments of "rupture," when the spectator resists "complete identification with the film's discourse." These ruptures define the relation between black spectators and dominant cinema prior to racial integration. Then, one's enjoyment of a film wherein representations of blackness were stereotypically degrading and dehumanizing coexisted with a critical practice that restored presence where it was negated. Critical discussion of the film while it was in progress or at its conclusion maintained the distance between the spectator and the image. Black films were also subject to critical interrogation. Since they came into being in part as a response to the failure of white-dominated cinema to represent blackness in a manner that did not reinforce white supremacy, they too were critiqued to see if images were seen as complicit with dominant cinematic practices.

Critical, interrogating black looks were mainly concerned with issues of race and racism, the way racial domination of blacks by whites overdetermined representation. They were rarely concerned with gender. As spectators, black men could repudiate the reproduction of racism in cinema and television, the negation of black presence, even as they could feel as though they were rebelling against white supremacy by daring to look, by engaging phallocentric politics of spectatorship. Given the real-life public circumstances wherein black men were murdered/lynched for looking at white womanhood, where the black male gaze was always subject to control and/or punishment by the powerful white Other, the private realm of television screens or dark theaters could unleash the repressed gaze. There they could "look" at white womanhood without a structure of domination overseeing the gaze, interpreting and punishing. The white supremacist structure that had murdered Emmet Till after interpreting his look as violation, as "rape' of white womanhood, could not control black male responses to screen images. In their role as spectators, black men could enter an imaginative space of phallocentric power that mediated racial negation. This gendered relation to looking made the experience of the black male spectator radically different from that of the black female spectator. Major early black male independent filmmakers represented black women in their films as objects of a male gaze. Whether looking through the camera or as spectators watching films, whether mainstream cinema or "race" movies such as those made by Oscar Micheaux, the black male gaze had a different scope from that of the black female.

Black women have written little about black female spectatorship, about our moviegoing practices. A growing body of film theory and criticism by black women has only begun to emerge. The prolonged silence of black women as spectators and critics was a response to absence, to cinematic negation. In "The Technology of Gender," Teresa de Lauretis, drawing on the work of Monique Wittig, calls attention to "the power of discourses to 'do violence' to people, a violence which is material and physical, although produced by abstract and scientific discourses as well as the discourses of the mass media." With the possible exception of early

race movies, black female spectators have had to develop looking relations within a cinematic context that constructs our presence as absence
that denies the "body" of the black female so as to perpetuate white
supremacy and with it a phallocentric spectatorship where the woman to
be looked at and desired is "white." (Recent movies do not conform to
this paradigm, but I am turning to the past with the intent to chart the
development of black male spectatorship.)

Talking with black women of all ages and classes, in different areas of
the United States, about their filmic looking relations, I hear again and
again ambivalent responses to cinema. Only a few of the black women I
talked with remembered the pleasure of race movies, and even those
who did felt that pleasure interrupted and usurped by Hollywood. Most
of the black women I talked with were adamant that they never went to
movies expecting to see compelling representations of black femaleness.
They were all acutely aware of cinematic racism—its violent erasure of
black womanhood. Anne Friedberg stresses in her essay "A Denial of
Difference: Theories of Cinematic Identification" that "identification
can only be made through recognition, and all recognition is itself an
implicit confirmation of the ideology of the status quo." Even when
representations of black women were present in film, our bodies and
being were there to serve—to enhance and maintain white womanhood
as object of the phallocentric gaze.

Commenting on Hollywood's characterization of black women in
Girls on Film, Julie Burchill described this absent presence:

> Black women have been mothers without children (Mammies—who can
> ever forget the sickening spectacle of Hattie MacDaniels waiting on the
> simpering Vivien Leigh hand and foot and enquiring like a ninny, "What's
> ma lamb gonna wear?").... Lena Horne, the first black performer signed to
> along term contract with a major (MGM), looked gutless but was actually
> quite spirited. She seethed when Tallulah Bankhead complimented her on
> the paleness of her skin and the non-Negroidness of her features.

When black women actresses like Lena Horne appeared in mainstream
cinema, most white viewers were not aware that they were looking at
black females unless the film was specifically coded as being about blacks.
Burchill is one of the few white women film critics who has dared to
examine the intersection of race and gender in relation to the construction of the category "woman" in film as object of the phallocentric gaze.
With characteristic wit she asserts: "What does it say about racial purity

that the best blondes have all been brunettes (Harlow, Monroe, Bardot?) I think it says that we are not as white as we think." Burchill could easily have said, "We are not as white as we want to be," for clearly the obsession to have white women film stars be ultra white was a cinematic practice that sought to maintain a distance, a separation between that image and the black female Other; it was a way to perpetuate white supremacy. Politics of race and gender were inscribed into mainstream cinematic narrative from *Birth of a Nation* on. As a seminal work, this film identified what the place and function of white womanhood would be in cinema. There was clearly no place for black women.

Remembering my past in relation to screen images of black womanhood, I wrote a short essay, "Do You Remember Sapphire?" that explored both the negation of black female representation in cinema and television and our rejection of these images. Identifying the character of Sapphire from *Amos 'n' Andy* as that screen representation of black femaleness I first saw in childhood, I write:

> She was even then backdrop, foil. She was bitch—nag. She was there to soften images of black men, to make them seem vulnerable, easygoing, funny, and unthreatening to a white audience. She as there as man in drag, as castrating bitch, as someone to be lied to, someone to be tricked, someone the white and black audience could hate. Scapegoated on all sides. *She was not us.* We laughed with the black men, with the white people. We laughed at this black woman who was not us. And we did not even long to be there on the screen. How could we long to be there when our image, visually constructed, was so ugly? We did not long to be there. We did not long for her. We did not want our construction to be this hated black female thing—foil, backdrop. Her black female image was not the body of desire. There was nothing to see. She was not us.

Grown black women had a different response to Sapphire; they identified with her frustrations and her woes. They resented the way she was mocked. They resented the way these screen images could assault black womanhood, could name us bitches, nags. And in opposition they claimed Sapphire as their own, as the symbol of that angry part of themselves white folks and black men could not even begin to understand.

Conventional representations of black women have done violence to the image. Responding to this assault, many black women spectators shut out the image, looked the other way, accorded cinema no importance in their lives. Then there were those spectators whose gaze was that of desire and complicity. Assuming a posture of subordination, they submitted to cinema's capacity to seduce and betray. They were cinematically "gaslighted." Every black woman I spoke with who was/is an ardent moviegoer, a lover of the Hollywood film testified that to experience fully the pleasure of that cinema she had to close down critique, analysis; she had to forget racism. And mostly those women did not think about sexism. What was the nature, then, of this adoring black female gaze—this look that could bring pleasure in the midst of negation? In her first novel, *The Bluest Eye*, Toni Morrison constructs a portrait of the black female spectator; her gaze is the masochistic look of victimization. Describing her looking relations, Miss Pauline Breedlove, a poor working woman, maid in the house of a prosperous white family, asserts:

> The onliest time I be happy seem like was when I was in the picture show. Every time I got, I went, I'd go early, before the show started. They's cut off the lights, and everything be black. Then the screen would light up, and I's over right on in them picture. White men taking such good care of they women, and they all dressed up in big clean houses with the bath tubs right in the same room with the toilet. Them pictures gave me a lot of pleasure.

To experience pleasure, Miss Pauline sitting in the dark must imagine herself transformed, turned into the white woman portrayed on the screen. After watching movies, feeling the pleasure, she says, "But it made coming home hard."

We come home to ourselves. Not all black women spectators submitted to that spectacle of regression through identification. Most of the women I talked with felt that they consciously resisted identification with films—that this tension made moviegoing less than pleasurable; at times it caused pain. As one black woman put, "I could always get pleasure from movies as long as I did not look too deep." For black female spectators who have "looked too deep" the encounter with the screen hurt. That some of us chose to stop looking was a gesture of resistance, turning away was one way to protest, to reject negation. My pleasure in the screen ended abruptly when I and my sisters first watched *Imitation of Life*. Writing about this experience in the "Sapphire" piece, I addressed the movie directly, confessing:

> I had until now forgotten you, that screen image seen in adolescence, those images that made me stop looking. It was there in *Imitation of Life*, that comfortable mammy image. There was something familiar about this hard-

working black woman who loved her daughter so much, loved her in a way that hurt. Indeed, as young southern black girls watching this film, Peola's mother reminded us of the hardworking, churchgoing, Big Mamas we knew and loved. Consequently, it was not this image that captured our gaze; we were fascinated by Peola.

Addressing her, I wrote:

> You were different. There was something scary in this image of young sexual sensual black beauty betrayed—that daughter who did not want to be confined by blackness, that "tragic mulatto" who did not want to be negated. "Just let me escape this image forever," she could have said. I will always remember that image. I remembered how we cried for her, for our unrealized desiring selves. She was tragic because there was no place in the cinema for her, no loving pictures. She too was absent image. It was better then, that we were absent, for when we were there it was humiliating, strange, sad. We cried all night for you, for the cinema that had no place for you. And like you, we stopped thinking it would one day be different.

When I returned to films as a young woman, after a long period of silence, I had developed an oppositional gaze. Not only would I not be hurt by the absence of black female presence, or the insertion of violating representation, I interrogated the work, cultivated a way to look past race and gender for aspects of content, form, language. Foreign films and U.S. independent cinema were the primary locations of my filmic looking relations, even though I also watched Hollywood films.

From "jump," black female spectators have gone to films with awareness of the way in which race and racism determined the visual construction of gender. Whether it was *Birth of a Nation* or Shirley Temple shows, we knew that white womanhood was the racialized sexual difference occupying the place of stardom in mainstream narrative film. We assumed white women knew it to. Reading Laura Mulvey's provocative essay, "Visual Pleasure and Narrative Cinema," from a standpoint that acknowledges race, one sees clearly why black women spectators not duped by mainstream cinema would develop an oppositional gaze. Placing ourselves outside that pleasure in looking, Mulvey argues, was determined by a "split between active / male and passive / female." Black female spectators actively chose not to identify with the film's imaginary subject because such identification was disenabling.

Looking at films with an oppositional gaze, black women were able to critically assess the cinema's construction of white womanhood as object of phallocentric gaze and choose not to identify with either the victim or the perpetrator. Black female spectators, who refused to identify with white womanhood, who would not take on the phallocentric gaze of desire and possession, created a critical space where the binary opposition Mulvey posits of "woman as image, man as bearer of the look" was continually deconstructed. As critical spectators, black women looked from a location that disrupted, one akin to that described by Annette Kuhn in *The Power of the Image*:

> ... the acts of analysis, of deconstruction and of reading "against the grain" offer an additional pleasure—the pleasure of resistance, of saying "no": not to "unsophisticated" enjoyment, by ourselves and others, of culturally dominant images, but to the structures of power which ask us to consume them uncritically and in highly circumscribed ways.

Mainstream feminist film criticism in no way acknowledges black female spectatorship. It does not even consider the possibility that women can construct an oppositional gaze via an understanding and awareness of the politics of race and racism. Feminist film theory rooted in an ahistorical psychoanalytic framework that privileges sexual difference actively suppresses recognition of race, reenacting and mirroring the erasure of black womanhood that occurs in films, silencing any discussion of racial difference—of racialized sexual difference. Despite feminist critical interventions aimed at deconstructing the category "woman" which highlight the significance of race, many feminist film critics continue to structure their discourse as though it speaks about "women" when in actually it speaks only about white women. It seems ironic that the cover of the recent anthology *Feminism and Film Theory* edited by Constance Penley has a graphic that is a reproduction of the photo of white actresses Rosalind Russell and Dorothy Arzner on he 1935 set of the film *Craig's Wife* yet there is no acknowledgement in any essay in this collection that the woman "subject" under discussion is always white. Even though there are photos of black women from films reproduced in the text, there is no acknowledgment of racial difference.

It would be too simplistic to interpret this failure of insight solely as a gesture of racism. Importantly, it also speaks to the problem of structuring feminist film theory around a totalizing narrative of women as

object whose image functions solely to reaffirm and reinscribe patriarchy. Mary Ann Doane addresses this issue in the essay "Remembering
Women: Psychical and Historical Construction in Film Theory":

> This attachment to the figure of a degeneralizible Woman as the product of
> the apparatus indicates why, for many, feminist film theory seems to have
> reached an impasse, a certain blockage in its theorization.... In focusing
> upon the task of delineating in great detail the attributes of woman as effect
> of the apparatus, feminist film theory participates in the abstraction of
> women.

The concept "woman" effaces the difference between women in
specific sociohistorical contexts, between women defined precisely as
historical subjects rather than as *a* psychic subject (or nonsubject).
Though Doane does not focus on race, her comments speak directly to
the problem of its erasure. For it is only as one imagines "woman" in the
abstract, when woman becomes fiction or fantasy, that race cannot be
seen as significant. Are we really to imagine that feminist theorists writing
only about images of white women, who subsume this specific historical
subject under the totalizing category "woman," do not "see" the whiteness of the image? It may very well be that they engage in a process of
denial that eliminates the necessity of revisioning conventional ways of
thinking about psychoanalysis as a paradigm of analysis and the need to
rethink a body of feminist film theory that is firmly rooted in a denial of
the reality that sex/sexuality may not be the primary and/or exclusive
signifier of difference. Doane's essay appears in the anthology, *Psychoanalysis and Cinema* edited by E. Ann Kaplan, where, once again, none of
the theory presented acknowledges or discusses racial difference, with
the exception of one essay, "Not Speaking with Language, Speaking with
No Language," which problematizes notions of orientalism in its examination of Leslie Thornton's film *Adynata*. Yet in most of the essays, the
theories espoused are rendered problematic if one includes race as a
category of analysis.

Constructing feminist film theory along these lines enables the
production of a discursive practice that need never theorize any aspect of
black female representation or spectatorship. Yet the existence of black
women within white supremacist culture problematizes, and makes
complex, the overall issue of female identity, representation, and spectatorship. If, as Friedberg suggests, "identification is a process which
commands the subject to be displaced by an other; it is a procedure

which breaches the separation between self and other, and, in this way, replicates the very structure of patriarchy," if identification "demands sameness, necessitates similarity, disallows difference"—must we then surmise that many feminist film critics who are "overidentified" with the mainstream cinematic apparatus produce theories that replicate its totalizing agenda? Why is it that feminist film criticism, which has most claimed the terrain of woman's identity, representation, and subjectivity as its field of analysis, remains aggressively silent on the subject of blackness and specifically representations of black womanhood? Just as mainstream cinema has historically forced aware black female spectators not to look, much feminist film criticism disallows the possibility of a theoretical dialogue that might include black women's voices. It is difficult to talk when you feel no one is listening, when you feel as though a special jargon or narrative has been created that only the chosen can understand. No wonder then that black women have for the most part confined our critical commentary on film to conversations. And it must be reiterated that this gesture is a strategy that protects us from the violence perpetuated and advocated by discourses of mass media. A new focus on issues of race and representation in the field of film theory could critically intervene on the historical repression reproduced in some arenas of contemporary critical practice, making a discursive space for discussion of black female spectatorship possible.

When I asked a black woman in her twenties, an obsessive moviegoer, why she thought we had not written about black female spectatorship, she commented: "We are afraid to talk about ourselves as spectators because we have been so abused by 'the gaze.'" An aspect of that abuse was the imposition of the assumption that black female looking relations were not important enough to theorize. Film theory as a critical "turf" in the United States has been and continues to be influenced by and reflective of white racial domination. Since feminist film criticism was initially rooted in a women's liberation movement informed by racist practices, it did not open up the discursive terrain and make it more inclusive. Recently, even those white film theorists who include an analysis of race show no interest in black female spectatorship. In her introduction to the collection of essays *Visual and Other Pleasures*, Laura Mulvey describes her initial romantic absorption in Hollywood cinema, stating:

> Although this great, previously unquestioned and unanalyzed love was put in
> crisis by the impact of feminism on my thought in the early 1970s, it also had

had an enormous influence on the development of my critical work and
ideas and the debate within film culture with which I became preoccupied
over the next fifteen years or so. Watched through eyes that were affected by
the changing climate of consciousness, the movies lost their magic.

Watching movies from a feminist perspective, Mulvey arrived at that
location of disaffection that is the starting point for many black women
approaching cinema within the lived harsh reality of racism. Yet her
account of being a part of a film culture whose roots rest on a founding
relationship of adoration and love indicate how difficult it would have
been to enter that world from "jump" as a critical spectator whose gaze
had been formed in opposition.

Given the context of class exploitation, and racist and sexist domination, it has only been through resistance, struggle, reading, and looking
"against the grain" that black women have been able to value our
process of looking enough to publicly name it. Centrally, those black
female spectators who attest to the oppositionality of their gaze deconstruct theories of female spectatorship that have relied heavily on the
assumption that, as Doane suggests in her essay "Woman's Stake: Filming the Female Body," "woman can only mimic man's relation to
language, that is, assume a position defined by the penis-phallus as the
supreme arbiter of lack." Identifying with neither the phallocentric gaze
nor the construction of white womanhood as black, critical black
female spectators construct a theory of looking relations where cinematic visual delight is the pleasure of interrogation. Every black woman
spectator I talked to, with rare exception, spoke of being "on guard" at
the movies. Talking about the way being a critical spectator of Hollywood films influenced her, black woman filmmaker Julie Dash
exclaims, "I make films because I was such a spectator!" Looking at
Hollywood cinema from a distance, from that critical politicized standpoint that did not want to be seduced by narratives reproducing her
negation, Dash watched mainstream movies over and over again for the
pleasure of deconstructing them. And of course there is that added
delight if one happens, in the process of interrogation, to come across a
narrative that invites the black female spectator to engage the text with
no threat of violation.

Significantly, I began to write film criticism in response to the first
Spike Lee movie, *She's Gotta Have It*, contesting Lee's replication of mainstream patriarchal cinematic practices that explicitly represent woman (in
this instance black woman) as the object of a phallocentric gaze. Lee's

investment in patriarchal filmic practices that mirror dominant patterns makes him the perfect black candidate for entrance to the Hollywood canon. His work mimics the cinematic construction of white woman-hood as object, replacing her body as text on which to write male desire with the black female body. It is transference without transformation. Entering the discourse of film criticism from the politicized location of resistance, of not wanting, as a working-class black woman I interviewed stated, "to see black women in the position white women have occupied in film forever," I began to think critically about black female spectator-ship.

For years I went to independent and/or foreign films where I was the only black female present in the theater. I often imagined that in every theater in the United States there was another black woman watching the same film wondering why she was the only visible black female spec-tator. I remember trying to share with one of my five sisters the cinema I liked so much. She was "enraged" that I brought her to a theater where she would have to read subtitles. To her it was a violation of Hollywood notions of spectatorship, of coming to the movies to be entertained. When I interviewed her to ask what had changed her mind over the years, led her to embrace this cinema, she connected it to coming to critical consciousness, saying, "I learned that there was more to looking than I had been exposed to in ordinary (Hollywood) movies." I shared that though most of the films I loved were all white, I could engage them because they did not have in their deep structure a subtext reproducing the narrative of white supremacy. Her response was to say that these films demystified "whiteness," since the lives they depicted seemed less rooted in fantasies of escape. They were, she suggested, more like "what we knew life to be, the deeper side of life as well." Always more seduced and enchanted with Hollywood cinema than me, she stressed that unaware black female spectators must "break out," no longer be imprisoned by images that enact a drama of our negation. Though she still sees Holly-wood films, because "they are a major influence in the culture"—she no longer feels duped or victimized.

Talking with black female spectators, looking at written discussions either in fiction or academic essays about black women, I noted the connection made between the realm of representation in mass media and the capacity of black women to construct ourselves as subjects in daily life. The extent to which black women feel devalued, objectified, dehumanized in this society determines the scope and texture of their looking relations. Those black women whose identities were constructed in resistance, by practices that oppose the dominant order, were most inclined to develop an oppositional gaze. Now that there is a growing interest in films produced by back women and that those films have become more accessible to viewers, it is possible to talk about black female spectatorship in relation to that work. So far, most discussions of black spectatorship that I have come across focus on men. In "Black Spectatorship: Problems of Identification and Resistance" Manthia Diawara suggests that "the components of 'difference'" among elements of sex, gender, and sexuality give rise to different readings of the same material, adding that these conditions produce a "resisting" spectator. He focuses his critical discussion on black masculinity.

The recent publication of the anthology *The Female Gaze: Women as Viewers of Popular Culture* excited me, especially as it included an essay, "Black Looks," by Jacqui Roach and Petal Felix that attempts to address black female spectatorship. The essay posed provocative questions that were not answered: Is there a black female gaze? How do black women relate to the gender politics of representation? Concluding, the authors assert that black females have "our own reality, our own history, our own gaze — one which sees the world rather differently from 'anyone else.'" Yet, they do not name/describe this experience of seeing "rather differently." The absence of definition and explanation suggests they are assuming an essentialist stance wherein it is presumed that black women, a victims of race and gender oppression, have an inherently different field of vision. Many black women do not "see differently" precisely because their perceptions of reality are so profoundly colonized, shaped by dominant ways of knowing. As Trinh T. Minha-ha points out in "Outside In, Inside Out": "Subjectivity does not merely consist of talking about oneself, ... be this talking indulgent or critical."

Critical black female spectatorship emerges as a site of resistance only when individual black women actively resist the imposition of dominant ways of knowing and looking. While every black woman I talked to was ware of racism, that awareness did not automatically correspond with politicalization, the development of an oppositional gaze. when it did, individual black women consciously named the process. Manthia Diawara's "resisting spectatorship" is a term that does not adequately describe the terrain of black female spectatorship. We do more than resist. We create alternative texts that are not solely reactions. As critical spectators, black women participate in a broad range of looking relations, contest, resist, revision, interrogate, and invent on multiple levels. Certainly when I watch the work of black women filmmakers Camille

Billops, Kathleen Collins, Julie Dash, Ayoka Chenzira, Zeinabu Davis, I do not need to "resist" the images even as I still choose to watch their work with a critical eye.

Black female critical thinkers concerned with creating space for the construction of radical black female subjectivity, and the way cultural production informs this possibility, fully acknowledge the importance of mass media, film in particular, as a powerful site for critical intervention. Certainly Julie Dash's film *Illusions* identifies the terrain of Hollywood cinema as a space of knowledge production that has enormous power. Yet, she also crates a filmic narrative wherein the black female protagonist subversively claims that space. Inverting the "real-life" power structure, she offers the black female spectator representations that challenge stereotypical notions that place us outside the realm of filmic discursive practices. Within the film she uses the strategy of Hollywood suspense films to undermine those cinematic practices that deny black women a place in this structure. Problematizing the question of "racial" identity by depicting passing, suddenly it is the white male's capacity to gaze, define, and know that is called into question.

When Mary Ann Doane describes in "Woman's Stake: Filming the Female Body" the way in which feminist filmmaking practice can elaborate "a special syntax for a different articulation of the female body," she names a critical process that "Undoes the structure of the classical narrative through an insistence upon its repressions." An eloquent description, this precisely names Dash's strategy in *Illusions*, even though the film is not unproblematic and works within certain conventions that are not successfully challenged. For example, the film does not indicate whether the character Mignon will make Hollywood films that subvert and transform the genre or whether she will simply assimilate and perpetuate the norm. Still, subversively, *Illusions* problematizes the issue of race and spectatorship. White people in the film are unable to "see" that race informs their looking relations. Though she is passing to gain access to the machinery of cultural production represented by film, Mignon continually asserts her ties to black community. The bond between her and the young black woman singer Esther Jeeter is affirmed by caring gestures of affirmation, often expressed by eye-to-eye contact, the direct unmediated gaze of recognition. Ironically, it is the desiring objectifying sexualized white male gaze that threatens to penetrate her "secret" and disrupt her process. Metaphorically, Dash suggests the power of black women to make films will be threatened and undermined by that white male gaze, which seeks to reinscribe the black female body in a narrative of voyeuristic pleasure where the only relevant opposition is male/female and the only location for the female is as a victim. These tensions are not resolved by the narrative. It is not at all evident that Mignon will triumph over the white supremacist capitalist imperialist dominating "gaze."

Throughout *Illusions*, Mignon's power is affirmed by her contact with the younger black woman whom she nurtures and protects. It is this process of mirrored recognition that enables both black women to define their reality, apart from the reality imposed upon them by structures of domination. The shared gaze of the two women reinforces their solidarity. As the younger subject, Esther represents a potential audience for films that Mignon might produce, films wherein black females will be the narrative focus. Julie Dash's recent feature-length film *Daughters of the Dust* dares to place black females at the center of its narrative. This focus caused critics (especially white males) to critique the film negatively or to express many reservations. Clearly, racism and sexism so overdetermine spectatorship—not only what we look at but who we identify with—that viewers who are not black females find it hard to empathize with the central characters in the movie. They are adrift without a white presence in the film.

Another representation of black females nurturing one another via recognition of their common struggle for subjectivity is depicted in Sankofa's collective work *A Passion of Remembrance*. In the film, two black women friends, Louise and Maggie, are from the onset of the narrative struggling with the issue of subjectivity, of their place in progressive black liberation movements that have been sexist. They challenge old norms and want to replace them with new understandings of the complexity of black identity, and the need for liberation struggles that address that complexity. Dressing to go to a party, Louise and Maggie claim the "gaze." Looking at one another, staring into mirrors, they appear completely focused on their encounter with black femaleness. How they see themselves is most important, not how they will be stared at by others. Dancing to the tune "Let's Get Loose," they display their bodies not for a voyeuristic colonizing gaze but for that look of recognition that affirms their subjectivity—that constitutes them as spectators. Mutually empowered they eagerly leave the privatized domain to confront the public. Disrupting conventional racist and sexist stereotypical representations of black female bodies, these scenes invite the audience to look differently. They act to critically intervene and transform conventional filmic practices, changing notions of spectatorship. *Illusions,*

Daughters of the Dust, and *A Passion of Remembrance* employ a deconstructive filmic practice to undermine existing grand cinematic narratives, even as they retheorize subjectivity in the realm of the visual. Without providing "realistic" positive representations that emerge only as a response to the totalizing nature of existing narratives, they offer points of radical departure. Opening up a space for the assertion of a critical black female spectatorship, they do not simply offer diverse representations, they imagine new transgressive possibilities for the formulation of identity.

In this sense they make explicit a critical practice that provides us with different ways to think about black female subjectivity and black female spectatorship. Cinematically, they provide new points of recognition, embodying Stuart Hall's vision of a critical practice that acknowledges that identity is constituted "not outside but within representation" and invites us to see film "not as a second-order mirror held up to reflect what already exists, but as that form of representation which is able to constitute us as new kinds of subjects and thereby enable us to discover who we are." It is this critical practice that enables the production of a feminist film theory that theorizes black female spectatorship. Looking and looking back, black women involve ourselves in a process whereby we see our history as countermemory, using it as a way to know the present and invent the future.

20

is paris burning?

There was a time in my life when I liked to dress up as a male and go out into the world. It was a form of ritual, of play. It was also about power. To cross-dress as a woman in patriarchy—then, more so than now—was also to symbolically cross from the world of powerlessness into a world of privilege. It was the ultimate intimate voyeuristic gesture. Searching old journals for passages documenting that time, I found this paragraph:

> She pleaded with him "Just once, well every now and then, I just want us to be boys together. I want to dress like you and go out and make the world look at us differently, make them wonder about us, make them stare and ask those silly questions like is he a woman dressed up like a man, is he an older black gay man with his effeminate boy/girl lover flaunting same-sex love out in the open? Don't worry I'll take it all very seriously, I want to let them laugh at you. I'll make it real, keep them guessing, do it in such a way that they will never know for sure. Don't worry when we come home I will be a girl for you again but for now I want us to be boys together."

Cross-dressing, appearing in drag, transvestism, and transsexualism emerge in a context where the notion of subjectivity is challenged, where identity is always perceived as capable of construction, invention, change. Long before there was ever a contemporary feminist moment, the sites of these experiences were subversive places where gender norms were questioned and challenged.

Within white supremacist capitalist patriarchy the experience of men dressing as women, appearing in drag has always been regarded by the dominant heterosexist cultural gaze as a sign that one is symbolically crossing over from a realm of power into a realm of powerlessness. Just to look at the many negative ways the word "drag" is defined reconnects this label to an experience that is seen as burdensome, as retrograde and retrogressive. To choose to appear as "female" when one is "male" is always constructed in the patriarchal mindset as a loss, as a choice worthy only of ridicule. Given this cultural backdrop, it is not surprising that many black comedians appearing on television screens for the first time included as part of their acts impersonations of black women. The black woman depicted was usually held up as an object of ridicule, scorn, hatred (representing the "female" image everyone was allowed to laugh at and show contempt for). Often the moment when a black male comedian appeared in drag was the most successful segment of a given comedian's act (for example, Flip Wilson, Redd Foxx, or Eddie Murphy).

I used to wonder if the sexual stereotype of black men as overly sexual, manly, as "rapists" allowed black males to cross this gendered boundary more easily than white men without having to fear that they would be seen as possibly gay or transvestites. As a young black female, I found these images to be disempowering. They seemed to allow black males to give public expression to a general misogyny, as well as to a more specific hatred and contempt toward black women. Growing up in a world where black women were, and still are, the objects of extreme abuse, scorn, and ridicule, I felt these impersonations were aimed at reinforcing everyone's power over us. In retrospect, I can see that the black male in drag was also a disempowering image of black masculinity. Appearing as a "woman" within a sexist, racist media was a way to become in "play" that "castrated," silly, childlike black male that racist white patriarchy was comfortable having as an image in their homes. These televised images of black men in drag were never subversive; they helped sustain sexism and racism.

It came as no surprise to me that Catherine Clément in her book *Opera, or the Undoing of Women* would include a section about black men and the way their representation in opera did not allow her to neatly separate the world into gendered polarities where men and women occupied distinctly different social spaces and were "two antagonistic halves, one persecuting the other since before the dawn of time." Looking critically at images of black men in operas, she found that they were most often portrayed as victims:

> Eve is undone as a woman, endlessly bruised, endlessly dying and coming back to life to die even better. But now I begin to remember hearing figures of betrayed, wounded men; men who have women's troubles happen to them; men who have the status of Eve, as if they had lost their innate Adam. These men die like heroines; down on the ground they cry and moan, they lament. And like heroines they are surrounded by real men, veritable Adams who have cast them down. They partake of femininity: excluded, marked by some initial strangeness. They are doomed to their undoing.

Many heterosexual black men in white supremacist patriarchal culture have acted as though the primary "evil" of racism has been the refusal of the dominant culture to allow them full access to patriarchal power, so that in sexist terms they are compelled to inhabit a sphere of powerlessness deemed "feminine" and have thus perceived themselves as emasculated. To the extent that black men accept a white supremacist sexist representation of themselves as castrated, without phallic power, and therefore pseudofemales, they will need to overly assert a phallic misogynist masculinity, one rooted in contempt for the female. Much black male homophobia is rooted in the desire to eschew connection with all things deemed "feminine," and that would, of course, include black gay men. A contemporary black comedian like Eddie Murphy "proves" his phallic power by daring to publicly ridicule women and gays. His days of appearing in drag are over. Indeed, it is the drag queen of his misogynist imagination that is most often the image of black gay culture he evokes and subjects to comic homophobic assault—one that audiences collude in perpetuating.

For black males, be they gay or straight, to take appearing in drag seriously is to oppose a heterosexist representation of black manhood. Gender bending and blending on the part of black males has always been a critique of phallocentric masculinity in traditional black experience. Yet the subversive power of those images is radically altered when the latter are informed by a racialized fictional construction of the "feminine" that suddenly makes the representation of whiteness as crucial to the experience of female impersonation as gender, that is to say, when the idealized notion of the female/feminine is really a sexist idealization of white womanhood. This is brutally evident in Jennie Livingston's new film *Paris Is Burning*. Within the world of the black gay drag ball culture she depicts, the idea of womanness and femininity is totally personified by whiteness. What viewers witness is not black men longing to imper-sonate or even to become like "real" black women but their obsession with an idealized fetishized vision of femininity that is white. Called out in the film by Dorian Carey, who names it by saying no black drag queen of his day wanted to be Lena Horne, he makes it clear that the feminin-ity most sought after, most adored, was that perceived to be the exclusive property of white womanhood. When we see visual representations of womanhood in the film (images torn from magazines and posted on walls in living space) they are, with rare exceptions, of white women. Significantly, the fixation on becoming as much like a white female as possible implicitly evokes a connection to a figure never visible in this film: that of the white male patriarch. And yet if the class, race, and gender aspirations expressed by the drag queens who share their deepest dreams is always the longing to be in the position of the ruling-class woman then that means there is also the desire to act in partnership with the ruling-class white male.

This combination of class and race longing that privileges the "femi-ninity" of the ruling-class white woman, adored and kept, shrouded in luxury, does not imply a critique of patriarchy. Often it is assumed that the gay male, and most specifically the "queen," is both anti-phallocen-tric and anti-patriarchal. Marilyn Frye's essay, "Lesbian Feminism and Gay Rights," remains one of the most useful critical debunkings of this myth. Writing in *The Politics of Reality*, Frye comments:

> One of the things which persuades the straight world that gay men are not really men is the effeminacy of style of some gay men and the gay institu-tion of the impersonation of women, both of which are associated in the popular mind with male homosexuality. But as I read it, gay men's effemina-cy and donning of feminine apparel displays no love of or identification with women or the womanly. For the most part, this femininity is affected and is characterized by theatrical exaggeration. It is a casual and cynical mockery of women, for whom femininity is the trapping of oppression, but it is also a kind of play, a toying with that which is taboo ... What gay male affectation of femininity seems to be is a serious sport in which men may

exercise their power and control over the feminine, much as in other sports ...
But the mastery of the feminine is not feminine. It is masculine ...

Any viewer of *Paris Is Burning* can neither deny the way in which its
contemporary drag balls have the aura of sports events, aggressive
competitions, one team (in this case "house") competing against
another, etc., nor ignore the way in which the male "gaze" in the audience is directed at participants in a manner akin to the objectifying
phallic stare straight men direct at "Feminine" women daily in public
spaces. *Paris Is Burning* is a film that many audiences assume is inherently
oppositional because of its subject matter and the identity of the filmmaker. Yet the film's politics of race, gender, and class are played out in
ways that are both progressive and reactionary.

When I first heard that there was this new documentary film about
black gay men, drag queens, and drag balls, I was fascinated by the title.
It evoked images of the real Paris on fire, of the death and destruction of
a dominating white Western civilization and culture, an end to oppressive Eurocentrism and white supremacy. Not only did this fantasy give
me a sustained sense of pleasure, it stood between me and the unlikely
reality that young white filmmaker offering a progressive vision of
"Blackness" from the standpoint of "whiteness" would receive the positive press accorded Livingston and her film. Watching *Paris Is Burning*, I
began to think that the many yuppie-looking, straight-acting, pushy,
predominantly white folks in the audience were there because the film
in no way interrogates "whiteness." These folks left the film saying it
was "amazing," "marvelous," "incredible funny," worthy of statements
like "Didn't you just love it?" and no, I didn't just love it. For in many
ways the film was a graphic documentary portrait of the way in which
colonized black people (in this case black gay brothers, some of whom
were drag queens) worship at the throne of whiteness, even when such
worship demands that we live in perpetual self-hate, steal, lie, go
hungry, and even die in its pursuit. The "we" evoked here is all of us,
black people / people of color, who are daily bombarded by a powerful
colonizing whiteness that seduces us away from ourselves, that negates
that there is beauty to be found in any form of blackness that is not
imitation whiteness.

The whiteness celebrated in *Paris Is Burning* is not just any old brand
of whiteness but rather that brutal imperial ruling-class capitalist patriarchal whiteness that presents itself—its way of life—as the only meaningful life there is. What could be more reassuring to a white public

fearful that marginalized, disenfranchised black folks might rise any day now and make revolutionary black liberation struggle a reality than a documentary affirming that colonized victimized, exploited black folks are all too willing to be complicit in perpetuating the fantasy that ruling-class white culture is the quintessential site of unrestricted joy, freedom, power, and pleasure? Indeed, it is the very "pleasure" that so many white viewers with class privilege experience when watching this film that has acted to censor dissenting voices who find the film and its reception critically problematic.

In Vincent Canby's review of the film in the *New York Times,* Canby begins by quoting the words of a black father to his homosexual son. The father shares that it is difficult for black men to survive in a racist society and that "if you're black and male and gay, you have to be stronger than you can imagine." Beginning his overwhelmingly positive review with the words of a straight black father, Canby implies that the film in some way documents such strength, is a portrait of black gay pride. Yet he in no way indicates ways this pride and power are evident in the work. Like most reviewers of the film, what Canby finds most compelling is the pageantry of the drag balls. He uses no language identifying race and class perspectives when suggesting at the end of his piece that behind the role playing "there is also a terrible sadness in the testimony." Canby does not identify fully the sources of this sadness; instead he states, "The queens knock themselves out to imitate the members of a society that will not have them." This makes it appear that the politics of ruling-class white culture are solely social and not political, solely "aesthetic" questions of choice and desire rather than expressions of power and privilege. Canby does not tell readers that much of the tragedy and sadness of this film is evoked by the willingness of black gay men to knock themselves out imitating a ruling-class culture and power elite that are one of the primary parents of their oppression and exploitation. Ironically, the very "fantasies" evoked emerge from the colonizing context, and while marginalized people often appropriate and subvert aspects of the dominant culture, *Paris Is Burning* does not forcefully suggest that such a process is taking place.

Livingston's film is presented as though it is a politically neutral documentary providing a candid, even celebratory look at black drag balls. And it is precisely the mood of celebration that masks the extent to which the balls are not necessarily radical expressions of subversive imagination at work undermining and challenging the status quo. Much of the film's focus on pageantry takes the ritual of the black drag ball and makes it spectacle. Ritual is that ceremonial act which carries with it meaning and significance beyond what appears, while spectacle functions primarily as entertaining dramatic display. Those of us who have grown up in a segregated black setting where we participated in diverse pageants and rituals know that those elements of a given ritual that are empowering and subversive may not be readily visible to an outsider looking in. Hence it is easy for white observers to depict black rituals as spectacle.

Jennie Livingston approaches her subject matter as an outsider looking in. Since her presence as white woman/lesbian filmmaker is "absent" from *Paris Is Burning*, it is easy for viewers to imagine that they are watching an ethnographic film documenting the life of black gay "natives" and not recognize that they are watching a work shaped and formed by a perspective and standpoint specific to Livingston. By cinematically masking this reality (we hear her ask questions but never see her), Livingston does not oppose the way hegemonic whiteness "represents" blackness but rather assumes an imperial overseeing position that is in no way progressive or counterhegemonic. By shooting the film using a conventional approach to documentary and not making clear how her standpoint breaks with this tradition, Livingstone assumes a privileged location of "innocence." She is represented both in interviews and reviews as the tenderhearted, mild-mannered, virtuous white woman daring to venture into a contemporary "heart of darkness" to bring back knowledge of the natives.

A review in the *New Yorker* declarers (with no argument to substantiate the assertion) that "the movie is a sympathetic observation of a specialized, private world." An interview with Livingston in *Outweek* is titled "Pose, She Said," and we are told in the preface that she "discovered the Ball world by chance." Livingston does not discuss her interest and fascination with black gay subculture. She is not asked to speak about what knowledge, information, or lived understanding of black culture and history she possessed that provided a background for her work or to explain what vision of black life she hoped to convey and to whom. Can anyone imagine that a black woman lesbian would make a film about white gay subculture and not be asked these questions? Livingston is asked in the *Outweek* interview, "How did you build up the kind of trust where people are so open to talking about their personal experiences?" She never answers this question. Instead she suggests that she gains her "credibility" by the intensity of her spectatorship, adding, "I also targeted people who were articulate, who had stuff they wanted to say and were very happy that anyone wanted to listen." Avoiding the difficult questions underlying what it means to be a white person in a white supremacist society creating a film about any aspect of black life, Livingston responds to the question "Didn't the fact that you're a white lesbian going into a world of Black queens and street kids make that [the interview process] difficult?" by implicitly evoking a shallowness of universal connection. She responds, "If you know someone over a period of two years, and they still retain their sex and their race, you've got to be a pretty sexist, racist person." Yet it is precisely the race, sex, and sexual practices of the black men who are filmed that are the exploited subject matter.

So far I have read no interviews where Livingston discusses the issue of appropriation. And even though she is openly critical of Madonna, she does not convey how her work differs from Madonna's appropriation of black experience. To some extent it is precisely the recognition by mass culture that aspects of black life, like "voguing," fascinate white audiences that creates a market for both Madonna's product and Livingston's. Unfortunately, Livingston's comments about *Paris Is Burning* do not convey serious thought about either the political and aesthetic implications of her choice as a white woman focusing on an aspect of black life and culture or the way racism might shape and inform how she would interpret black experience on the screen. Reviewers like Georgia Brown in the *Village Voice* who suggest that Livingston's whiteness is "a fact of nature that didn't hinder her research" collude in the denial of the way whiteness informs her perspective and standpoint. To say, as Livingston does, "I certainly don't have the final word on the gay black experience. I'd love for a black director to have made this film" first to oversimplify the issue and to absolve her of responsibility and accountability for progressive critical reflection, and it implicitly suggests that there would be no difference between her work and that of a black director. Underlying this apparently self-effacing comment is cultural arrogance, for she implies not only that she has cornered the market on the subject matter but that being able to make films is a question of personal choice, like she just "discovered" the "raw material" before a black director did. Her comments are disturbing, because they reveal so little awareness of the politics that undergird any commodification of "blackness" in this society.

Had Livingston approached her subject with greater awareness of the way white supremacy shapes cultural production—determining not only what representations of blackness are deemed acceptable, marketable, as well as worthy of seeing—perhaps the film would not so easily have turned the black drag ball into a spectacle for the entertainment of those presumed to be on the outside of this experience looking in. So much of what is expressed in the film has to do with questions of power and privilege and the way racism impedes black progress (and certainly the class aspirations of the black gay subculture depicted do not differ from those of other poor and underclass black communities). Here, the supposedly "outsider" position is primarily located in the experience of whiteness. Livingston appears unwilling to interrogate the way assuming the position of outsider looking in as well as interpreter can, and often does, pervert and distort one's perspective. Her ability to assume such a position without rigorous interrogation of intent is rooted in the politics of race and racism. Patricia Williams critiques the white assumption of a "neutral" gaze in her essay "Teleology on the Rocks," included in her new book *The Alchemy of Race and Rights*. Describing taking a walking tour of Harlem with a group of white folks, she recalls the guide telling them they might "get to see some services," since "Easter Sunday in Harlem is quite a show." Williams's critical observations are relevant to any discussion of *Paris Is Burning*:

> What astonished me was that no one had asked the churches if they wanted to be stared at like living museums. I wondered what would happen if a group of blue-jeaned blacks were to walk uninvited into a synagogue on Passover or St. Anthony's of Padua during high mass—just to peer, not pray. My feeling is that such activity would be seen as disrespectful, at the very least. Yet the aspect of disrespect, intrusion, seemed irrelevant to this well-educated, affable group of people. They deflected my observation with comments like "We just want to look," "No one will mind," and "There's no harm intended." As well-intentioned as they were, I was left with the impression that no one existed for them who could not be governed by their intentions. While acknowledging the lack of apparent malice in this behavior, I can't help thinking that it is a liability as much as a luxury to live without interaction. To live so completely impervious to one's own impact on others is a fragile privilege, which over time relies not simply on the willingness but on the inability of others—in this case blacks—to make their displeasure heard.

This insightful critique came to mind as I reflected on why whites could so outspokenly make their pleasure in this film heard and the many black viewers who express discontent, raising critical questions about how the film was made, is seen, and is talked about, who have not named their displeasure publicly. Too many reviewers and interviewers not only assume that there is no need to raise pressing critical questions about Livingston's film but act as though she somehow did this marginalized black gay subculture a favor by bringing their experience to a wider public. Such a stance obscures the substantial rewards she has received for this work. Since so many of the black gay men in the film express the desire to be big stars, it is easy to place Livingston in the role of benefactor, offering these "poor black souls" a way to realize their dreams. But it is this current trend in producing colorful ethnicity for the white consumer appetite that makes it possible for blackness to be commodified in unprecedented ways, and for whites to appropriate black culture without interrogating whiteness of showing concern for the displeasure of blacks. Just as white cultural imperialism informed and affirmed the adventurous journeys of colonizing whites into the countries and cultures of "dark others," it allows white audiences to applaud representations of black culture, if they are satisfied with the images and habits of being represented.

Watching the film with a black woman friend, I was disturbed by the extent to which white folks around us were "entertained" and "pleasured" by scenes we viewed as sad and at times tragic. Often individuals laughed at personal testimony about hardship, pain, loneliness. Several times I yelled out in the dark: "What is so funny about this scene? Why are you laughing?" The laughter was never innocent. Instead it undermined the seriousness of the film, keeping it always on the level of spectacle. And much of the film helped make this possible. Moments of pain and sadness were quickly covered up by dramatic scenes from drag balls, as though there were two competing cinematic narratives, one displaying the pageantry of the drag ball and the other reflecting on the lives of participants and value of the fantasy. This second narrative was literally hard to hear because the laughter often drowned it out, just as the sustained focus on elaborate displays at balls diffused the power of the more serious critical narrative. Any audience hoping to be entertained would not be as interested in the true life stories and testimonies narrated. Much of the individual testimony makes it appear that the characters are estranged from any community beyond themselves. Families, friends, an the like are not shown, which adds to the representation of these black gay men as cut off, living on the edge.

It is useful to compare the portraits of black gay male lives in *Paris Is Burning* with those depicted in Marlon Riggs's compelling film *Tongues Untied*. At no point in Livingston's film are the men asked to speak about their connections to a world of family and community beyond the drag ball. The cinematic narrative makes the ball the center of their lives. And yet who determines this? Is this the way the black men view their reality, or is this the reality Livingston constructs? Certainly the degree to which black men in this gay subculture are portrayed as cut off from a "real" world heightens the emphasis on fantasy, and indeed gives *Paris Is Burning* its tragic edge. That tragedy is made explicit when we are told that the fair-skinned Venus has been murdered, yet there is no mourning of him/her in the film, no intense focus on the sadness of this murder. Having served the purpose of "spectacle" the film abandons him/her. The audience does not see Venus after the murder. There are no scenes of grief. To put it crassly, her dying is upstaged by spectacle. Death is not entertaining.

For those of us who did not come to this film as voyeurs of black gay subculture, it is Dorian Carey's moving testimony throughout the film that makes *Paris is Burning* a memorable experience. Carey is both historian and cultural critic in the film. He explains how the balls enabled marginalized black gay queens to empower both participants and audience. It is Carey who talks about the significance of the "star" in the life of gay black men who are queens. In a manner similar to critic Richard Dyer in his work *Heavenly Bodies*, Carey tells viewers that the desire for stardom is an expression of the longing to realize the dream of autonomous stellar individualism. Reminding readers that the idea of the individual continues to be a major image of what it means to live in a democratic world, Dyer writes:

> Capitalism justifies itself on the basis of the freedom (separateness) of anyone to make money, sell their labor how they will, to be able to express opinions and get them heard (regardless of wealth or social position). The openness of society is assumed by the way that we are addressed as individual—as consumers (each freely choosing to buy, or watch, what we want), as legal subjects (equally responsible before the law), as political subjects (able to make up our minds who is to run society). Thus even while the notion of the individual is assailed on all sides, it is a necessary fiction for the reproduction of the kind of society we live in.... Stars articulate these ideas of personhood.

This is precisely the notion of stardom Carey articulates. He emphasizes the way consumer capitalism undermines the subversive power of the drag balls, subordinating ritual to spectacle, removing the will to display unique imaginative costumes and the purchased image. Carey speaks profoundly about the redemptive power of the imagination in black life, that drag balls were traditionally a place where the aesthetics of the image in relation to black gay life could be explored with complexity and grace.

Carey extols the significance of fantasy even as he critiques the use of fantasy to escape reality. Analyzing the place of fantasy in black gay subculture, he links that experience to the longing for stardom that is so pervasive in this society. Refusing to allow the "queen" to be Othered, he conveys the message that in all of us resides that longing to transcend the boundaries of self, to be glorified. Speaking about the importance of drag queens in a recent interview in *Afterimage*, Marlon Riggs suggests that the queen personifies the longing everyone has for love and recognition. Seeing in drag queens "a desire, a very visceral need to be loved, as well as a sense of the abject loneliness of life where nobody loves you," Riggs contends "this image is real for anybody who has been in the bottom spot where they've been rejected by everyday and loved by nobody." Echoing Carey, Riggs declares: "What's real for them is the realization that you have to learn to love yourself." Carey stresses that one can only learn to love the self when one breaks through illusion and faces reality, not be escaping into fantasy. Emphasizing that the point is not to give us fantasy but to recognize its limitations, he acknowledges that one must distinguish the place of fantasy in ritualized play from the use of fantasy as a means of escape. Unlike Pepper Labeija, who constructs a mythic world to inhabit, making this his private reality, Carey encourages using the imagination creatively to enhance one's capacity to live more fully in a world beyond fantasy.

Despite the profound impact he makes—Riggs would call him "a visual icon of the drag queen with a very dignified humanity"—Carey's message, if often muted, is overshadowed by spectacle. It is hard for viewers to really hear this message. By critiquing absorption in fantasy and naming the myriad ways pain and suffering inform any process of self-actualization, Carey's message mediates between the viewer who longs to voyeuristically escape into film, to vicariously inhabit that lived space on the edge by exposing the sham, by challenging all of us to confront reality. James Baldwin makes the point in *The Fire Next Time* that "people who cannot suffer can never grow up, can never discover who they are." Without being sentimental about suffering, Dorian Carey urges all of us to break through denial, through the longing or an illusory star identity, so that we can confront and accept ourselves as we really are—only then can fantasy, ritual be a site of seduction, passion, and play where the self is truly recognized, loved, and never abandoned or betrayed.

"whose pussy is this?"

a feminist comment

Before I see Spike Lee's film *She's Gotta Have It*, I hear about it. Folks tell me, "It's black, it's funny, it's something you don't want to miss." With all this talk, especially coming from black folks who don't usually go to the movies, I become reluctant, even suspicious. If everybody is liking it, even white folks, something has got to be wrong somewhere! Initially, these are the thoughts that keep me from seeing the film but I don't stay away long. When I receive letters and phone calls from black women scholars and friends telling me about the film and wanting to talk about whether it portrays a liberated black woman, I make my way to the movies. I don't go alone. I go with my black women friends Beverly, Yvette, and Maria, so we can talk about it together. Some of what was said that evening in the heat of our discussion informs my comments.

A passionate viewer of films, especially the work of independent film-makers, I found much to appreciate in the technique, style, and overall

production of *She's Gotta Have It*. It was especially refreshing to see images
of black people on-screen that were not grotesque caricatures, images
that were familiar, images that imaginatively captured the essence,
dignity, and spirit of that elusive quality known as "soul." It was a very
soulful film.

Thinking about the film from a feminist perspective, considering its
political implications, I find it much more problematic. In the article
"Art vs. Ideology: The Debate Over Positive Images," Salim Muwakkil
raises the question of whether a "mature African-American community" can allow "aesthetic judgments to rest on ideological or political
criteria," commenting:

> The black cultural nationalists of the 60s and 70s demonstrated anew the
> deadening effect such ideological requirements have on creative expression.
> Their various proscriptions and prescriptions aborted a historical moment
> pregnant with promise. It seems clear that efforts to subordinate the
> profound and penetrating creative process of black people to an ideological
> moment suffocates the community's creative vitality.

While I would emphatically assert that aesthetic judgments should
not rest *solely* on ideological or political criteria, this does not mean that
such criteria cannot be used in conjunction with other critical strategies
to assess the overall value of a given work. It does not imply a devaluation
to engage in critical discussion of those criteria. To deny the validity of an
aesthetic critique that encompasses the ideological or political is to mask
the truth that every aesthetic work embodies the political, the ideological
as part of its fundamental structure. No aesthetic work transcends politics
or ideology.

Significantly, the film *She's Gotta Have It* was advertised, marketed, and
talked about in reviews and conversations in a manner that raised political and ideological questions about both the film and the public
responses to it. Was the film "a woman's story"? Did the film depict a
radically new image of black female sexuality? Can a man really tell a
woman's story? One viewer posed the question to me as "Is Nola Darling
a liberated woman or just a WHORE?" (This is the way this sentence
was written in a letter to me by a black woman professor who teaches
film, who wrote that she was "waiting for the feminist response.") There
has been no widespread feminist response to the film, precisely because
of the overwhelming public celebration of that which is new, different,
and exciting in this work. Given the pervasive antifeminism in popular

culture, in black subculture, a feminist critique might simply be aggressively dismissed. Yet for feminist thinkers to avoid public critique is to diminish the power of the film. It is a testimony to that power that it compels us to think, to reflect, to engage the work fully.

Recently, the film version of Alice Walker's *The Color Purple* evoked more discussion among black folks of feminist issues (sexism, freedom of sexual expression, male violence against women, etc.) than any theoretical and/or polemical work by feminist scholars. *She's Gotta Have It* generated a similar response. Often these discussions exposed grave ignorance about feminist political movement, revealing the extent to which shallow notions of feminist struggle disseminated by nonfeminists in popular culture shape and influence the way many black people perceive feminism. That all feminists are man-hating sexually depraved, castrating, power-hungry, and so forth, are prevailing stereotypes. The tendency to see liberated women as sexually loose informed the way many people viewed the portrayal of black female sexuality in *She's Gotta Have It*. To some extent, this perception is based on a narrowly defined notion of liberation that was acceptable in some feminist circles at one time.

During the early stage of contemporary women's movement, feminist liberation was often equated with sexual liberation by both feminist activists and nonfeminists. At that time, the conceptualization of female sexual liberation was informed by a fierce heterosexist bias that saw sexual liberation primarily in terms of women asserting the right to be sexually desiring, to initiate sexual relationships, and to participate in casual sexual encounters with varied male partners. Women dared to assert that female sexuality was not passive, that women were desiring subjects who both longed for and enjoyed sex as much if not more than men. These assertions could have easily provided the ideological framework for the construction of a character like Nola Darling, the main female character in *She's Gotta Have It*. Nola expresses again and again her eagerness and willingness to be sexual with men as well as her right to have numerous partners.

Superficially, Nola Darling is the perfect embodiment of woman as desiring subject—a representation that does challenge sexist notions of female sexual passivity. (It is important to remember that from slavery on, black women have been portrayed in white racist thought as sexually assertive, although this view contrasts sharply with the emphasis on chastity, monogamy, and the male right to initiate sexual contact in black culture, a view held especially among the middle classes.) Ironically and unfortunately, Nola Darling's sexual desire is not depicted as an autonomous gesture, as an independent longing for sexual expression, satisfaction, and fulfillment. Instead her assertive sexuality is most often portrayed as though her body, her sexually aroused being, is a reward or gift she bestows on the deserving male. When bodybuilder Greer Childs tells Nola that his photo will appear on the cover of a popular men's magazine, she responds by removing her clothes, by offering her body as a token of her esteem. This and other incidents suggest that Nola, though a desiring subject, acts on the assumption that heterosexual female sexual assertion has legitimacy primarily as a gesture of reward or as a means by which men can be manipulated and controlled by women (what is vulgarly called "pussy power"). Men do not have to objectify Nola's sexuality, because she objectifies it. In so doing, her character becomes the projection of a stereotypical sexist notion of a sexually assertive woman—she is not in fact liberated.

While Nola is not passive sexually, her primary concern is pleasing each partner. Though we are led to believe she enjoys sex, her sexual fulfillment is never the central concern. She is pleasured only to the extent that she is able to please. while her partners enjoy being sexual with her, they are disturbed by her desire to have frequent sex with several partners. They see her sexual longing as abnormal. One male partner, Mars, says, "All men want freaks (in bed), we just don't want 'em for a wife." This comment illustrates the sexist stereotypes about female sexuality that inform Mars's perceptions of Nola. When Jaime, another partner, suggests that Nola is sick, evoking sexist stereotypes to label her insane, depraved, abnormal, Nola does not respond by asserting that she is sexually liberated. Instead she internalizes the critique and seeks psychiatric help. Throughout the film, she is extremely dependent on male perceptions of her reality. Lacking self-awareness and the capacity to be self-critical, she explores her sexuality only when compelled to do so by a man. If Nola were sexually liberated, there would be no need for her to justify or defend herself against male accusations. It is only after the men have passed judgment that she begins the process of coming to consciousness. Until that point, we know more about how the men in the film see her than about how she sees herself.

To a very grave extent the focus of the film is not Nola but her male partners. Just as they are the center of attention sexually, they are also central personalities in the film. In telling us what they think about Nola, they tell us more about themselves, their values, their desires. She is the object that stimulates the discourse, they are its subjects. The narrators are male and the story is a male-centered, male-biased patriarchal tale. As such, it is not progressive nor does it break away from the traditional portrayal of female sexuality in film. *She's Gotta Have It* can take its place alongside a growing body of contemporary films that claim to tell women's stories while privileging male narratives, films that stimulate audiences with versions of female sexuality that are not really new or different (*Paris, Texas*, for example). Another recently acclaimed film, *Mona Lisa*, objectifies black womanhood and black female sexuality in a similar way.

Overall, it is the men who speak in *She's Gotta Have It*. While Nola appears one-dimensional in perspective and focus, seemingly more concerned about her sexual relationships than about any other aspect of her life, the male characters are multidimensional. They have personalities. Nola has no personality. She is shallow, vacuous, empty. Her one claim to fame is that she likes to fuck. In the male pornographic imagination she could be described as "pure pussy," that is to say that her ability to perform sexually is the central, defining aspect of her identity.

These sexually active, sexually hungry men are not "pure penis," because there is no such category. They are each defined by unique characteristics and attributes—Mars by his humor, Greer by his obsession with bodybuilding, Jaime by his concern with romance and committed relationships. Unlike Nola, they are not always thinking about sex, do not suffer from penis on the brain. They have opinions on a variety of topics: politics, sports, lifestyles, gender, and so on. Filmmaker Spike Lee challenges and critiques notions of black male sexuality while presenting a very typical perspective on black female sexuality. His imaginative explorations of the black male psyche is far more probing, far more expansive, and finally much more interesting than his exploration of black femaleness.

When Nola testifies that there have been "dogs" in her life—men who were only concerned with getting into bed—a group of black men appear on the screen in single file delivering the lines they use to seduce women, to "get it." In this brief segment, sexist male objectification of females is exposed along with the falseness and superficiality of the men. This particular scene more than any other in the film, is an excellent example of how cinema can be effectively used to raise consciousness about political concerns—in this case sexist male objectification of females. Without any particular character making a heavy-handed statement about how shallowly these black men think about women and sexuality, this point is powerfully conveyed. Filmmaker Spike Lee acknowledges that he intended to focus critically on black male behavior in the film, stating, "I know that black men do a lot of things that are fucked up and I've tried to show some of the things that we do."

While his innovative portrayal of black men in this scene (which is shot in such a way as to assume a documentary stance—the men appearing in single file before a camera as though they were being individually interviewed—acts to expose and, by implication, critique black male sexism, other scenes reinforce and perpetuate it. The deconstructive power of this scene is undermined most glaringly by the rape scene that occurs later.

Often talking with folks about the movie, I found my people did not notice that there was a rape scene, while others questioned whether what happened could be accurately described as a rape. Those of us who understand rape to be an act of coercive sexual contact, wherein one person is forced by another to participate without consent, watched a rape scene in *She's Gotta Have It*. When I first saw the film with the black women friends mentioned earlier, we were surprised and disturbed by the rape scene, yet we did not yell out in protest or leave the theater. As a group, we collectively sunk in our seats as though hiding. It was not the imaginative portrayal of rape that was shocking and disturbing but the manner and style of this depiction. In this instance, rape as an act of black male violence against a black woman was portrayed as though it was just another enjoyable sexual encounter, just another fuck. Rape, the film implies, is a difficult term to use when describing forced sexual intercourse with a sexually active female (in this case it is called a "near rape"). After all, as many black folks—women and men—stressed in conversation with me, she called him—she wanted to be sexual—she wanted it." Embedded in such thinking is the sexist assumption that woman as desiring subject, as active initiator, as sexual seducer is responsible for the quality, nature, and content of male response.

Not surprisingly, Nola sees herself as accountable, yet her ability to judge situations clearly has been questioned throughout the film. While she is completely in character when she labels the rape a "near rape," the fact remains that she is raped. Though she is depicted as deriving pleasure from the act, this does not alter the fact that she is forced to act sexually without her consent. It is perfectly compatible with sexist pornographic fantasies about rape to show a woman enjoying violation. Since the sexist mindset places responsibility on the female, claiming that she is really in control, such a fantasy allows that she (who is in actuality a victim) has the power to change this violent act into a plea-surable experience.

Hence the look on Darling's face during the rape, which begins as a grimace, reflecting pain, ends as a game of pleasure, satisfaction. This is most assuredly a sexist imaginative fantasy of rape—one that we as passive, silent viewers condone by our complicity. Protests from the audi-ence would have at last altered passive acceptance of this depiction of rape. In keeping with the reality of patriarchy, with sexism in our culture, viewers who were pleased with the rape cheered and expressed their approval of Jaime's action when I saw the film.

As Jaime rapes Nola and aggressively demands that she answer the question "Whose pussy is this?" we arrive at the moment of truth—the moment when she can declare herself independent, sexually liberated, the moment when she can proudly assert through resistance her sexual autonomy (for many partners, to belong to no one). Ironically, she does not resist the physical violence. She does not assert the primacy of her body rights. She is passive. It is ironic because until this moment we have been seduced by the image of her as a forceful woman, a woman who dares to be sexually assertive, demanding, active. We are seduced and betrayed. When Nola responds to the question "Whose pussy is this?" by saying, "Yours," it is difficult for anyone who has fallen for the image of her as sexually liberated not to feel let down, disappointed both in her character and in the film. Suddenly we are not witnessing a radi-cal questioning of female sexual passivity or a celebration of female sexual self-assertion but a reconstruction of the same old sexist content in a new and more interesting form. While some of us were passively disgusted, disturbed, sexist male viewers feeling vilified cheered, express-ing their satisfaction that the uppity black woman had been put in her place—that male domination and patriarchal order were restored.

After the rape, Nola ceases to be sexually active, chooses to be in a monogamous relationship with Jaime, the partner who has coerced her. Ideologically, such a scenario impresses on the consciousness of black males, and all males, the sexist assumption that rape is an effective means of patriarchal social control that it restores and maintains male power over women. It simultaneously suggests to black females, and all females, that being sexually assertive will lead to rejection and punish-ment. In a culture where a woman is raped every eighteen seconds, where there is still enormous ignorance about rape, where patriarchy and sexist practices promote and condone the rape of women by men as a way to maintain male domination, it is disturbing to witness this scene, not only because it reinforces dangerous stereotypes (a central one being that women enjoy rape), but because it suggests that rape does not have severe and grave consequences for victims. Without counseling, without support, Nola is restored to her cool, confident self by the end of the movie. Silent about her sexuality throughout much of the film, she suddenly speaks. It is she who will call the rape a "near rape," as though it was really no big deal.

Yet it is the rape that shifts the direction of the film, of Nola Darling's fictional self-exploration. As an expression of her newly acquired self-assertion, she calmly denounces the "near rape," explains that the relationship with Jaime has not worked, and stresses her right to be autonomously self-defining. Expressed without the bravado and zest that has characterized that we have witnessed a woman being disempowered and not a woman coming to power. This perception seems to be reconfirmed when Nola's choice to be truly self-defining means that she will be alone, with no sexual partner.

In perfect contrast to *The Color Purple*, wherein same-sex relationships between women are depicted as a source of mutual, nonexploitive erotic affirmation and serve as catalysts for self-development, the lesbian sexuality in *She's Gotta Have It* is negatively portrayed. It does not represent an alternative to destructive heterosexual practice. The lesbian character is predatory, as much a "dog" as any of the men. Significantly, Nola does not find it difficult to reject unwanted sexual advances from another woman, to assert her body rights, her preferences. Utterly male-identified, she does not value her women friends. Though they are underdeveloped characters in the film, her two female friends are compelling and interesting. The apparent dedication and discipline the bass player shows in relationship to her music stand in sharp contrast to Nola's lackadaisical approach to her art, whereas the bass player appears comfortable with her autonomy in a way that Nola is not.

Autonomy is not depicted as a life-enhancing, empowering choice for Nola. Her decision to be self-defining leaves her as vacuous and as empty as she has previously appeared without the savvy she had in her role as vamp. Finally we see her at the end of the film alone, wrapped in her sheets, a familiar image that does not suggest transformation. Are we to imagine that she has ceased to long for the "it" she's gotta have? Are we to think that the "it" is multiple in implication after all, that it may not be sex but a sense of self she is longing for? She has had sex throughout the film; what she has not had is a sense of self that would enable her to be fully autonomous and sexually assertive, independent, and liberated. Without a firm sense of self her attempts at becoming a desiring subject rather than an object are doomed to fail. Nola cannot enter the sexual power struggle between women and men as object and become subject. Desire alone is not enough to make her a subject, to liberate (the film does make this point, but this is no new revelation). A new image, the one we have yet to see in film, is the desiring black woman who prevails, who triumphs, not desexualized, not alone, who is "together" in every sense of the word. Joan Mellen in her introduction to *Women and Their Sexuality in the New Film* emphasizes that the recent attempt to portray radical and transformative images of female sexuality has proven to be a disappointment, in most instances a failure:

> The language of independent women may be reluctantly allowed, but the substance goes unaltered. If lip service provides a pseudo-anticipation of challenge to old values and images, the real business at hand is to refurbish the established view, now strengthened by nominal reference to "awareness." This sleight of hand is the method of co-option. Cinema is an arena in which the process had been refined. Thus the very image of liberated or self-sufficient women, when it is risked on the screen, is presented unpalatably and deployed to reinforce the old ways.

Even though filmmaker Spike Lee may have intended to portray a radical new image of black female sexuality, *She's Gotta Have It* reinforces and perpetuates old norms overall. Positively the film does show us the nature of black male-female power struggles, the contradictions, the craziness, and that is an important new direction. Yet it is the absence of compelling liberatory reconciliation that undermines the progressive radical potential of this film. Even though nude scenes, scenes of sexual play constitute an important imaging of black sexuality on-screen since they are not grotesque or pornographic, we still do not see an imaging of mutual, sexually satisfying relationships between black women and men in a context of nondomination. It does not really matter if the woman is dominating and a male submitting—it is the same old oppressive scenario. Ultimately, it is a patriarchal tale—one in which woman does not emerge triumphant, fulfilled. While we can applaud Nola's feeble attempt to tell a new story at the end of the film, it is not compelling, not enough—it is not satisfying.

index